WATER

law

DATE DUE   5 / 02

1/23/07			
Red Ink Top Edge noted 05/03			
GAYLORD			PRINTED IN U.S.A.

MEMORIES
AND
ADVENTURES

MEMORIES AND ADVENTURES

Winston S. Churchill

WEIDENFELD & NICOLSON
New York

Published by Weidenfeld & Nicolson, New York
A Division of Wheatland Corporation
841 Broadway
New York, New York 10003-4793

Published in Canada by General Publishing Company, Ltd.

First published in Great Britain
by George Weidenfeld Limited, London

Library of Congress Cataloging-in-Publication Data

Churchill, Winston S. (Winston Spencer), 1940–
Memories and adventures / Winston S. Churchill.—1st ed.
p. cm.
Includes index.
ISBN 1-55584-168-6 (alk. paper)
1. Churchill, Winston S. (Winston Spencer), 1940–
2. Great Britain. Parliament. House of Commons—Biography.
3. Legislators—Great Britain—Biography. 4. Journalists—Great
Britain—Biography. 5. Churchill family. I. Title.
DA591.C48A3   1989
328.41'092—dc20
[B]
89-34128
CIP

Manufactured in the United States of America

This book is printed on acid-free paper

First Edition

1 3 5 7 9 10 8 6 4 2

To

Minnie
Randolph, Jennie
Marina and Jack

Contents

Illustrations

Preface

Next year will mark the twenty-fifth anniversary of the death of my grandfather Winston Churchill, whose name I am so proud to bear. With this in mind, and the fact that I shall myself soon be entering the second half-century of my life, I feel the time may be ripe to make a record of the memories and adventures of my youth for the benefit of my own children, who have themselves either entered adult life or newly become teenagers, as well as for a wider public.

I am indebted to my friend George Weidenfeld for suggesting this book and, thereby, giving me the opportunity of exploring my early memories of wartime Chequers and the London Blitz, as well as of my parents and grandparents, of rediscovering numerous letters from my grandfather and of reliving the adventures of my youth, which included piloting a single-engine plane 20,000 miles round Africa, and reporting conflicts from the Middle East and Southeast Asia as a newspaper correspondent. I certainly found retracing the early years of my life a lively and invigorating experience, and I trust that in the pages that follow I have been able to convey something of their flavour.

I would like to place on record my gratitude to my wife, Minnie, for her loyal and unstinting support and encouragement in the completion of this work which, as with all my previous books, we wrote as a team. Many were the mornings when she was manning the typewriter before 6 am which, most will agree, comes in the category of devotion beyond the call of duty. In this venture, as in all our life together, she has been a tower of strength and inspiration.

I am most grateful to my mother, Pamela Harriman, for her many reminiscences of my childhood, especially during the war years, and for her permission to publish her correspondence with my father and grandparents. My thanks are also due to my aunt, Lady Soames, and to Anthony Montague Browne, who was for many years my grandfather's private secretary, for their kindness in reading and commenting on the proofs.

I wish also to express my appreciation to the Prime Minister for giving me the opportunity of revisiting the room where I was born at Chequers and the 'prison suite' where I stayed during my many visits in the wartime years, enabling me to confirm my very first childhood memories.

Finally, I wish to thank my secretary, Mrs Alison Hiller, for typing the numerous redrafts and corrections with commendable efficiency and good humour.

WINSTON S. CHURCHILL
24 January 1989

· I ·

Chequers: 1940

With a sense of occasion appropriate to one who was to aspire to a career in journalism, where being at the right place at the right time is of the essence, I was born on 10 October 1940 at Chequers in Buckinghamshire, the official country residence of Britain's prime ministers. My grandmother recorded the event in the visitors' book in her own hand:

'Winston' 4.40 am October the 10th 1940

The night before, a German bomb had landed in the field a bare 100 yards from the house, causing great consternation among those charged with ensuring the Prime Minister's security. Had the Luftwaffe succeeded, they wondered, in pinpointing Chequers, where he worked most weekends?

Shortly afterwards, with the German bomber offensive continuing in spite of the whipping they had received in the Battle of Britain, which had forestalled Hitler's planned invasion, the straight half-mile long drive that led to the large Elizabethan mansion, and made it easily identifiable from the air, was dug up and grassed over. The Prime Minister was strenuously urged no longer to spend weekends there when the moon was full. Instead he stayed as the guest of Mr and Mrs Ronald Tree at Ditchley, their elegant country home nearby. But no further attack materialized and the explosion that heralded my birth was presumed to have been a 'hung' bomb which fell accidentally from a German bomber returning from a raid on the industrial cities of the Midlands or the north-west of England, both of which had been hit that same night.

The next 'bombshell' to arrive was me, and at a most inconvenient predawn hour. So far as I can discover I was the only baby to have had the presumption to be born at Chequers this century – certainly the only one since 1920, when Lord Lee of Fareham gave his home to the nation as a country retreat for the prime minister of the day.

My parents had met on a blind date barely a year before and within three weeks had married. It had been one of those whirlwind wartime courtships that, in response to the human instinct for survival, were taking place throughout the country as, for the second time in a quarter century, the nation's youth prepared to march off to war. On 3 September 1939 Britain and her Dominions had declared war on Nazi Germany. (How many have forgotten that it was *we* who declared war, not the other way around!) In the starkness of the hour, with a conviction that – like their fathers before them in the trenches in the Great War – millions were destined never to return, young men and women were propelled by a sense of urgency into decisions about their lives and their futures that might in other circumstances, have been postponed or even never taken.

My father, Randolph, was twenty-eight years old. Journalist, lecturer and would-be politician, he had acquitted himself creditably in three unsuccessful attempts to enter Parliament in noisy, controversial by-elections, two in Lancashire and one in the Western Highlands of Scotland. He had made himself an outrider in his father's campaign to re-arm Britain in the face of the menace of Hitler's rise to power and the growing military might of Nazi Germany. He had been strident in his denunciation of the infamous Munich Agreement whereby, to buy time, the British Prime Minister, Neville Chamberlain, and the French Premier Daladier had betrayed the people of Czechoslovakia to Hitler, whose Nazi storm troopers invaded and occupied that country soon afterwards. But the policy of throwing friends and allies to the wolves in the hope of appeasing their appetite was doomed to failure. Now the war that he and his father had campaigned together for seven long years to prevent was upon them and was about to engulf the people of Britain who, like their cousins in the Great Republic across the seas – as my grandfather was fond of calling the United States – had slumbered on, heedless of the dramatic developments in Europe which they were determined should not involve them but which they made no attempt to forestall.

Sensing that war was inevitable my father, in the summer of 1938, had joined his father's old regiment. As he recalled in an unpublished memorandum dated 12 June 1954 which I found among his papers following his death in 1968:

When the Second War started, I was serving as a 2nd Lieutenant with the 4th Queen's Own Hussars at Tidworth. I was a Supplementary Reserve Officer and when Hitler marched into Poland I was doing my three weeks annual training. We were a cavalry regiment but had been officially mechanized about 18 months before. This meant that our horses had been taken away from us but that no tanks had been supplied in their place. So we did not have very much to do.

About ten days after war was declared, the First Lord of the Admiralty [his father Winston] telephoned to me and asked whether I could get three or four days' leave so that I could act as his representative on a mission. This was easily arranged...

My father received specific instructions about his secret mission from his father who on 3 September 1939, the very day of the outbreak of the Second World War, had returned to the Admiralty as First Lord in Neville Chamberlain's government, thus being entrusted, for the second time within a quarter of a century, with the momentous responsibility of preparing the British Fleet for war with Germany:

Private and Personal   Admiralty,
                                                        Whitehall

My dearest Randolph,
    Please be at the house of the Captain-in-Charge at Portland at a quarter to nine on Tuesday morning. He will be expecting you, and I am told his house is well-known. You should wear uniform and look your best. You will have to travel over in the day and sleep on board on the way back. I believe you will land at the other place I mentioned.
    I enclose you a letter which you should hand to our friend saying that you have been sent to represent me. You may tell the Colonel, but the whole matter must be regarded as very secret.
    I hope you will enjoy your *mission spécial.*

                    Your loving father,
                    Winston S. Churchill

My father takes up the story:

    Pursuant to the instructions which I received from the First Lord, I went on board HMS *Kelly* at Portsmouth and reported to the ship's Commanding Officer, Captain Lord Louis Mountbatten. The First Lord had instructed me to wear boots and breeches and my sword. I knew that military officers should not wear spurs on board His Majesty's ships; but I thought they might be needed in the course of my mission and I had therefore brought them with me in my suitcase.
    The 'object of the exercise', it transpired, was to proceed to Cherbourg and to bring back to England the Duke and Duchess of Windsor. The Duchess had not been in England since she left a week before the abdication. Both Lord Louis and myself were friends of the Windsors and it seemed to both of us in this phoneyest part of the 'phoney war', a very agreeable and jolly expedition.
    We arrived at Cherbourg in the morning. I had put on my spurs before going on shore. Otherwise I would have been 'improperly dressed'. We were conducted to a large saloon on the first floor of the naval headquarters where we were received by what seemed to be at least seven or eight French Admirals. The whole affair was conducted most ceremoniously. After a quarter of an hour, the Duke and Duchess arrived by train from Paris. A *vin d'honneur* was served and toasts were drunk to everyone and everything that seemed appropriate in September 1939. We then sat down, eleven or twelve of us, in large over-stuffed

3

armchairs in a large circle. I was almost immediately opposite the Duke of Windsor and perhaps at a distance of some eight or nine yards. Suddenly, with eagle eye and an accent of triumph, he interrupted the general buzz of stilted conversation: 'Randolph, you have got your spurs on upside down.' Bending my portly figure uneasily and uncomfortably over my Sam Browne belt, and knocking over with my sword a half-filled glass of champagne which I had put by my side on the floor, I found that the Duke was correct in his diagnosis of my military turnout. I made abject and ineffective gestures of apology and exculpation, but it was no good. When royalty can discover a medal put on in the wrong order or any error in dress, it makes their day and they are not to be denied. This occasion was a gala day.

My father goes on to describe what I well recall him telling me was the most embarrassing moment of his life:

He [the Duke of Windsor] strode across the floor and said: 'Let me put them right, Randolph.' Scarlet, expostulating and miserable I rose and sought to deter him. 'Sit down, sit down,' he said, 'let me do it.' Obedience is said to be the highest form of politeness and down I sat, and there in the presence of all the French Admirals, scandalized and uncomprehending, the Duke of Windsor knelt down and spent three or four of the happiest moments of his life fussing and fiddling about with the straps by which my spurs were attached to my boots. I kept trying ineffectively to relieve him of his task; all to no avail.

After what I suppose was only three or four minutes but seemed like several aeons of time, the spurs were adjusted to the satisfaction of His Royal Highness. Fortunately the tide proclaimed and compelled our departure and we went aboard HMS *Kelly*. I at once removed the offending spurs in the forlorn hope that I should be twitted no more. It was not to be. The cup was not allowed to pass and all the way through luncheon the Duke continued to tease me about my extraordinary solecism. I bore it with such good nature as I could muster, but eventually as he is a kind man and saw that I had received sufficient punishment, he turned upon Captain Lord Louis Mountbatten and said: 'Dickie, I know you are only a simple sailor man, but you have played a lot of polo in your time. You must have noticed that Randolph's spurs were on upside down. Why didn't you tell him?' 'Well sir,' replied Lord Louis with that disingenuous charm which has served him so well in his various careers, 'of course I noticed it, but I didn't want to spoil your fun.'

We got back to Portsmouth alright. Eighteen months later HMS *Kelly* was torpedoed. Lord Louis had to swim for it and survived to have two other destroyers sunk under him and to do a number of other things which are a matter of history.

Shortly after his return from his secret mission of 12 September Randolph telephoned the London flat of his friends Philip and Mary Dunne, only to discover that Philip had already left to join his regiment. As fate would have it, the telephone was answered instead by Pamela Digby, the nineteen-year-old daughter of Lord and Lady Digby of Minterne in Dorset. Pamela, a beautiful redhead, was working at the Foreign Office doing

4

translations from German and French for which she was earning all of £6 per week. Having nowhere to live in London she had arranged to rent the Dunnes' flat for two pounds ten shillings (£2.50) a week and she later recalled:

Philip had gone and Mary was showing me round the flat when the telephone rang. She was by the drinks cupboard so I answered the telephone. A voice said: 'This is Randolph Churchill.'
'Do you want to speak to Mary?' I asked.
'No', he replied firmly, 'I want to speak to you.'
'But you don't know me,' I protested.
At that moment Mary came over from the far side of the room, nodding her head vigorously. Meanwhile he continued: 'As a matter of fact I was wondering if you would come and have dinner with me tonight.' Mary was interjecting: 'Please do! Please do!' So I said, 'Alright – come and pick me up at 7 o'clock', put down the telephone and demanded, 'Mary, what's all this about?' – 'Oh, he's an old friend of mine,' she replied, 'He's great fun, he's a bit too fat, but very amusing. I told him that you were taking our flat and that I couldn't dine with him but I would try and persuade you to dine with him. Please do – you'll have a very good time!'
I agreed because at that point the war had already started and I found it all so depressing. Anytime one went to the Four Hundred whoever you were with, instead of asking the head waiter to keep his whiskey bottle until his next visit, as was the custom, would end the evening by presenting the bottle to the head waiter and saying: 'Take this, I won't be coming again – I'm going out to get killed.' I was getting so terribly upset by seeing all my friends going off, as they dramatically thought, to be killed, and I thought how marvellous it was to be going out with somebody about whom I didn't give a damn...

In the whirlwind courtship stakes, my parents must have been front-runners even in those heady days of swift proposals and instant marriages. Within two weeks of their first meeting they became engaged and just a week later they married. Many of my mother's friends tried to dissuade her from the enterprise and even one of my father's closest friends, Ed Stanley – later Lord Stanley of Alderley – tried to put her off. According to my mother:

Ed Stanley called me up to complain: 'You stood me up for dinner last night and I find you dining at a restaurant with Randolph Churchill. He's a very, very bad man and you shouldn't go out with people like that.'
'But he's one of your best friends,' I protested.
'Yes, he is one of *my* best friends – but he shouldn't be one of *yours*.'

'That,' as my mother later confessed, 'rather egged me on though there were moments, every time Randolph disappeared, when I became anxious and said to myself: "This is absolutely idiotic – I don't know him, he doesn't know me and there's a war on." But while everyone else was so scared and so uncertain of what was to happen to us all and to the world,

Randolph was totally confident that, though the war was going to be bloody and millions would be killed, we would survive it and we would win. It gave one great confidence.'

Opposition to the match was not confined to Ed Stanley. My Grandmother Churchill as well as my mother's parents, the Digbys, thought the suggestion quite ridiculous. 'She's too young!' 'They don't have any money or anywhere to live!' 'They don't even know each other!' 'The whole thing is absurd – they must not be allowed to do it!' It seemed that everyone was against the match – everyone, that is, except Grandpapa Churchill. Brushing aside all such arguments he declared: 'Nonsense! All you need to be married are champagne, a box of cigars and a double-bed!' He even confided to my mother that he, himself, had nearly married a 'Pamela' – Pamela Plowden, who later became Countess of Lytton, with whom he had had a romance while serving as a subaltern in the 4th Hussars in India before the turn of the century.

The wedding took place on 4 October 1939 at the beautiful Wren church of St John's, Smith Square, which, later in the war, was to be hit by a German bomb. The next day the *Daily Mirror* devoted a whole page to a report and photographs of the wedding:

CROWD CHEERS WINSTON AT SON'S WEDDING

Mr Winston Churchill, First Lord of the Admiralty, was cheered again and again yesterday when he arrived at St John's Church, Smith Square, Westminster, with his wife for the wedding of their only son, Mr Randolph Churchill. Large crowds had gathered outside the church and even the guests, standing in the porch, cheered ...

It was a real war wedding, with the bridegroom, who is a subaltern in the cavalry corps, wearing uniform ... All the guests carried gas-masks and Canon F.R. Barry, Rector of St John's, who performed the ceremony, arrived at the church with his own slung over his shoulder in a scarlet satchel.

After the ceremony my parents left the church, passing under an arch of drawn swords held high above their heads by two rows of my father's brother officers from his regiment. Following a reception at Admiralty House given by Grandpapa and Grandmama Churchill, they spent a brief honeymoon at Belton, near Grantham in Lincolnshire, as the guests of Lord Brownlow, the Duke of Windsor's Equerry, whom my father had befriended at the time of the abdication crisis. The marriage got off to a faltering start when Father tried to read his teenage bride Gibbon's *Decline and Fall of the Roman Empire* in bed on their honeymoon. My mother later commented: 'Fancy trying to read me *Decline and Fall!* Even worse, he would stop and say: "Are you listening?" When I said: "Yes I am", he would demand: "Well, what was the last sentence?" Can you imagine! Hilaire Belloc was fine, but Gibbon was too much!'

On 30 November Grandpapa Churchill celebrated his sixty-fifth birthday, qualifying him for the Old Age Pension, though he had yet to become Prime Minister for the first time. At a quiet family celebration at Admiralty House my parents presented him with a gold fountain pen, with which he was to sign all his wartime documents as the momentous events of the Second World War unfolded.

From Tidworth, my father's regiment was moved North to near Hull in Yorkshire, where my parents lived in a small semi-detached house. My mother does not have happy memories of their time in Hull:

It was the hardest winter – the winter of 1939–40. There was snow and more snow. It was cold, there was ice everywhere – it really was ghastly. It was a desperately frustrating time for Randolph. Other regiments were being sent abroad, but not his – he was stuck in Hull. All the sergeants' wives were saying: 'Of course we have nothing to worry about as long as Mr Churchill's son is in the regiment – none of our husbands will be sent abroad.' One thing that Randolph never lacked was courage. He was desperate to go abroad, yet it seemed that every regiment except the Fourth Hussars was sent.

Such criticisms were grossly unfair. From the very outset of war he had been pressing his father to use his influence to get him to the front, conscious that, in his day, Winston had ensured that no string within reach of his very resourceful mother, Jennie Jerome, had remained unpulled, so determined was he to see action on the North-west Frontier of India, the Sudan and the Boer War. But he was adamant he would pull no strings on his son's behalf:

15 September 1939   Admiralty

Dearest Randolph,

I am sure yr best & indeed *only* course is to obey with good grace, & do whatever duty is assigned to you. In this way you will win the confidence of those in whose power you lie.

I will write to General Barnes about yr grief at being detached from yr regiment for training duties; & of yr desire to accompany them to the front. Such feelings are in no way discreditable; but the good officer wd take care not to show them, while hoping for a better turn of events.

I am always on the look out for any compliment or pleasure I can give you, as you know; but so far as the service is concerned you must make yr own way. I am always thinking about yr interests & yr fortunes.

> Your loving father,
> Winston S. Churchill

My father had joined the 4th Hussars, his father's old regiment, to please him. Had he joined a territorial regiment with his friends, like Seymour Berry and Basil Dufferin – killed in action in Burma at the very end of the war – they would all have been junior officers together. As it was, by joining a regiment of the Regular Army, my father, already twenty-eight years old,

7

found himself with a group of lieutenants all of whom were nearly ten years his junior.

While at Hull, these young officers taunted him about his lack of physical fitness, provoking a typical Randolphian response: 'Rubbish – I am tougher than the lot of you!' They thereupon challenged him to prove it, betting him £50 that he could not walk to York and back – a distance of 104 miles – in twenty-four hours. For three weeks my father trained, taking long walks at a brisk pace every afternoon, when he got home. My mother vividly recalls the time:

> He went on to special foods and took to rubbing his feet with methylated spirits to toughen them up. He took it all terribly seriously and kept on saying how useful the £50 was going to be, how it would pay off so many bills – in fact it wouldn't have paid off a tenth of them.
>
> In between times, Randolph was on to White's Club and Evelyn Waugh and all his other friends who were only too anxious to give him advice. Obviously Evelyn's was of the worst type: 'You know you mustn't start in the middle of the night!', 'you shouldn't march in the midday sun,' etc. There never was any midday sun in Hull anyway! Finally, the great day arrived and Randolph set off at a brisk pace for York where he had taken a room at the Station Hotel so he could grab three hours' rest. It was the return journey that was most painful. We set off at two or three in the morning. I had to follow him with the car headlights on and toot if ever he dropped below 4 mph or was doing more than 6 mph. After many, many hours of walking, Randolph was in such agony from blisters and sores that he finally took off his boots and walked in his socks – two pairs. Then his socks hurt and we had to stop and pad the socks with cotton wool. Then that got wet. It was a desperate struggle. I think we made it into the camp just twenty-two minutes under the time limit.
>
> The young officers greeted him with hoots of derisive laughter. They were furious he had succeeded and determined not to pay. Randolph always thought they would – but they never paid a single penny. The Army then put him on fatigue duties for his trouble ...

In April 1940, Hitler launched a furious attack against Norway. In spite of naval support and seaborne landings, Britain was unable to prevent Norway falling under the Nazi jackboot. This failure provoked a political crisis at home and, by the conclusion of the Commons debate on 8 May, it had become clear that Neville Chamberlain, though he had narrowly survived what amounted to a vote of censure, no longer commanded the support of the House of Commons or even the Conservative Party. Chamberlain thereupon held consultations with the leaders of the Labour and Liberal Parties to see if they would join in the formation of a national government under his leadership. Clement Attlee, the leader of the Labour Party, had already pointed out that it would be difficult to get his party to serve under Chamberlain when, on the morning of 10 May, the grave and momentous news broke that Hitler had invaded Belgium and Holland.

8

Chamberlain informed King George VI that he could no longer carry on.

It was Chamberlain's wish, and the King's, that Lord Halifax succeed him as Premier. But the Labour Party was adamant. The Party's leaders, Clement Attlee and Arthur Greenwood, abandoned their party conference at Bournemouth to make clear that the only Conservative under whom the Labour Party was willing to serve in a national government was Churchill. Thus, at 6 pm that day, the King summoned Churchill to Buckingham Palace and invited him to form a government. My grandfather always regarded it as a supreme irony that it had taken the combined efforts of Hitler and the Labour Party to make him Prime Minister, and in his *Second World War* memoirs he movingly records his emotion at that historic moment:

> Thus then, on the night of the tenth of May, at the outset of this mighty battle, I acquired the chief power in the State, which henceforth I wielded in ever-growing measure for five years and three months of world war ...
> ... as I went to bed at about 3 am, I was conscious of a profound sense of relief. At last I had the authority to give directions over the whole scene. I felt as if I were walking with destiny, and all my past life had been but a preparation for this hour and for this trial.

My grandparents moved from Admiralty House to 10 Downing Street where, almost immediately, my grandfather had to grapple with the plight of the British Expeditionary Force in France, whose position was becoming rapidly untenable in the face of the momentum of the German *blitzkrieg*. Hitler's tanks were smashing through the Low Countries, and nearly cut off the British forces before they could be evacuated from the beaches of Dunkirk.

In June my mother, who was five months pregnant with me, moved into Downing Street with my grandparents to be near her doctor, and would spend weekends with them at Chequers. By this time Hitler had made himself master of continental Europe, where no organized resistance remained to the Hun soldiery, every country having either been occupied or remained neutral.

Great Britain alone, succoured by her Dominions and Empire, remained in the field to challenge Hitler's supremacy and thwart his ambition. But even the friends of Britain abroad believed it would only be a matter of weeks before she, too, would be forced to run up the white flag of surrender, and then all effective resistance would be at an end. Hitler was already marshalling thousands of vessels, landing-craft and barges in the ports and estuaries of the French, Dutch and Belgian coasts, ready to launch his invasion armies against Britain. His plan for the conquest of Britain, code-named Operation Sea-Lion, awaited only the achievement of air superiority by the Luftwaffe to be put into effect.

My mother recalls an evening during this anxious time when, as was often the case, she dined alone with my grandparents at Downing Street. My grandfather warned them both in the sternest terms that Britain could be invaded at any moment. Suddenly he turned to my mother and grandmother across the dining table and declared: 'If that should happen, I am counting on each of you to take at least one German with you!' When my mother protested that she did not have a gun and would not know how to fire one anyway, my grandfather retorted: 'But my dear, you can always use a carving knife!' It was with this single-minded, even ruthless, determination to resist the enemy, however hopeless the situation might seem, that he was able to inspire the British nation to feats of which it did not know it was capable.

This was a time when, because of the neglect of Britain's defences over two decades, the British Army was almost entirely lacking in modern equipment. My father's cavalry regiment was a prime example: though their horses had been removed they still had no tanks. Meanwhile the Home Guard stood ready to repel invaders, armed only with a ramshackle collection of rifles of Boer War vintage, shotguns and pitchforks. The Royal Navy would, of course, play its part, but my grandfather had no illusions but that the fate of Britain would be decided by the battle in the air.

As the German air raids against Britain built towards a crescendo in what was to be known as the Battle of Britain, a makeshift air raid shelter was created in the wine cellar below Downing Street. My mother and grandmother, together with an increasingly grumbling Prime Minister, were forced to spend several nights underground. This was some months before the elaborate network of bunkers under the Number 10 Annexe by Storey's Gate, now known as the Cabinet War Rooms and recently opened to the public, had been built. My mother recounts:

At the far end of the wine cellar, there was a little room where they put two bunks one above the other. At the other end there was a room with a single bed. So Clemmie [my grandmother] had the single bed and Winston and I – together with the 'Baby Dumpling' [the author, as yet unborn] – shared the double-decker. We used to have dinner at 8 pm because, most evenings, the sirens would go at 9 pm and I would immediately be sent below. I would fall sound asleep until about 1 or 1.30 in the morning when Papa [as my mother called Grandpapa] would come down and climb up the narrow ladder into the top bunk. That was the end of my sleep because, within two minutes of arriving in his bunk, he would be snoring. He would snore most of the night and the 'Baby Dumpling' would kick for the rest of it. So between the two of them the only sleep I got was before Winston arrived and after about 6 am when he got up and went back to his own bed when the raids were over.

Meanwhile my father, still with his unit in training in Yorkshire, was growing more and more frustrated at seeing no action and at the failure of the 4th Hussars to be posted overseas. Then, out of the blue, he received an invitation to stand as a candidate for the Parliamentary seat of Preston in Lancashire. He leapt at the opportunity and, following his speech on 12 September addressed to the Preston Conservative Association, found himself unanimously adopted as their candidate for the forthcoming by-election. In his address, according to the account in the *Lancashire Daily Post*:

Mr Churchill explained that if he was adopted and returned, so long as the war lasted, the Army naturally would have first call upon his time. (Applause). He might not, therefore, be able to come to Preston as often as he would wish. He had spent that morning walking round the streets of London, in the City and in the East End, surveying the havoc that had been wrought by the German air bombardment. It was, particularly in the East End, a pathetic and terrible sight to see the houses of so many poor people blasted to bits – whole walls blown away, all their personal belongings and possessions, the results of the savings of a lifetime, scattered and strewn about the roads. But what really moved him was not the spectacle of the damage, but the courage and cheerfulness of the people subjected to this disaster and, in particular, of the people who had been rendered homeless ...

'I am sure from what I saw this morning (observed Mr Churchill) that every Londoner would rather see the entire City razed to the ground in a rubble heap than be under the heel of Hitler.' (Loud applause.) These feelings he believed were shared by all the people of the country ... Fear was the quality that brought ruin to a nation. No nation was ever ruined by courage, sacrifice or suffering. A great nation placed sacrifice and heroism above destruction and death, and if that was their spirit today there could not be the slightest doubt about their ultimate triumph ...

It was an ironic twist of fate that my father, who was always looking for a fight and who, though not yet thirty years of age, had contested no fewer than three very lively by-elections, should finally find himself returned to the House of Commons without so much as a contest, as a party truce had come into force with the creation of the National Government. After all the drama of Wavertree, the hurly-burly of West Toxteth and the tramping through the snows of Ross and Cromarty in the Western Highlands, it must have been something of an anticlimax for him to arrive in Parliament without enduring any of the excitement of the hustings.

On 8 October my father took his seat in the House of Commons where he was introduced by his father. John Carvel reported in the *Star* the next day:

Yesterday was a big Churchill occasion at Westminster. In addition to his review of the war in which he [the Prime Minister] dealt with home and foreign affairs, he introduced his son to Parliament. Mr Randolph Churchill took his seat for Preston. It was a rare spectacle to see a Prime Minister act as one of the sponsors for his son; the other was the Chief Whip. In fact, the last occasion on which a Prime Minister stood sponsor to a new Member was in 1919, when Mr

Lloyd George and Lord Balfour escorted Lady Astor – the first woman to take her seat – to the table.

Yesterday's cheers left no doubt about the esteem in which the Prime Minister is held in every part of the House. Here came the third generation of Churchills to a Chamber which has been successively dominated by his grandfather and father. Lord Randolph arrived in 1847, the Prime Minister in 1900. With two short intervals the family have had one prominent member at least for more than sixty years.

How true is the classic saying that the new MP is his father's son. So far his career has run parallel with that of his father. I have seen him battle away in a by-election with the assurance of a mature Winston. He was only 23 when he fought his first by-election in Wavertree. It was also in Lancashire that his father made his first attempt to enter Parliament when he was 24. He went into that contest in Oldham in 1899, already known as a dashing officer and a dashing war correspondent, with a cavalryman's *élan*. Yesterday the son took his seat in the uniform of a subaltern in his father's former regiment the 4th Hussars ... One great quality at least the young man has – audacity ...

My father's old friend Quintin Hogg [later Lord Hailsham and Lord Chancellor of England] – against whom he had once campaigned in the wake of the Munich Agreement with the slogan 'A Vote for Hogg is a vote for Hitler!' – greeted his arrival at Westminster with the accolade: 'Well, Randolph, it took a major war to get *you* into the House of Commons!'

Two days after my father took his seat in the House of Commons I was born at Chequers and, three weeks later, on Sunday 1 December – the morning after my grandfather had celebrated his 66th birthday – I was christened at the nearby Parish Church of Ellesborough by the Rector, the Rev. C. N. White. It was my grandfather's wish, as well as that of my parents, that, born in an hour when Britain's survival depended, more than ever before in our nation's history, upon one man, I should bear his name. However, a drama had arisen a short while before when the Duke of Marlborough's wife, Mary, who had given birth to a son in July, announced that she was going to name him Winston. My mother, on learning of this, went to my grandfather in floods of tears, imploring him to intervene, which he agreed to do. Mary, even when confronted by a Prime Minister, was no pushover and demanded tartly: 'How does Pamela know that hers will be a boy?' To which my grandfather replied with assurance: 'If it isn't this time, it will be next time!' Thus I was christened Winston Spencer Churchill, while the Marlborough's son was named Charles. My grandfather could never know the scrapes that bearing his name would lead me into in later life, including being arrested at sub-machine gun point in North Africa and being beaten up by Mayor Daley's police in Chicago at the time of the Democratic National Convention in 1968.

The name Spencer derived from the fact that John Churchill, the great Duke of Marlborough who first brought glory to the family name, had no male heir to reach marriageable age. By Act of Parliament the dukedom was allowed to pass through the female line by way of his daughter Henrietta Godolphin who succeeded to the Dukedom as 2nd Duchess in her own right, when her son died the succession passed through her sister, Anne, who married Charles Spencer, Earl of Sunderland. We are in reality not Churchills at all but Spencers. However, in 1817 George, 5th Duke of Marlborough (about whom my aunt, Mary Soames, has recently written a most entertaining life entitled *The Profligate Duke*) was granted a Royal Licence to combine the arms of Churchill (a lion rampant) with those of Spencer (a griffin's head) and revive the name of Churchill by hyphenating it with that of Spencer. Spencer-Churchill remains to this day the correct family name, although my great-grandfather, Lord Randolph Churchill, who regarded hyphenated names as an abomination, dropped the hyphen, retaining the Spencer as a middle name, a style which his heirs have followed to this day.

I had three godfathers. Max Beaverbrook, the remarkable, buccaneering newspaper tycoon who had arrived in England from Canada in 1910 and within a few years was making and breaking British governments, had recently been appointed Minister of Aircraft Production, charged with speeding the flow of fighter-aircraft from the factories to the RAF. Brendan Bracken, an eccentric Irishman with a wild shock of red hair who hailed from Australia and, after befriending my grandfather, entered Parliament where he became his Parliamentary Private Secretary and, subsequently, Minister of Information. The third was Lord Brownlow, former Equerry to the Duke of Windsor. My godmother, Virginia Cowles, was a distinguished American war correspondent whom my father had met while reporting the Spanish Civil War. She was one of the very few to cover that conflict from both sides and went on to report the Finnish–Soviet war as well as the North African campaign of the Second World War, accompanying US Forces up through Italy and into France. In her book *Winston Churchill – the Great Man* she recalls her surprise at the emotion shown by my grandfather at my christening:

I had always heard that the PM's emotions were easily stirred and that at times he could be as sentimental as a woman. On this occasion I had proof of it, for he sat throughout the ceremony with tears streaming down his cheeks. 'Poor infant,' he murmured, 'to be born into such a world as this.'

· II ·

The Blitz

Shortly before my birth my mother, desperate to find a home they could call their own, had managed to lease a small Queen Anne rectory, Ickleford House, near Hitchin in Hertfordshire some 30 miles North of London. She recalls that it had pretty white panelling, a single bath and the rent was £52 a year. In late October, while still staying at Chequers, she wrote my father a letter bubbling with excitement and anticipation:

Oh! My darling how lovely to get into our own house. Too much officialness is getting me beat.

The news the German Press Agency have put out about Vichy France ... couldn't be blacker. Papa [my grandfather] is very upset & says it will lengthen the war considerably – all the fleet, bases, colonies, all to be used against us. Alsace-Lorraine and Savoy all to become German – it's unbelievable isn't it. 'For the French a blush, for France a tear', I only hope it frightens the Americans into action ...

We had a bomb near here last night – a terrific noise, it even woke Baby Winston up ... Papa came and saw Winston this afternoon & was very sweet with him. He has so much character now, & I'm getting to know him quite well. Oh! Randy everything would be so nice, if only you were with us all the time ... Soon, so soon now, I shall be settled in a home of my own, our home – yours & mine & baby Winston's – Oh my darling isn't it rather thrilling – our own family life – no more living in other people's houses.

Shortly after my christening my mother and I moved from Chequers into our new home, where my father joined us when he was able to get a few days leave from the Army. The first guests were the Maiskys, the Russian Ambassador and his wife, who described the house as 'very cold and uncomfortable'. Other early visitors were Cecil Beaton and Lord and Lady Melchett. My mother got back her old nanny, Nanny Hall, who had looked after her from her birth at Farnborough twenty years before.

Shortly after arriving at Ickleford my mother volunteered for war work, helping the local Women's Voluntary Services run a soup kitchen for factory workers from the nearby town of Hitchin. This was one of the 'Communal Feeding Centres', to whose name my grandfather had taken the strongest exception, prompting on 21 March 1941 one of his pithy wartime minutes, this one addressed to the Minister of Food: 'It is an odious expression, suggestive of Communism and the workhouse. I suggest you call them "British Restaurants". Everybody associates the word "restaurant" with a good meal, and they may as well have the name if they cannot get anything else.'

On 26 November, my father made his maiden speech in the House of Commons. His father was on the Treasury Bench for the occasion, and both my mother and Grandmother Churchill were in the Gallery to hear him. *The Times*, which carried a lengthy report the next day, recorded:

The debate in the House of Commons today on the Address in reply to the King's Speech ranged over many topics and was enlivened by an admirable maiden speech by Mr Randolph Churchill. Mr Churchill, wearing Army uniform, spoke of war aims as seen by the younger generation . . .

In the course of his speech my father spoke of 'the very great patience which the army has been able to show under such trying and difficult conditions of inaction'. But patience was a virtue with which my father was not overly endowed and such as he had was being tried to the limit. After more than a year of war he had yet to hear a shot fired in anger.

When, therefore, he learned that his friend Lt-Col. Robert Laycock was forming a Commando unit to be trained for special operations and that many of his friends – in fact most of the White's Club brigade including Peter Beatty (younger son of Admiral of the Fleet Sir David Beatty who had commanded at the Battle of Jutland in the First War), Dermot Daly, Philip Dunne, Peter Milton, Harry Stavordale, Robin Campbell and Evelyn Waugh – were joining, my father could not restrain himself and put in for an immediate transfer. Number 8 Commando, which was undergoing training at Largs on the Ayrshire coast near Glasgow, consisted of ten troops of 50 men, each commanded by a captain and two subaltern section leaders. The men were drawn from the Household Cavalry, Grenadiers, Coldstream, Scots Greys, Irish and Welsh Guards as well as some specialists from the Royal Engineers, Royal Artillery and Royal Marines. On top of this tough, efficient bunch of soldiers was superimposed the command structure recruited from the bar of White's Club, whose members were more noted for their high gambling and heavy drinking than for their military prowess.

Evelyn Waugh, who had been seconded to Number 8 Commando from the Royal Marines, recorded in his diary:*

> The smart set drink a very great deal, play cards for high figures, dine nightly in Glasgow, and telephone to their [racehorse] trainers endlessly ... The standard of efficiency and devotion to duty, particularly among the officers is very much lower than in the Marines. There is no administration or discipline ...
>
> The indolence and ignorance of the officers seemed remarkable, but I have since realized they were slightly above normal army standards. Great freedom was allowed in costume; none even pretended to work outside working hours ... Two night operations in which I acted as umpire showed great incapacity in the simplest tactical ideas. One troop leader was unable to read a compass. The troops, however, had a smarter appearance on inspection parades, arms drill was good, the officers were clearly greatly liked and respected. The men had no guard duties. After parade they were free from all restraint and were often disorderly. There was already a slight undercurrent of impatience that they had not yet been put into action ...

Number 8 Commando were training for an operation code-named Workshop, for the proposed seizure of the Mediterranean island of Pantellaria near the heel of Italy. This involved several assault-landing exercises and, especially, night operations. My mother had an even more jaundiced view of their efficiency than Evelyn:

> They used to go out on these night raids at about three in the morning. At 0500 hours Troop A were supposed to make their assault landing on the beaches by landing craft. Troop B were to try and catch them at it. Peter Beatty – he was impossible at anything, even worse than Evelyn – was given a stopwatch and was put in charge of the landing group. '0500 hours will be the moment your troops will land,' Bob Laycock had ordered. 5 am came and went, and 5.30, but still nothing had happened. So Bob radioed to Peter Beatty to demand what had become of the assault party. Peter feebly explained: 'It's dark and I can't see my watch.'
>
> That was the sort of thing Bob was up against. Soon they gave up the water expeditions and started up the mountains. When they got to the other side of the mountains they of course didn't know what they were supposed to do next – how those poor soldiers stood for it!
>
> In the meantime, the war was going on and the Commandos remained uncommitted. Evelyn was cooking up more and more devious plots while Randolph would telephone his father to demand: 'Aren't there a few more technical weapons that we ought to have? Hasn't the Prof. [Professor Lindemann, the Prime Minister's Scientific Adviser] come up with any new devices?'

'Then,' my mother relates, 'the worst happened. No sooner had Randolph joined the Commandos than the 4th Hussars were sent overseas. Their wives naturally said it was because Randolph Churchill had been

---

* *The Diaries of Evelyn Waugh*, Weidenfeld & Nicolson 1976.

given another posting that their husbands were being sent overseas to their deaths. Randolph was most upset at this and was on the point of trying to get transferred back to his old regiment when it was learned that the Commandos were to be sent to the Middle East. In fact, the 4th Hussars were sent to Crete – an operation which proved disastrous and resulted in practically all of them being wiped out.'

Meanwhile the bombing of London and the Home Counties was intensifying and my father became concerned for our safety. He wrote on 30 December 1940: 'We have just heard the news of the blitz on London ... Do please stay quietly & buy a shovel & a bucket of sand for dealing with incendiaries ...'

Just before Christmas, my mother reported to my father from Chequers: 'We saw *The Great Dictator* with Charlie Chaplin as Hitler. Papa adored it and thought it frightfully funny when Mussolini & Hitler began throwing food in each other's faces!' That was my first Christmas, and I spent it with my parents and grandparents at Chequers where we were joined by my Aunt Sarah, with her husband Vic Oliver, Aunt Diana with her husband Duncan Sandys and Aunt Mary. It was to be the last Christmas the family was to spend together for many years.

Early in the new year of 1941 Number 8 Commando was ordered to Egypt to do battle with the German–Italian army under the command of Field Marshal Rommel. Due to the presence of German U-boats and the lack of friendly air cover, it was impossible for the troopships to take the direct route through the Straits of Gibraltar and the Mediterranean. Instead they had to take the long way round Africa by way of Cape Town and the Suez Canal.

In early February they set sail from England in the *Glenroy*. Evelyn Waugh records in his wartime diary:

The conditions of overcrowding were worse than ever. Number 11 Commando were very young and quiet, over-disciplined, unlike ourselves in every way but quite companionable. They trained indefatigably all the voyage. We did very little except PT and one or two written exercises for the officers. Bob [Laycock] took me for Force HQ as Adjutant, to be promoted to Brigade Major if we became a brigade. There was very high gambling, poker, roulette, chemin-de-fer, every night. Randolph lost £850 in two evenings. We stopped at Cape Town where people treated all ranks with the most notable hospitality. Harry [Stavordale] ill-treated the ostriches in the zoo. Randolph lunched with Smuts [the South African Premier]. Dermot [Daly] got very drunk.

On 8 March we reached Suez and proceeded up the Canal, which was reported to be mined, to Kabrit in the Bitter Lakes ... At Kabrit General Evetts came on board and spoke to the officers. He said we were to serve with his Division (6th) and promised us a bellyful of fighting.

When my father sailed for the Middle East my mother, to economize, invited my Aunt Diana Sandys, together with her children, to share our house at Ickleford. She had £12 per week to keep the two of us and was continuing her work at the communal kitchen where 200-300 people were being fed each day.

According to my mother, my father told her before leaving: 'It's going to be terrible, being parted like this. But with you living very economically and I living off my Army pay we will at least be able to pay off some of the bills and that will be glorious.' Sadly, that was not the way things turned out. 'The house was very cold,' my mother recalls. 'We didn't have much heat and so I used to go to bed at 6.30, so as to turn off the gas fires. By day I settled down to life at my communal kitchen.' But within three weeks of my father's departure, my mother received devastating news in a telegram followed up by a letter from Cape Town. It was a bombshell which was to shatter their marriage. In the letter my father confessed that he had lost a fortune gambling with his rich friends on the troopship. He enjoined her on no account to tell his father but to arrange payment 'in the best way possible', suggesting 'payments on the instalments plan of perhaps £10 per month to each of the following ...'

Until her marriage, my mother had never been even a penny in debt, but since then worries about bills, debts and people threatening to sue had been endless. To my mother, not yet twenty-one, this letter was the last straw. In tears she went to see their close friend, my godfather, Max Beaverbrook. But Beaverbrook, who was generously continuing to pay my father's £1,500 a year salary with the *Evening Standard*, was adamant. He would give my mother a cheque as a present but he would not advance one penny of my father's salary. She thereupon decided to rent out the house at Ickleford, park me with a nanny at Cherkley, Beaverbrook's country home, so that my Churchill grandparents would not know what had happened, and took a £12 a week job at the Ministry of Supply.

My mother paid off the debts, but things were never to be the same between my parents. Looking back on that time she recalls: 'I sold all my wedding presents, including some diamond earrings and a couple of nice bracelets. We eventually got it all paid, but it was a lesson. I suddenly realized that if there was to be any security for Baby Winston and me, it was going to be on our own ...'

On 8 June my grandfather wrote to inform my father that Averell Harriman, President Roosevelt's personal representative who had been a frequent visitor at Chequers and Downing Street in recent weeks, would shortly be arriving in Egypt on a fact-finding mission to report on the progress of the campaign in the Middle East:

Darling Randolph,

Averell Harriman is travelling out to the Middle East, and I take the opportunity of sending you a line. There is so much to say. One hardly knows where to begin.

Harriman's daughter [Kathy, who later was to marry Stanley Mortimer], who is charming, and Pamela have made friends and are going to take a small house together while he is away. It seems a pity that the house that was furnished at Ickleford is not available. Still, you are getting a very good rent.

A gigantic 4000 pound bomb fell just outside the building of your flat in Westminster Gardens, obliterating the fountain and cracking the whole structure on one side. Unluckily it is the wrong side for you. The CIGS [Chief of the Imperial General Staff, Field Marshal Sir John Dill] who was sleeping quite close, in fact about twenty yards away, seems to have had a marvellous escape and is greatly exhilarated by the explosion. I am trying to get a similar stimulus applied in other quarters, but it is difficult to arrange.

The [Downing Street] Annexe is now becoming a very strong place, but we have only once been below the armour during a raid. Your mother is now insisting upon becoming a fire watcher on the roof, so it will look very odd if I take advantage of the securities provided. However, I suppose everybody must do their duty ...

I see Pamela from time to time, and she gives me very good accounts of Winston. I have not seen him as he is living in Max's domains.

The air attack has greatly lessened, and the Air Force are very disappointed that this moon-phase should have been spoiled by clouds, as they were hoping to make an impression upon the raiders. On the whole, I think the attack will not be so successful as it has been in the past, and at the moment we are having very little of it. Anyhow, I think the Baby is quite safe where he is ...

Our old House of Commons has been blown to smithereens. You never saw such a sight. Not one scrap was left of the Chamber except a few of the outer walls. The Huns obligingly chose a time when none of us were there. Oddly enough, on the last day but one before it happened I had a most successful Debate and wound up amid a great demonstration. They all got up and cheered as I left. I shall always remember this last scene. Having lived so much of my last forty years in this building, it seems very sad that its familiar aspect will not for a good many years be before me. Luckily we have the other place in good working order, so that Parliamentary institutions can function 'undaunted amid the storms'. We are now going to try the experiment of using the House of Lords. The Peers have very kindly moved on into the big Robing Room, and handed over their Debating Chamber to us. In about a fortnight I expect we shall be there. I never thought to make speeches from those red benches, but I daresay I shall take to it all right ...

Meanwhile, in the larger sphere, not only are we gaining mastery over the air attack, but making good progress in the Battle of the Atlantic. The United States are giving us more help every day, and longing for an opportunity to take the plunge. Whether they will do so or not remains an inscrutable mystery of American politics ...

Everything is very solid here, and I feel more sure than ever that we shall beat the life out of Hitler and his Nazi gang ... It looks to me more and more likely that Hitler will go for Stalin. [Precisely two weeks later, German forces with 150 divisions invaded the Soviet Union, its erstwhile ally.] I cannot help it. All my sympathies are already fully engaged.

I am having this letter left for you at the Embassy, Cairo, and am asking them to tell you that it has arrived. I do not want it to go up the line, and after you have received it, you should not take it there. Leave it at the Embassy, or burn it. Do not show it to strangers. I am glad that Lampson [Sir Miles Lampson, British Ambassador to Egypt] and his wife have been nice to you, and I am sure it is a comfort to have a good hot bath and a clean bed there when you come in from the Desert.

All good luck.

> My very best wishes
> Your loving father
> Winston S. Churchill

PS I send you a cheque for £100 which I expect you can get cashed in Cairo.

My father, who had been asked by my grandfather to look after Harriman during his visit to Cairo, reported to my mother on 5 July:

This letter will be brought to you by Averell Harriman who will be able to tell you all my news direct. And I am sending back by him a long dictated letter to Papa which you might get him to show you. So I won't give you a long account of our travels. I found him absolutely charming & it was lovely to be able to hear so much news of you & all my friends. He spoke delightfully about you & I fear that I have a serious rival!

Little could my father know the truth of his words. Indeed, thirty years on, in 1971, Averell and my mother were to marry and, although he was by then nearly eighty years of age, they were to enjoy fifteen years of happy marriage together before his death. The second letter Averell carried back with him was addressed to my grandfather.

> Alexandria
> 5 July 1941

My dear Papa,

This letter should reach you very speedily through the hands of Averell Harriman, with whom I have spent the last 10 days.

I was suddenly summoned from a place of which he will give you the name to report to GHQ in Cairo ...

It was indeed kind of you to suggest that I should be attached to the Harriman Mission. I have thereby not only obtained all the latest news of you and Pamela, and all my friends in London, but have also had a wonderful opportunity of learning about things out here. I have been tremendously impressed by Harriman, and can well understand the regard which you have for him. In 10 very full and active days he has definitely become my favourite American. He seems to me to possess a quite extraordinary maturity of judgment that is almost on a par with F.E.'s [F.E. Smith, the 1st Earl of Birkenhead]. He got down to work out here with amazing ease and sure-footedness, and has won the confidence of everyone he met. I have become very intimate with him and he has admitted me to all the business he has transacted. I am sure you would do well to back his opinions on the situation out here to the limit.

We had a very interesting trip down south, of which he will tell you, with Wavell . . .

It has been most cheering to hear from Harriman how well and vigorous you are. I am sure you know what a tremendous admiration he has for you. He clearly regards himself more as your servant than Roosevelt's. I do hope you will keep him at your side as I think he is the most objective and shrewd of all those who are around you. I hope too you will take his advice about American public opinion. I am convinced his view is right.

Thank you so much for your cheque & also for the very generous help you extended to Pamela. That has been a great help.

> Your loving son
> Randolph

For some time my father had been urging upon my grandfather in numerous letters and telegrams the need for a shake up in the whole of Britain's military establishment in North Africa. While the Prime Minister did not find the advice of a junior lieutenant invariably helpful, he nonetheless paid close attention to my father's reports and suggestions. He had a natural inclination to prefer the view from the 'front line' to that conveyed by the rear echelons. One specific point on which he acceded to my father's suggestion was in the decision to appoint a Resident Minister with Cabinet rank in Cairo to supervise and direct the war effort on behalf of the War Cabinet. It was my father's good fortune that the man chosen for the job was Oliver Lyttelton, later Lord Chandos, who was a friend with a high regard for his talents as a journalist. Soon after his arrival in Cairo, Lyttelton appointed my father to the post of Director of Propaganda with responsibility for handling the Press.

This was a task to which my father's talents were admirably suited. He was a natural communicator – something that, in later years, Cabinet ministers were to discover to their cost when roused from their slumbers by calls from my father in his quest for news. In addition to his general duties, he launched a weekly news sheet called *The Desert News*, later known as *Eighth Army News*, to combat the dearth of news among the troops in North Africa. Ken Downs of United Press International recalls: 'With almost ferocious energy and great skill, he began to transform the inept information section into the most efficient operation of its sort that I saw throughout the war. His experience in journalism and his personal acquaintance with the correspondents, particularly the Americans, paid off handsomely.'

In a letter to my mother dated 21 September from General Headquarters, Cairo, my father reported:

I am enjoying it very much & think I am beginning to make some headway: but the forces of obstruction are very strong ...

I am sending you some parcels of foodstuffs which with luck should arrive about Xmas. One v. large tin of honey, which an Egyptian gave me for Winston and three smaller parcels each containing sugar, jam, sweets and marmalades. I hope they will be a help. It seems frightful living in this land of plenty while you are all so tightly rationed at home.

Darling, the picture you sent of Baby W. was divine! He certainly doesn't seem to be starving ...

Darling, I am so glad that you are hearing good accounts of my work. I do terribly want to do something of which you can be proud.

In the spring of 1942 my father, recently promoted to the rank of Captain and anxious to escape from his desk duties in Cairo and see some action, volunteered to join a detachment of the Special Air Service that was being formed by his friend David Stirling. This involved some rigorous training, including parachuting.

Very soon after joining the SAS he took part with David Stirling and five other members of the Long Range Desert Group on a raid against Benghazi, several hundred miles behind enemy lines, with the aim of blowing up ships in the harbour, which was the major resupply point on the Libyan coast for the German–Italian Army. Returning from the raid their vehicle was hit by an Army lorry on the road from Alexandria to Cairo, and rolled over twice. The *Daily Telegraph* war correspondent, Arthur Merton, to whom they had given a lift in Alexandria, was killed and everyone else, including my father, was fairly seriously injured. The exception was David Stirling, the driver, who in my father's words, 'had the luck of the devil' and was unscathed, setting off the very next morning on another sabotage raid.

My father reported his progress in a letter to my mother:

> 4, Sharia El Gabalaya,
> Gezira
> 1 July 1942

My Darling Pamela,

... The new photographs of Winston which arrived 3 days ago are enchanting – particularly those of him walking in the street.

I have now been out of hospital about a week but I still have to take things fairly easily. I stay in bed all morning & when I get up I have to wear a brace which is pretty uncomfortable ...

It is vile being immobilised at a time like this. I just sit here getting scraps of news, hearing rumours & hoping that all will be well. It is difficult not to be gloomy.

Bless you darling. Don't worry about me, I love you so much. Kiss Baby Winston from me. And be nice to Alexander!

> All my love darling
> Randy

Alexander, named after the Field Marshal, was a beautiful white Pekinese. Like many small dogs, Alexander was inclined to be snappy and one day he nipped me, for which offence, and to my dismay, he was sent away. Thereafter the only pet I had during the wartime years was a magnificent blue-grey Persian cat named Eisenhower but which I knew as 'Kitty-Winks'.

It was not until late October that my father was declared fit and able to return to his unit. By this time the war was going better for the Allies. The Americans, having been bombed into the war by the Japanese at Pearl Harbor in December 1941, were now arriving in Britain and North Africa in strength. They brought with them vast quantities of military equipment. With the victorious Battle of Alamein, the tide in the desert war had turned in Britain's favour and, soon after, the landing of American forces in Tunisia, in an operation code-named Torch, rendered Rommel's position in North Africa untenable.

Grandpapa gave an account of the drastically improved situation in a hastily written note to my father:

> Lyneham Air Port,
> Midnight 19-xi-42

Dearest Randolph,
I have come down here to see F.M. Smuts off, & I take the chance of sending you a line.

All is well here at home, & Winston & his mother are completely installed in their flat. He is coming to see me next week. From all I hear he flourishes.

Our affairs have gone wonderfully well, & I have had most enthusiastic messages from Uncle Joe [Stalin]. Rommel's remnants are in the toils & it may well be a clear mop-up for them.

But the key to the future is the Tunis leg & that I hope you will be taking a hand in yourself. All good luck attend you. Write to me when you can. One of these fine days you will see me turn up from somewhere.

> Your mother sends her love
> Ever your loving father
> Winston S. Churchill

The early years of my childhood were dominated by the war. My very first memories are of Chequers. I vividly recall lying awake at night, watching the flak and tracer from the ack-ack guns firing up into the night sky, framed by the little window at the foot of my bed. The thunderous crashing of the gunfire would send cold shivers of fear down my spine as I huddled under the bed clothes.

My room was at the very top of the house in what is known as the 'Prison Suite', where the tragic Lady Mary Grey, sister of Lady Jane Grey

(Queen of England for ten days following the death of Edward VI and executed with her husband for treason by Queen Mary in 1554), was imprisoned by Queen Elizabeth I. One of its two small windows looks out towards Beacon Hill where, in the woods about a mile from the house, an anti-aircraft battery had been established for the protection of Chequers. Hidden behind the panelling was a very narrow secret staircase, which came up from the floor below.

President Roosevelt's wife, Eleanor, in her book *This I Remember*, recalls of the autumn of 1942:

> I spent a weekend at 'Chequers', the country estate given by Lord Lee to the British Government for the use of British Prime Ministers. There I watched Prime Minister Churchill playing a game on the floor with his grandson and noticed the extraordinary resemblance between the two. Mr Churchill once remarked that his grandson didn't look like him, *he* just looked like all babies.

I thoroughly enjoyed the time I spent at Chequers. It was a wonderful house for a small child to run riot in. On one occasion, which I will never forget, I tried to play a trick on a maid who was hoovering in an adjacent room. Because in those days power-points were few and far between, the Hoover had an inordinately long flex so that it could be used in one room while plugged in in another. As I was playing on the floor with my toys my attention was drawn to a large connector joining two lengths of flex moving jerkily across the floor, pulled by a snake of flex from the adjoining room. I could not resist the temptation to unplug the connector to see what would happen. I got more than I had bargained for. Suddenly there was an incredible blue flash and I got a fierce belt from the 240 volt electric current, the shock and pain of which I have not forgotten to this day. It was possibly this piece of mischief to which my grandfather was alluding in a letter he wrote to my father in North Africa:

10, Downing Street,
Whitehall
April 16, 1943

My dearest Randolph,

... I am glad of your decision to join the North Irish Horse, as it seems to me that you must have been well forward in the small-scale continuous fighting of the First Army, and will no doubt want to see the greater operations of the finale. There is not much scope for Commando work now the Armies are so closely locked and the theatre has become so restricted. Do write & tell me about the fighting you have seen ...

Baby Winston is extremely well. He came to stay at Chequers the week-end before last [marginal note: 'He is coming again tomorrow'], and shows proficiency at bagatelle though he has not yet reached your Casablanca standard. Naturally, as he gets older he develops more personality, which takes the form of 'naughtiness'. But his mother takes infinite pains with him, and with extreme patience makes him yield his point of view. He is very handsome with a noble air. He has got the Eighth Army firmly in his mind, but is not yet apparently aware of the feats of the First . . .

Randolph dear, I see no reason why the war should not be very long, and it would be folly to indulge in comfortable hopes of an early ending. Nevertheless the rascals are getting it pretty hot from the Air as well as from the Russians. They probably have a big disaster facing them in Africa, & I think they are now convinced they cannot win. What a change this is from the days when Hitler danced his jig of joy at Compiegne! [Where in 1940 the French had been required to surrender on the spot where Germany had signed the Armistice in 1918.]

Your mother sends her love. Sarah continues her toil in the Photographic Section [of the RAF]. Mary has been posted to the heavy battery in Hyde Park, & Diana's event* is expected in June. I am going to spend Easter at Chartwell which I have not seen for many months. The valley must be lovely now.

> Always yr loving father
> Winston S. Churchill

Soon after my second birthday, at the end of 1942, my mother and I moved to London where she took a flat at 49 Grosvenor Square, barely five minutes' walk from Hyde Park. Our flat was on the sixth and top floor with spectacular views over the London skyline; '49' was to be our home for nearly ten years, though I was moved to the country when the bombing became particularly intense and continued to spend weekends from time to time with Grandpapa at Chequers.

Having been parked for some considerable time at Lord Beaverbrook's home at Cherkley in Surrey, I was thrilled when I moved, with my mother, into our new flat in the heart of London. At '49' I had a bedroom of my own which combined as a playroom. It had a single dormer window looking west over the rooftops towards Hyde Park where a heavy anti-aircraft battery was stationed and which, like the one at Chequers, provided me with an almost nightly fireworks display.

Those who, like myself were born and brought up during the war – Blitz babies, as we were known – will never forget the piercing, spine-chilling wail of the air raid sirens, shrieking their urgent warning of another German bombing raid. I suppose to conserve electricity, or possibly to avoid people becoming stuck during one of the frequent power cuts, the lift in the building was out of commission. Every time the sirens would sound, which seemed to be most nights, Nanny Hall – 'Old Nanny', as she came to be known – would grab me from my bed, wrap me in a blanket, bundle me down six flights of stairs, out into the street and down some steps to the air raid shelter in the basement.

I enjoyed air raids. They were a great excitement as, no doubt, had been the Zeppelin raids in my father's childhood during the First World War when air raids had been rare and still something of a novelty. Londoners on their way to or from work late at night or returning from the

* Celia, the youngest of the Sandys' three children, was born on 8 May 1943.

theatres (many of which never closed for the war) would dive down into our shelter for safety. As a result there would be a different crowd every night, though the atmosphere seemed always the same. The dank, musty air of the shelter would soon become warm with the crush of forty or fifty people huddled together in the semi-darkness. There would be hot sweet tea and biscuits and frequently sing-songs when all the old music hall songs of the First War ('Pack Up your Troubles in your Old Kit Bag!' and 'It's a Long Way to Tipperary') were rehearsed. What I remember most of all was the warmth of feeling and the friendliness of total strangers facing a common danger. The traditional stuffy British reserve was supplanted by a wonderfully happy community spirit which banished all fears. Inevitably as a small child I was particularly fussed over.

While I relished these nocturnal adventures and excitements and was delighted with my gas mask with a 'Mickey Mouse' face, 'Old Nanny', already sixty years of age, was less amused by them. Indeed she got it into her head that the Germans were playing their games quite deliberately to make more work and inconvenience for her. She thereupon conceived it as her duty not to give in to them. When the next air raid came Nanny 'went on strike', resolutely refusing to take me down to the shelter. My mother, when she learned of this, was furious and raced me downstairs herself. It was at that point that 'Old Nanny' was given her marching orders and was retired. Her place was taken by a governess, Mrs Raiker, known as 'Bobbie', who looked after me from the age of two-and-a-half until I was just four.

With the entry of the Americans into the war and their arrival in large numbers in Britain, my mother, at the suggestion of Brendan Bracken, founded a club – known as the Churchill Club – to enable professional men and women from the US and Canadian armed forces to meet their British counterparts, when off-duty in London, for a meal and a drink or at concerts and lectures. She found premises in Ashburton House, in the precincts of Westminster School, adjacent to Westminster Abbey, and became actively involved in the running of the Club, which was a huge success.

In addition to the excitement of the air raids and the nights spent underground in the air raid shelter, Bobbie would take me for walks to Hyde Park. If there had been any bombs that had fallen nearby in the night, I would insist on being taken to view the damage and see the fire-engines hosing down the smouldering ruins of what had been a block of flats or an office building. But, best of all, were the visits I paid to my Aunt Mary (later Lady Soames) at the heavy anti-aircraft battery in the Park near Marble Arch, where, aged twenty-one, she was one of the ATS officers commanding the guns.

To a three-year-old, having a grandfather who was Prime Minister and running the entire war was a concept difficult to grasp, though I knew he was very important by the way he bossed about all those Generals who were constantly in attendance in their smart uniforms. But to have an aunt who had four huge guns of her very own – that was *something!* I thoroughly enjoyed watching her give the orders as the girls operated the instruments and the man manning the great gun turned the wheels furiously with their hands to swivel the gun and train its barrel up to the sky.

Following a dinner party given by my mother at '49', Max Beaverbrook wrote to remonstrate at my precocious behaviour:

> Cherkley
> Leatherhead
> Surrey
> 13 December 1943

My darling Pamela,

It shocked me a bit when Winston ran down the hall on Thursday to ask me to have a cocktail with him!

I feel that I must intervene at once, on account of the pledges that I made at the altar at the Church at Chequers on a cold winter day.

So I send you £100 for the benefit of Winston, and I hope you will spend the money on his religious instruction.

But if religious instruction should be free – which I have always been led to believe, then of course the £100 had better be spent for his account, and on his behalf, in some other direction.

With love and affection abounding,

> I am,
> Yours ever,
> Max

Then, and right up to his death in 1964, he was always the most generous of godfathers.

Around this time my mother received a touching, somewhat wistful, letter from General de Gaulle, who, following the fall of France, had raised the standard of the Free French in London. In view of my grandfather's quip that 'The greatest cross I have to bear is the Cross of Lorraine!' – the symbol of the Free French adopted by de Gaulle – the General was most generous in his tribute to my grandfather in this letter (which I have translated from the French original) which accompanied a picture-book entitled *L'Histoire de Marlborough:*

LE GENERAL DE GAULLE

> 4 Carlton Gardens,
> London SW1
> Le   194[3?]

Dear Madame,

Permit me to send you for your son Winston an old picture book on Marl-borough. It is almost the only thing I brought from France.

If, later, the young Winston Churchill looks through these drawings of Caran d'Ache, perhaps he will spare a moment's thought for a French General who was, in the greatest war in history, the sincere admirer of his grandfather and the faithful ally of his country.

I beg you to accept, dear Madame, my respectful homage,

C. de Gaulle

Early in the new year of 1944 my father parachuted into Yugoslavia with Fitzroy Maclean to fight with the partisans in the mountain fastnesses of Bosnia. Their mission was to work alongside the partisan leader, Marshal Tito, and to assist his guerrilla fighters, especially with the air-dropping of supplies and equipment from RAF bases in newly liberated Southern Italy. My father, in a letter to my grandfather dated 26 March 1944, described Tito as living 'in an eyrie with a rocky and precipitous approach. His office is all lined with parachute silk and looks more like the *nid d'amour* of a luxurious courtesan than the office of a guerrilla leader.' My father's accommodation in the remote mountain village of Drvar was clearly not quite so commodious for in a letter of 14 May, thanking my grandmother for a parcel of books, he reported: 'I got back here to find a new born baby in the house in which I live with the pig, the six Bosnian girls and the intelligence officer ...'

Some ten days later the Germans made a large-scale attack on Drvar with parachute forces, backed up by Stuka dive-bombers, in the hope of capturing Tito as well as, no doubt, the British Prime Minister's only son whom they knew to be there. After some stiff fighting the partisans, together with the small British mission, managed to escape into the hills. My father later told me how, with the Germans hard on their heels, they nonetheless found time to pick the wild strawberries that were to be found in abundance in the woods.

On my father's thirty-third birthday my grandfather sent him a line by the hand of General Ira Eaker, Commander-in-Chief of Allied Air Forces in the Mediterranean:

10 Downing Street
Whitehall
Sunday, May 28, 1944

Dearest Randolph,

Eaker is here and is starting immediately, so this is a chance to send you a line. We are naturally following with some anxiety the news of the attack on Tito's Headquarters. But today the report is that the airborne Huns have been liquidated, and there only remain the forces trying to surround you. I cannot do more than wish you good luck, but you are ever in my thoughts and in those of all (repeat all) here. We have a lovely day at where we live from time to time [Chequers], and all is fair with the first glory of summer. The War is very fierce and terrible, but in these sunlit lawns and buttercup meadows, it is hard to conjure up its horrors.

Baby Winston, as you will no doubt have been told by Pamela, has developed German measles. I am ashamed to say I told him it was the fault of the Germans, but I shall labour to remove this impression quite soon.

> With all my love
> Yr loving father
> Winston S. Churchill

General Eaker made a very favourable impression upon me. This was, doubtless, not unconnected with the fact that, while at Chequers, he presented me with a splendid model of a Flying Fortress bomber which I knew as 'General Eaker's plane'.

An intimate glimpse of life at Chequers at this time is afforded by the diary of one of my grandfather's secretaries, Marion Walker Spicer:

Saturday, 22nd April 1944. Chequers
Arrived at midday ... The Maharajah of Kashmir came to lunch with the PM and there was a Guard of Honour in the Court Yard for him. The official photographers ... took several in the office and some outside of us with Baby Winston. General Doolittle, who led the first air attack on Tokyo was here. The after-dinner films started at 11.30 – *This Happy Breed* by Noël Coward, wonderful entertainment. Film finished at 1.45 am. The PM worked on until 3.30 am. It was quiet in the Office. He was studying a document when he suddenly said 'There's a pussy mewing.' It turned out to be General Ismay wheezing. Apparently he is sometimes known as 'the whispering strategist'.

I find it quite remarkable, looking back from the vantage point of middle life, the amount of time that my grandfather found to devote to me and my doings amidst all his worries and responsibilities of the war. Later that summer Marion Spicer recorded the usual Monday morning dash back from Chequers to Downing Street:

Monday, 17th July 1944. Chequers
Played with Baby Winston and [my cousin] Edwina Sandys in the Rose Garden. Accompanied the PM in the car. The children were waving goodbye and yelling 'Don't go Grandpa!' The PM said 'What a world to bring children into!' The chauffeur touched 70 mph and the PM was dictating. Quite a balancing act with the despatch boxes and papers. The PM dictated a letter to Baby Winston and asked if I would type it on the new electric typewriter [the D-Day gift of President Roosevelt]. For posterity? ...

Shortly after D-Day on 6 June 1944 and the invasion by Anglo-American forces one million strong, my father came back from Yugoslavia to report to my grandfather on the situation there. However, a month later, as he was returning to Yugoslavia, the Dakota transport in which he was flying with his friend Evelyn Waugh, whom he had recruited to the Yugoslav mission, crashed on landing in the hills near Topusco and caught fire. Although injured himself, my father went back into the blazing wreckage in a vain attempt to rescue his batman, Douglas Sowman who, earlier in the year had on his own initiative undertaken a parachute course so as to be able to join my father in Yugoslavia.

The crew of four, together with six of the fifteen passengers, perished and most of the survivors suffered injuries or burns. On learning of the crash my grandmother sent my father a telegram which reached him a fortnight later:

PAMELA WENT DOWN TO COLWORTH TO SEE LITTLE WINSTON AND HAS SICKENED THERE WITH SCARLET FEVER. THE CHILD IS ISOLATED.

YOUR FATHER AND I BOTH HOPE THAT YOU ARE MAKING GOOD PROGRESS. I HAVE WRITTEN TO MRS SOWMAN.

MAMA

Possibly due to the intensified bombing of London, I had been sent to stay for a while with Henry and Gwen Melchett at Colworth, their home in Bedfordshire. From there my governess, Bobbie, wrote a letter on my behalf to my father:

Colworth House,
Sharnbrook,
Bedford
August 3rd [1944]

My darling Father,

I hope you are better. When are you coming home? I hope it will be soon. We all had a lovely weekend together when you were here. Bobbie and I are staying with Auntie Gwen and Uncle Henry for a few weeks. We are having a very nice time fishing, swimming, punting and going out in the pony-cart ... Mummy has got a cottage in Sussex on Mrs Wallace's estate. We are going there about the first week in September to live. Uncle Henry is going to take us to Chequers on Sunday to see my grandfather ...

Will you please take us to the sea when you come home. Mummy said she does not like it there. But I would like to go very much. I wonder if you will be in England for my birthday in October. With my love and a big hug and kiss. Love from everybody at Colworth to you.

From your
Winston

Some three weeks earlier, again with the help of Bobbie, I had written to Grandpapa telling him how much I enjoyed being with him at Chequers. Grandpapa replied in the first letter I have from him:

10 Downing Street
Whitehall
July 17, 1944

Darling Winston,

I was delighted to get your charming letter last week. It is always a pleasure to me to hear from you. I hope particularly to have a letter from you in your new home, which I hope you will enjoy.

I shall look about and see if I can find either the train or the bicycle motorcar. Owing to the war, it may be difficult finding what you want. You should also write often to your papa as I know your letters are very welcome, especially now that he is at the wars.

> I remain,
> Your loving grandfather
> Winston S. Churchill

Grandpapa was true to his word and my greatest excitement was the arrival that summer of a wonderful clockwork train set which Grandpapa and Grandmama Churchill had scoured London to find for me secondhand, as no such thing existed in the shops in wartime. Those who never knew him will find it astonishing that, even in his seventieth year with all his weighty responsibilities, he could find time to play trains with his small grandson, getting down on his hands and knees to adjust the track or attend to a derailment. For corroboration of this memory I am indebted to Mrs Kathleen Hill who came to Chartwell in 1937 as Personal Secretary to my grandfather and after the war served as Curator of Chequers, serving six prime ministers up to her retirement in 1969. She recalls a day when her teenage son, Richard, on 'embarkation leave' before setting sail with his regiment for the Far East, was asked by my grandmother to come over to her room in the Downing Street Annexe, now known as the Cabinet War Rooms. The Royal Marine sentries looked askance at a mere private soldier from the Infantry seeking entry. He was shown to my grandmother's room where, still in bed, she asked him to unpack the toy train set intended for me and check that it was in working order. According to Mrs Hill:

The train set consisted of two clockwork engines, some rolling stock and some gauge rails. Richard knelt upon the floor, and arranged the rails to form a circle. While engaged upon this, he noticed close beside him a pair of velvet slippers initialled 'WSC'. He looked up to find looming over him the figure of the Prime Minister wearing his 'siren-suit' [an all-in-one suit with zippered front which he had devised himself and in which he spent much of the war and post-war years] and smoking a large cigar. Richard's efforts to stand up were in vain and he was firmly instructed: 'Carry on with what you are doing.'

Once the circle of rails was completed the Prime Minister ordered: 'Put one of the engines on the track.' This was done and the engine ran around the circle until the clockwork ran down. He then said: 'I see you have two engines. Put the other one on the track as well.' So both engines ran around the circle. When they had stopped, the Prime Minister got down upon his hands and knees on the floor and declared, 'Now, let's have a crash!' Richard, as he was bidden, wound up the two engines and put them on the track, back to back. Of course they duly crashed, much to the Prime Minister's satisfaction! Fortunately, neither engine was damaged. In thanking Richard the Prime Minister said: 'I believe you are going off to India. I have been there!' Then he called for one of the private secretaries to fetch him a copy of 'The Malakand Field Force' which he proceeded to inscribe for Richard who to this day treasures it as one of his proudest possessions.

The train was evidently a great success as confirmed by my mother in a letter to Grandmama of 14 August: 'Winston enjoyed his weekend so much ... but the arrival of the much talked about train is the climax of his life so far. I have never before seen him so excited ...'

Amazingly it survived several months' hard service for, later that autumn, Grandpapa was able to report to my father who was still in Yugoslavia:

> 10 Downing Street
> Whitehall
> November 23, 1944

Dearest Randolph,

... I have only seen Winston once all these months, but he seems very lively and very well, and I am informed that the train is still running. Considering all the railways that have been cut and the general breakdown of communications over large areas, this peculiarly threatened sector seems to have done well, especially as I am assured there has been a good deal of traffic ...

Mary has been promoted to Junior Commander with 3 pips, equal to Captain. She is back at the Hyde Park Battery commanding 230 women. Not so bad at 21! The Battery is to go to the front almost immediately, and will be under a somewhat stiffer rocket fire than we endure with composure here. Mary is very elated at the honour of going to the front, and at the same time bearing up against her responsibilities. So far we are proceeding on the voluntary basis in regard to young women sent into the fight. If we do not get enough that way, they will have to be directed. Many of them have troubles at home with their papas and mamas. When Mary sounded her girls out as to whether they wished to go overseas, the almost universal reply was, 'Not 'arf!'...

God protect us all, especially the young who are retrieving the follies of the past and will, I pray, ward off the worse follies that threaten us in the future.

> All my love
> Yr affectionate father
> Winston S. Churchill

Although plans had been laid for Christmas at Chequers, these had to be changed when Grandpapa, deeply concerned at the way in which Communist guerrillas in Greece were threatening to take over that country, decided to take personal charge of the situation in Athens, where he spent the last Christmas of the war. I went instead with my mother to spend Christmas at Cherkley with Lord Beaverbrook. However, Grandpapa had not forgotten me and sent me a copy of *Aesop's Fables*.

By early 1945, the worst of the bombing was over and I was allowed to move back to 49 Grosvenor Square. The latest threat to London came from the flying-bomb or Doodle-Bug, as the V-Is were known. From our sixth-floor vantage point – and there were few buildings in London at the time much higher than that – we had a grandstand view of London at night. I would stand and point in excitement at the Doodle-Bugs which lit up the night sky like fireworks, oblivious of the devastation and death that they caused. At the same time that I moved back to London, Bobbie left us. Instead I came to be looked after by my mother's Scottish housekeeper, Marion Martin, who had come to work at '49' when I was just two.

'Mrs M', as I called her, was a widow, whose husband had died of leukaemia a few years before and, of all those who looked after me during my childhood, it was her whom I loved most dearly. Not that she could not be quite fierce if I got under her feet in the kitchen while she was preparing a dinner. Many were the times that she would chase me with her rolling-pin wielded above her head. But I was able to outrun her and would dash down the long corridor, out through the front door, across the landing to a back passage where there were some staff bedrooms and would dive into a bathroom. 'Mrs M' would arrive breathless just as I slammed the door locked. But it was all a game and she was never unkind to me. She was to remain with us for more than thirty years, not retiring until she was eighty years of age.

In the spring I wrote my first surviving letter in my own hand to my father who was in hospital in Rome, where he was undergoing operations on his knees which had been damaged in the plane crash in Yugoslavia the year before:

Garden Cottage

MY DARLING FATHER,
   THANK YOU FOR MY LOVELY PRESENTS. PLEASE MAY I HAVE MY SCOOTER SOON. I HOPE YOU WILL BE HOME SOON.

   WITH LOVE FROM
   WINSTON
   XOXOXOXO

[Picture of a scooter]

This prompted Father to write to my mother from his hospital bed on 18 April: 'I had a charming letter from Winston the other day asking in most peremptory terms for the scooter I told him I was sending. I hope by now it has arrived.'

As an only child, brought up at a time when children had virtually no parties or outings and television did not exist, I had no choice but to involve grown-ups in my games and mischief. Sometimes they became the targets of my high spirits and, if the following account by David Stirling of a luncheon at 10 Downing Street on 31 May 1945 is to be believed, even the Prime Minister was not immune:

33

This occasion turned out to be a fascinating luncheon confined to Sir Winston, Randolph and young Winston, apart from myself.

One of the highlights of the lunch with three generations of the Churchill family was young Winston from behind the sofa planting an accurate shot with a cushion upon his grandfather's face and lighted cigar as he entered the room. He disappeared behind it [the sofa], so that the old boy, while exonerating me, presumed it was Randolph who had thrown it, until the giggles from the sofa revealed the real culprit.

At last the war was over. VE-Day was a day which none of my generation will ever forget. Following the unconditional surrender of Germany to the Allies on 8 May 1945, the entire British nation, after more than five long years of war, launched into a great and spontaneous celebration of victory. Aged four and a half, waving my paper Union Jack on a stick and with my hand firmly held by 'Mrs M', I joined the half-million strong crowd that gathered outside Buckingham Palace on that joyful day. I was not in the least surprised to see Grandpapa appear on the balcony with King George VI, the Queen and other members of the Royal Family, as we all cheered them to the echo. What could be more natural? I always knew he was the most important Grandpapa in the whole world.

· III ·

Life with Father

Though VE-Day marked the end of the war in Europe, the war in the Far East was not over, with the fighting against Japan promising to be long and costly in Allied lives. However, following the dropping of the Atom bombs on Hiroshima and Nagasaki some three months later, the Japanese surrendered on 14 August. The celebrations for VJ-Day – Victory over Japan – were, if anything, even more full-hearted than those that had marked Victory in Europe, for now the war was truly over.

VJ-Day marked the first clear memories I have of my father. Though I was by then nearly five years of age I – in common with most of the 'Blitz Baby' generation – hardly knew my father. There had been a moment when, at the age of about three, a large parcel had arrived for me from North Africa. My excitement was intense as I unwrapped the box, only to discover it contained some large unappetizing bright green objects called bananas – something that did not exist in wartime London and the like of which I had never seen before. I was told they had been sent by someone called 'Father'. Though far from ripe, my nanny made me eat them all. As a result, I have never liked bananas to this day and I suspect that their sour taste left me somewhat prejudiced against this being called 'Father'.

On his return from Yugoslavia Father had taken steps to regain possession of the Old Rectory at Ickleford which had, for much of the war, been sub-let to the Waifs and Strays Society of the Church of England. Meanwhile in July 1945 a General Election was called in which he defended his seat at Preston. But the Tories were trounced at the polls, Grandpapa lost the premiership and Father his seat. Following the great victory secured on the battlefield and the bitter defeat sustained on the hustings so soon afterwards, Father retreated to Ickleford to take stock of the situation.

On the night of VJ-Day there were tremendous celebrations in the

35

village and Father built a huge bonfire, in the embers of which we baked potatoes. There was also a fireworks display, of a rather rudimentary nature by today's standards no doubt but to a child brought up in the Blackout, it was magical. We had staying with us at the time a funny little fat man, whom I learned was Evelyn Waugh, together with his red-headed son Auberon, who was a year older than me. Auberon alleges more than forty years after the event and with, I suspect, scant regard for the truth, that I pushed him into the bonfire. His father in his diary* entry for Thursday 16 August 1945 exonerates me of the charge: 'Another public holiday. Hangover. Winston a boisterous boy with head too big for his body. Randolph made a bonfire and Auberon fell into it. American came to luncheon and signed R. for highly profitable daily column. Some village sports, a damp bonfire and floodlit green.'

The house at Ickleford had a walled garden with a large tree overhanging the wall, making it ideal for climbing. We played 'Bears', with Father chasing me up the tree while I tried to escape into the branches. Less happy were the hours spent being made to read aloud – at the age of not yet five – the leading article in each day's *Times*. I never did understand why he attached so much importance to what seemed to me to be mumbo-jumbo especially when, as I learned later, it was a journal of which he disapproved strongly since it had endorsed Chamberlain's surrender at Munich.

'Munich' was a theme that was to recur in my father's conversation over the years, though its significance remained a mystery to me. Eventually, when I was about fourteen years old, I summoned up the courage to ask: 'Father, what *was* Munich?' No sooner had I asked the question than I wished I had not. Face flushed red with anger and voice quivering with rage, Father exploded: 'What is Munich? You ask! For years I have hired the most gifted teachers that money can buy to teach you, yet you do not know what was Munich!' He was so angry that he became quite incoherent and I do not believe I ever did get the answer to my question. But I did realize that it was a matter to which he attached inordinate importance. For him, Munich was the touchstone of any political figure's honour or good sense. He would applaud those of his generation as patriots who had sided with Grandpapa against the policy of Appeasement. Those who had not, he branded 'Filthy *Munichois*', charging them with encouraging Hitler and responsibility for leading us into World War. For them no obloquy was too damning.

Meanwhile I continued to live for the most part with my mother at '49' and that October she gave a party to celebrate my fifth birthday. Amid all the excitement of the occasion at the Churchill Club, I was scarcely aware that Queen Mary, the widow of King George V, had chosen the same afternoon to visit the Club. In a letter a few days later Queen Mary's Lady-

* *The Diaries of Evelyn Waugh*, Weidenfeld & Nicolson 1966.

in-Waiting, Lady Cynthia Colville, wrote by command of the Queen to thank my mother, adding: 'Her Majesty felt some remorse impinging on such a high festival as Winston's 5th birthday! and hoped that the appropriate celebrations were not unduly interfered with.'

Following the tea party my friends and I were taken to a private cinema where the cinema mogul Alexander Korda, a friend of my grandfather's, had arranged a screening of the Disney film *Bambi*. It was the first film that I or any of my friends had seen and we all cried our eyes out at the scenes of the baby deer caught in the forest fire – perhaps not the best choice for a party, but it is a film that has remained firmly in my memory to this day.

Now I was five, I was sent to a small day school just off Sloane Square called Mitford Colmer where the benches were hard and the classrooms gloomy. I was taken there each morning on the 74 bus by Sam Hudson, my mother's butler. Sam was an old soldier of the First World War who had served as batman to Colonel Freddie Cripps and I recall him telling me how, aboard a troopship in the Mediterranean bound for the Middle East, they had been torpedoed at night and many on board had been dragged down to a watery grave. Sam would be waiting for me outside the school, come rain or shine, to collect me when classes were over. He and I became best friends and would often kick a football in Hyde Park together. He also took me to football matches, and I remember seeing Arsenal play Fulham. It was long before hooliganism had wrecked the game and it was completely safe even for the smallest children to go to the matches, which began with the singing of the National Anthem and finished with a rendition of 'Abide with me'. Everyone knew the words and the whole stadium sang as one. I found it very moving and memorable.

Those were the days before there was any control on pollution and, with almost the only heating in homes or offices being provided by coal-fires or coke-boilers, the Thames Valley fog would, in winter months, combine with the smoke to make a thick dark yellow-brown 'smog' which stung my eyes and cut visibility to four or five yards. One foggy morning, our big red double-decker bus skidded on sheet-ice as it turned from Knightsbridge into Sloane Street, crashing into a lamp-post. Lots of people were hurt, including Sam, who had a nasty gash to his head. Like so many five-year-olds I just bounced and escaped unscathed. I accompanied Sam in the ambulance to nearby St George's Hospital where I looked after him while he had several stitches put in his head.

That Christmas I spent in the small village of Cerne Abbas in Dorset with my Digby grandparents whom, up till then, I scarcely knew but with whom I was to spend much of my childhood in the years to come. After Christmas Grandma Digby, who like my mother was also called Pamela, gave an account of our festivities in a letter to Grandpapa Churchill:

Cerne Abbey
Dorchester
Dorset
Dec. 28th [1945]

My Dear Winston,

I thought it might amuse you to hear little Winston's remarks at lunch on Xmas day. He was talking about his presents & was especially pleased with the soldiers you sent him and suddenly said: 'Aren't I lucky to have two such nice grandfathers & I've got another grandfather too!' Someone said he must be thinking of Mr Attlee again, but he said, 'No. My other grandfather comes first. I can't remember his name, but he is the one what fighted with the soldiers Grandfather Churchill sent me. He is my great-great-grandfather!' So my short explanation about Marlborough had evidently sunk in!

He is being so good & sweet & is getting very keen on riding. Jacquetta [my aunt, later Mrs David James] takes him out on Twinkle every day & he can guide him quite well.

We also should like to tell you how very nice Randolph has been lately – quite charming to me & very nice to Pamela. The divorce is very sad, but I feel it will be so much better for the little boy if they continue to be on friendly terms as they are at present.

Winston had an Xmas cable from Randolph from Rome & from Pamela [my mother] from New York. With all best wishes for 1946 to you & Clemmie from Kennie & myself.

Yours v. sincerely
Pamela Digby

Though I was quite oblivious of the fact, my parents had divorced as soon as the war was over. This development made no impression on me whatever as, with my father away at war for the first four and a half years of my life, I had no recollection of them ever being together.

Many years later father was to observe that theirs was a marriage 'made and broken by Hitler'. While my parents faced up to it philosophically and resolved at least to put on a show of friendship for my benefit whenever they met, Grandpapa Churchill was deeply distressed that the marriage should have foundered – a sorrow which shows through in his letter to my Grandmother Digby:

28 Hyde Park Gate
London SW7
6.1.46

My dear Pamela,

I was so glad to hear from you about Winston.

I grieve vy much for what has happened wh put an end to so many of my hopes for the future of Randolph & Pamela. The war strode in havoc through the lives of millions. We must make the best of what is left among the ruins. Everything must be centred upon the well-being & happiness of the Boy. Pamela has brought him up splendidly. There must be friendship to shield him from the defects of a broken home.

It is a comfort that the relations between our families remain indestructible.

Yours affectionately,
W

P.S. My warm regards to Kennie [Grandpa Digby].

As a result of my parents' divorce, my holidays came to be divided between my mother, my father and my Churchill and Digby grandparents, with both of whom I came to spend an increasing amount of time.

Life with Father was liable to be tempestuous. Being with him as a small boy was like going around hand in hand with a walking volcano. All would be calm, serene and happy one moment; the next, there would be an earth-quaking eruption. There was absolutely no means of foretelling when the next would be, though I came to recognize tell-tale signs in his demeanour if there was any hint of dilatoriness, inefficiency or surliness by a waiter, taxi driver or, especially, any employee of British Railways.

One day, when I was about six, Father, who had by now given up Ickleford and taken a small house in London, invited me to lunch with him. Mrs Martin delivered me at the appointed hour into the custody of the hall porter of White's Club, which occupies magnificent premises at the top end of St James's and is one of the oldest and most renowned of London's gentlemen's clubs, having begun life in 1693 as White's Chocolate House, established by an Italian, implausibly called Francis White, whose original name is believed to have been Francesco Bianco.

White's was strictly 'men only' and the bar on women – which exists to this day – was rigorously enforced and extended also to children. I was to come to know the outer hall of White's Club very well over the coming years, as I waited for Father to 'finish his drink' ('How long could it take,' I asked myself, to 'finish one drink?') or to complete dictating an article through to the *Evening Standard* by telephone. Suddenly, Father would appear in his beige camelhair overcoat clutching, as always, a cigarette in his nicotine-stained fingers: 'Let's go to lunch!' he would announce. While most men's clubs have a Ladies' Annexe, the members of White's have never felt the need for one since, a stone's throw across the street, there is the Ritz Hotel, whose Grillroom serves this function admirably.

The war had only ended some eighteen months before. London was still littered with gaping bomb-sites, which were not finally cleared up until fifteen or twenty years later. Rationing of food and other necessaries, including sweets – a matter of particular concern to me – was still very much in force, and remained so until Grandpapa's return to office in 1951.

While, therefore, the bill of fare even at the Ritz was somewhat restricted, to a small boy who had never before been to a restaurant or been offered a choice of food it was truly amazing. Father and I lunched alone, facing

39

each other across a small round table covered in a crisp white tablecloth. He enquired if I would like a steak. I was not sure, never having had a steak before in my life. I fear my look must have betrayed my uncertainty, but a steak was ordered all the same. I suppose 30 minutes must have passed and still nothing had arrived. I could see my father eyeing his watch. Suddenly, out of the blue, came a tremor: 'Waiter!' As the head waiter approached, the tremor gave way to a full-scale eruption. After delivering himself of a pithy lecture on how the standards of service had fallen since the pre-war years, he bellowed at the wretched man: 'Bring my son some steak!' The high-ceilinged room with its elaborate gilt decor resounded, even the chandeliers seemed to quiver and, in the instant, the heads of everyone at the other tables turned in our direction and an icy silence descended upon the establishment. I was mortified. I felt it must be my fault for having ordered something difficult or out of the ordinary but, as I was soon to learn, this was part and parcel of life with Father.

I must confess that I found such episodes traumatic and would avert my gaze in embarrassment at his abuse of people who were not in a position to answer back. When, later, I discovered that he was in the habit of heaping equal abuse on powerful figures, such as Press barons who could indeed answer back and had armies of hacks and flunkies to do so on their behalf, I felt that this was at least more excusable. But the thunder clouds would clear almost as quickly as they had gathered and he would resume his conversation as if nothing had happened, becoming once again an enchanting companion full of fun and stories.

Sometimes at weekends Sam Hudson would collect me from school in an old shooting brake with wooden sides to it and we would drive down to stay with American friends of my mother's, Madeleine and Bob Sherwood – a playwright, biographer of Harry Hopkins and sometime speech-writer for FDR – at Great Enton in Surrey, where Averell Harriman, who was at the time US Ambassador to Britain, was a frequent guest. I thoroughly enjoyed weekends there with my mother. Someone had given me a pedal car in the shape of a jeep painted khaki with a huge white US Army star on the bonnet. I would take my jeep up to the road and, with my feet off the pedals as I could not keep up with them, I would career down the hill at speed towards the house. One of my favourite pastimes at Enton was to disappear beneath the strawberry-nets where one day, to my embarrassment, I was caught literally red-handed by my hostess. I thought I would be in trouble but, instead, she thought it a huge joke and came to join me under the netting where we munched strawberries together – an incident she has not forgotten to this day.

After some eighteen months at Mitford Colmer I was moved to Gibb's, an all boys school just off Queen's Gate. We wore grey uniforms with short trousers and red caps and, in addition to Latin, I found myself launched off on the hieroglyphics of Greek. In contrast to Mitford Colmer's, here we played a lot of sport, including football and boxing. My best friend was Jonathan Dudley and, almost invariably, I would be drawn to box against him, even though he was some six inches taller than me and had a longer reach. I regularly got a bloody nose, but he remained my friend and came to stay with me in the holidays at Chartwell. I well remember one cold morning in November of 1948 as we sat in class hearing the guns booming nearby in Hyde Park to announce the birth of our future sovereign, Prince Charles.

In 1948 I acquired my first passport and was taken abroad for the first time. Father took me to the island of Porquerolles, one of the Iles d'Hyères off the coast of Southern France. There we were joined by a beautiful lady with long blonde hair called June Osborne who, I learned, was to become my stepmother. She was very kind to me, especially when I was foolish enough to have an argument with a sea urchin on which I trod while paddling in the sea. She spent long hours plucking the painful needles out of my foot. Later that year they were married at Caxton Hall and, in October of the following year, 1949, my sister Arabella was born.

Summer holidays with Father were usually spent in England by the seaside. Diana and Duff Cooper, who had won his spurs with the Churchill family by being a staunch anti-*Munichois* and was later to become Ambassador in Paris, had a small house at Bognor on the Sussex coast which they would lend us for a couple of weeks. I loved the seaside and thoroughly enjoyed the holidays at Bognor. We would sometimes be invited over to tea at the vast medieval castle of Arundel by my cousin on my mother's side, Lavinia, Duchess of Norfolk, whose husband Bernard, as hereditary Earl Marshal of England, was to have responsibility for organizing the Coronation of Queen Elizabeth II as well as my grandfather's state funeral. The Norfolks had children of my age and there could be no better place for games of hide-and-seek than the castle, with its seemingly limitless number of rooms, miles of passages, vast chambers with vaulted ceilings and numerous suits of armour behind which to hide.

One summer an American movie mogul, who had apparently seen my picture in the paper, descended upon us at Bognor to invite me to play the twin roles of the Prince and the Pauper in the film of Mark Twain's book of that name. Father was appalled and did not think much of the idea, judging – no doubt rightly – that it would disrupt my schooling. Thus my brilliant career in the movies was over before it had ever begun!

Other summers we went to Bembridge on the Isle of Wight where we stayed at the Royal Spithead Hotel, which stands by the small harbour and looks out over a vast expanse of the most lovely golden sands. From here we would see the great Cunarders making their way majestically in and out of Southampton water on their New York run. At low tide more than a mile of sand would be uncovered and, just as his father had done for him on the East coast beaches of Frinton and Cromer after the First War,

Father would organize the construction of vast sand fortresses on the beach. There was no question of making mud pies with upturned buckets. Father would commandeer a large shovel and conscript at least half a dozen other youngsters to the enterprise. We would all dig furiously to create the moats, battlements and keeps of our fortress, which we would then proceed to man and defend against the incoming tide which would rush in across the flat sands and completely encircle us.

When Father married June, Grandpapa as a wedding present had given him a London house, 12 Catherine Place, in a quiet backwater two minutes' walk from Buckingham Palace and St James's Park. The street was so peaceful that one summer's evening we carried all the tables and chairs outside and gave a large dinner-party in the middle of the roadway. There was another more dramatic occasion that I recall while staying at Catherine Place. I must have been about twelve and, since June was ill in bed with flu, father took me to dine with him at White's. By now I was old enough to be admitted to this holy of holies.

Even more so than most men's clubs, White's has the firmest of rules that the staff are never to divulge to any lady who may telephone whether a particular member is, or is not, in the club, lest any carefully laid alibis be upset. They will not therefore call a member directly to the telephone. Messages may be left and it could be some time before a call was returned, especially if the member were engaged in a game of bridge or poker. On this particular evening as we dined in the ornate first-floor dining room with its large eighteenth-century windows overlooking St James's, the head porter suddenly arrived breathless at our table. He reported that Mrs Churchill had just telephoned to say that the house was on fire and would we come urgently. With me hard on his heels, Father raced downstairs and out into the street where he hailed the first passing taxi. With the promise of a £5 note – you could go a long way by taxi for a fiver in those days – he urged the startled driver to crash every red light that stood in our path. We arrived in three minutes flat, just as the first fire engine was turning into the narrow street, to be greeted by clouds of dark smoke billowing from the top of the house.

It seems that in a strange ordering of priorities June had telephoned White's Club even before the Fire Brigade. The fire had started when, feeling cold, she had reached from her bed to switch on the wall socket to which the electric fire was connected, not realizing that the fire had been left behind the curtains when they had been drawn closed. Within two or three minutes the heavy curtains erupted in flames. In panic, June dashed to grab baby Arabella from her bed in the adjoining room and carried her downstairs where she telephoned for assistance. By the time we and the Fire Brigade had arrived on the scene the fire had taken a good hold and the flames were shooting up the staircase. The firemen, using a turntable ladder, quickly climbed with their hoses on to the roof where one of them, in the darkness and smoke, crashed through the skylight above the staircase. I recall his yell as he fell four storeys down the stairwell. Fortunately the staircase was narrow and he was able to break his fall on the banisters before crashing on to a chair at the bottom of the stairs, which probably saved his life.

Whereas Grandmama Churchill liked to arrive for any function at least fifteen minutes early, preferring to arrive calm and collected, Father was quite the opposite. He believed that trains should be given a 'sporting chance' of getting away, a habit which led to reckless dashes by car or taxi on two wheels to railway stations where sometimes we would arrive in time to wave the train goodbye. Whenever Grandmama made the mistake (which was not often) of allowing Father to collect her for a function to which they had both been invited, she would get into a terrible fluster as she waited. When, finally, he showed up she would upbraid him for his tardiness and he would grandly retort: 'Punctuality does not rest in being early!' Nobody seems to have told him that it did not rest in being late either.

On one occasion, in the late Fifties, he had an appointment to see the then US Ambassador, David Bruce, at the Embassy in Grosvenor Square. I too had been bidden to the meeting and, as usual, I met Father in advance at White's Club, where he would spend long hours on the telephone or trading gossip at the bar over whiskies and soda, and which would invariably be the jump-off point for any such sortie. Father, who had a high regard for David Bruce, was determined not to be late. Alas, when the time came for us to leave for the Embassy, it was bucketing with rain and there was not a taxi in sight. Without umbrellas or raincoats – I don't think my father ever possessed either – we set forth on foot for Grosvenor Square in the hope of catching a taxi on the way. By the time we entered Berkeley Square we were soaked through and Father, who was very out of breath, realized we were going to be quite badly late. He thereupon strode out into the street and flagged down the first car that happened to be passing, which turned out to be a Mini Minor. Sticking his head in through the window, Father announced to the dumbfounded driver: 'I'm Randolph Churchill. This is my son Winston. We are late for an appointment with the American Ambassador. Will you drive us to Grosvenor Square?' The poor fellow, quite bowled over with the brashness of the approach, obligingly agreed and my father squeezed his bulky form into the front seat of the Mini while I bundled into the back.

Life with Father was certainly different!

· IV ·

Minterne

As a result of my parents' divorce I came to spend the greater part of my school holidays with my grandparents – with the Digbys in Dorset and the Churchills in Kent. My father had, meanwhile, resumed his career as an author and journalist and would make almost annual forays to America to boost his finances, which were invariably strained, on the US lecture circuit. My mother had gone to live abroad in Paris, but kept on Mrs Martin and the flat in Grosvenor Square as a home base for me. This was eventually sold for a smaller one, 11 Hyde Park Gardens, overlooking the Park.

I was fortunate to have not one, but two remarkable grandfathers, both of whom were a powerful influence on me during my formative years. If I say that one was a bricklayer and the other a milkman, I tell no lie, though I have to admit that these were not their sole occupations. Only too eagerly, I became the brickie's and the milkman's mate. Grandpapa Churchill had just ceased being Prime Minister – clearly a most important job, though I was not quite sure exactly what this and 'beating Hitler' had entailed. However, every bit as important in my life, was my Grandpa Digby who – at least so far as I was aware – was the local milkman!

What fun we had together! Grandpa Digby and I would get up at cock-crow and by six in the morning we would be on our way in his small dark blue electric milk float – the only vehicle he was able to drive, as he had never mastered the mysteries of gearshift vehicles. The wagon, which was kept plugged in 'on charge' overnight, would be laden down with milk from his own pedigree Guernsey herd and with the richest butter and cream in the land. In addition there would be plentiful supplies of fresh eggs and vegetables – commodities almost unknown in ration-bound London. No wonder all the villagers were so pleased to see us! 'Good

44

morning, M'Lord! Good morning, Master Winston!' they would greet us in their broad Dorset accents. It never struck me as incongruous that the Lord of the Manor should be doing the milk round. I would deliver the bottles of milk to the door while Grandpa put the few pence per pint into his old leather cartridge bag which he wore slung across his shoulder on top of his white milkman's coat.

It was not until much later that I came to appreciate that this 'other' grandfather of mine had also had a remarkable career. In the First World War, at the age of 21, he had been the youngest officer ever to command a battalion of the Brigade of Guards – the Coldstream – in action. All the more senior officers had been killed and he, a mere lieutenant, together with a sergeant, were the most senior left alive and unwounded. In the Second War, too old for active service, he had been Inspector-General of Infantry Training. A tall portly figure – a sharp contrast to the ramrod-thin soldier who, on return from the trenches of Flanders, had been told that he only had months to live if he did not force himself to eat – he was a warm smiling character, much loved by all who knew him. He achieved eminence in the fields both of agriculture and horticulture, becoming famous for the quality and variety of the rhododendrons which he grew in the renowned shrubbery at Minterne. He came to be nicknamed 'Carnation' Digby for the superb home-grown blooms he would invariably sport in his button-hole. As President of the Royal Agricultural Society he would be in charge of the Royal Show, attended most years by the Queen. But the crowning accolade of his life came when Queen Elizabeth created him Knight of the Garter. There are few, if any, outside the Royal Family who can lay claim, as I proudly can, to having not one, but two grandfathers who were Knights of the Garter. One of the oldest and certainly the most distinguished order of chivalry, it was conceived by Edward III in 1344 as a revival of King Arthur's mythical order of Knights of the Round Table and remains in the sole gift of the Sovereign.

When, at the end of the war, I first went to stay with my Digby grandparents, the main house at Minterne was shut up, having at my grandmother's suggestion been converted into a Royal Naval hospital for the war years. As a result, they had moved into the old but much smaller house of Cerne Abbey, three miles down the valley.

By a most remarkable coincidence the Digby family home of Minterne had, some three hundred years before, been the home of the Churchills, who themselves were of West Country stock. Though my grandfather enjoyed the idea of tracing the family's origins to one Wandril, Lord of Courcelle (later Anglicized to 'Churchill'), who had come over with William the Conqueror, evidence for this is tenuous. The historian A. L. Rowse in *The Early Churchills* thinks it more likely that the family derives from small freeholders in Somerset, possibly from a line of blacksmiths, a circumstance which my grandfather viewed as 'very suspicious and even disquieting'. I prefer to take the part of my ancestress Duchess Sarah, wife of John, 1st Duke of Marlborough who, on reading Lediard's life of her husband, bluntly declared: 'This history takes a great deal of pains to make the Duke of Marlborough's extraction very ancient. That may be true for aught I know; but it is no matter, whether it be true or not, in my opinion, for I value nobody for another's merit.'

From the mid-seventeenth century for three generations the Churchills had leased Minterne which, with its lake and streams, nestles in the valley amid the wooded hillsides above the village of Cerne Abbas, midway between Sherborne and Dorchester. John Churchill, a lawyer in the Middle Temple who rose to be Deputy-Registrar of Chancery, married Sarah, daughter of Sir Henry Winston of Standish in Gloucestershire, and subsequently acquired the leasehold to the estate from Winchester College. His son Winston – the first to combine the names of 'Winston' and 'Churchill' which, in a later generation were to reverberate around the world – made Minterne his home at the end of the Civil War in which he had fought gallantly as a Captain of Horse. Following the Restoration of the monarchy in 1660 under Charles II, he served eighteen years in Parliament as Member for Weymouth (1661–79) and was knighted for his services to the Crown. It was at Minterne that the first Sir Winston Churchill, progenitor of the Churchill line, and his wife Elizabeth (née Drake) brought up their four surviving children, Arabella, John, George and Charles. A staunch Royalist, whose fortunes had suffered under Cromwell, he had high hopes of the Restoration. When these were not fulfilled he defiantly adopted as the family motto: *Fiel pero desdichado*, Spanish for 'Faithful but unfortunate'.

His elder son, John, was to become the foremost military genius of the age – perhaps the only commander, in a military career spanning several decades, of whom it can be said: He never fought a battle he did not win, nor besieged a city he did not take. Charles, also a general, was to lead the British infantry, under his elder brother's overall command, at the Battle of Blenheim – the first of a series of victories masterminded by Marlborough, that were to humble the power of France's 'Sun King', Louis XIV, in the War of the Spanish Succession. George rose to be Admiral in the Royal Navy, while their sister, Arabella, became mistress to King James II, bearing him a royal bastard called James, Duke of Berwick and Alba – who, intriguingly, became the most celebrated military commander of his day next only to his uncle, Marlborough. While Marlborough played a key part in the 'Glorious Revolution' of 1688 which led to the replacement of James II and his Stuart successors by William of Orange, and later Queen Anne, Berwick fought on the side of France and Spain in the War of the Spanish Succession, winning the famous Battle of Almanza.

I find it strange to reflect that, nearly three hundred years before me, John, George, Charles, and Arabella played in the same valley as I did in my childhood. But, sadly for them, the Churchills never owned the freehold of Minterne. However, they left behind them a set of the large and very splendid Flemish tapestries depicting their great campaigns and victories, which Marlborough had given to each of his four key military commanders including his younger brother, General Charles, who became Governor of Brussels. They also left a magnificent mirror-topped table, surmounted by a spectacular wall mirror, in *verre églomisé* emblazoned with the Churchill cipher of a lion rampant and with reversed 'C's for Charles Churchill and an 'M' for Marlborough. On his death, my Grandfather Digby bequeathed this to me in his will and it is now one of my most treasured possessions, having been restored to the Churchill family after a quarter of a millennium with the Digbys. The latter explained the crack across one corner of the mirror-top as being due to General Charles' fury on discovering – having completed a fine house on the property – that the Churchills only owned the leasehold to the estate, not the freehold. They claim that he slammed down his sword on the table in a rage, causing it to crack. He died in 1714 and has a fine memorial in the tiny church at Minterne where he is buried alongside his grandfather John. The Digbys finally took over Minterne from the Churchills in 1765 when they bought the freehold from Winchester College.

The Digbys trace their ancestry to Aelmar the Saxon in the eleventh century and to one Sir Diggeby de Tilton from Lincolnshire. The Digbys number among their ancestors John Digby, who served as Ambassador in Madrid under King James I and who, for his services to the Crown, was allowed to buy Sherborne Castle, following the execution of Sir Walter Raleigh whose property it had previously been. He was created Baron Digby of Sherborne and 1st Earl of Bristol. Intriguingly his granddaughter Anne Digby married Robert Spencer, 2nd Earl of Sunderland, and, in turn, their son Charles, 3rd Earl of Sunderland, married Anne Churchill, second daughter of John, 1st Duke of Marlborough. By Act of Parliament, the Marlborough dukedom was, exceptionally, allowed to pass by way of his daughters Henrietta and Anne. It is from Anne's marriage to Charles Spencer, through their sons Charles (3rd Duke of Marlborough) and John (father of the 1st Earl Spencer), that are descended all the Spencer-Churchills, including Sir Winston Churchill, as well as the Earls Spencer and the present Princess of Wales. Thus my Churchill grandfather, eight generations back, was also descended from the Digbys.

The first Digby to live at Minterne was Admiral Sir Robert Digby who bought the property in 1765. As Admiral of the Blue he served on the Americas Station and married Eleanor Elliot, daughter of the Governor of New York. He had a natural son, Robert Sherbourne, who established the first plate glass factory in England, near St Helens in Lancashire.

Admiral Robert's nephew, Admiral Sir Henry Digby, was one of Nelson's Captains at the Battle of Trafalgar, commanding HMS *Africa*. He made a great reputation for himself, capturing in the course of his naval career no fewer than 57 prizes, which earned him the accolade of the 'Silver Captain'. So popular was he with his sailors that, contrary to the custom of the day, he never had to use the Press Gang to recruit his crew. His richest trophy was the capture of the Spanish treasure ship *Santa Brigada* in 1799, which was carrying gold coins minted in Spain to her colonies in the Americas. This was the greatest prize ever captured by the Royal Navy and his portion of the bounty amounting to £40,000 (approx. £5 million in today's money) was to be the foundation of the Digby fortune. My Uncle Eddie, the present Lord Digby, tells me that the family kept one sack of the 'Pieces of Eight' – Spanish 8-*real* coins minted in gold – right up to 1914 when all except one of the coins were given towards the war effort.

Admiral Sir Henry Digby married Lady Andover, daughter of Thomas Coke of Norfolk, 1st Earl of Leicester. Their daughter, Jane, whose romantic adventures were to become one of the greatest scandals of Victorian times, was divorced by her husband Lord Ellenborough – something which, at the time, required an Act of Parliament. She then married successively Baron Carl-Theodore von Venningen from Bavaria, a Greek Count by the name of Spyridon Theotoky and finally Sheikh Abdul Medjuel el Mezrab. In between she had several dalliances, among them with King Ludwig I of Bavaria and with his son King Otto of Greece. For twenty-five years, up to her death at the age of seventy-four, she remained at the side of Medjuel and, with him, led his Bedouin tribesmen on horseback in battles and skirmishes through the Syrian desert. She lies buried in the Protestant cemetery in Damascus. I recall, as a child, my Grandfather Digby speaking of the wayward Jane in hushed tones which combined both shock and a certain admiration. He would occasionally go to the large safe in his study, where he stored many family treasures, and would read a passage from Jane's diaries which had been carefully preserved and which cast a new perspective on those supposedly strait-laced Victorian days.

Another ancestor – of whom the family never spoke even in hushed tones – was Sir Everard Digby who, as a very young man and a recent convert to Catholicism, became embroiled with Guy Fawkes in the Gun Powder Plot to blow up the Houses of Parliament and King James I during the State Opening of Parliament on 5 November 1605. He was imprisoned in the Tower of London where, the following year, he was hanged, drawn and quartered.

To a boy who had spent much of his life cooped up in a London flat, being taken for walks in Hyde Park only under the watchful gaze and in the firm hand of a keeper, life at Cerne was a wonderful freedom. There was a large working farm with some 200 pedigree Guernsey and Jersey cows. I used to spend much of my time helping in the farmyard and riding on the tractors. My favourite toy was a small milk trolley which, when it was not being used for trundling churns of milk around, I would appropriate as my personal go-cart. I would pull the four-wheel trolley up the drive, which was on quite a slope, perch myself on the front with the handle doubled back towards me serving as a steering wheel and would head off downhill, rapidly gathering speed. The contraption had no brakes and the trick was to turn on to the level before hitting the house but without tipping over – a feat at which I became quite expert with practice.

It was here too that I learnt to ride on a small but very spirited Shetland pony called Twinkle. When my Aunt Jacquetta, my mother's youngest sister, was not around to take me riding I would go out with Twinkle in a small pony trap made for two. For my visits, he would be stabled in the old Gate House which formed part of the tenth-century Benedictine abbey which once stood nearby. Clearly Twinkle did not think much of this arrangement, for I well remember an occasion when we were no sooner through the farmyard and starting up the lane than he took off, high-tailing it for home. We careered out of control into the main Dorchester to Sherborne road – fortunately a very underused lane in those days – and flew the three miles up hill and down dale to Minterne, where Twinkle only stopped when he reached his friends in the stable yard. Whitelock, the groom, leapt for safety as we spun round the corner on one wheel.

It was about this time that there arrived at Minterne a remarkable man, also a groom, a Hungarian by the name of Laznick who, with a string of magnificent Lippizaners at his heel, had made his way on foot from Hungary across a devastated war-stricken Europe. He had many a tale of how he had evaded the Nazis, and others besides who would willingly have had his precious charges for horse meat, before he was able to bring them to safety in England, where he arrived with a letter of introduction from his former employer to my Grandfather Digby. At Minterne he was given charge of Grandpa's magnificent jet-black stallion, implausably called Whiteway, which had won the Cesarewitch at Newmarket in 1947 and would be walked by the faithful Laznick many miles along the lanes of the West Country to pay his stud calls.

Grandpa Digby was an avid follower of horseracing and a shrewd judge of form on the turf. Over the years he did very well at the expense of the bookies. He is possibly the only person to have been paid twice in the same year for a Derby winner. It happened in the summer of 1914 when he was a very young man. He had backed two horses in the race and, when the results were declared, he was thrilled to discover that he had backed a winner. The bookie was clearly less enthused with the result and promptly attempted to welsh. Grandpa, realizing what was happening and being long of limb and fleet of foot, gave chase, catching the man and securing payment before he could decamp. A few minutes later an objection was lodged and, after a Stewards' Enquiry, another horse was declared the winner. As it happened this was the second horse which Grandpa had backed, fortunately with a different bookie, for the other was nowhere to be seen.

In 1938 he won the Daily Double on the Tote in the Grand National which was won by Battleship. With the only winning ticket he scooped the pool which was worth £6,025. With the proceeds he restored the church at Minterne and purchased a maroon Buick and a Ford station wagon. Thus it was that in the summer of 1949 Grandpa Digby took the whole family on a wonderful expedition to Ireland in these two splendid cars, which were vast by comparison with anything that was to be found in post-war Britain. Together with my Aunts Jacquetta and Sheila, the latter with her newly acquired American husband, Charles Moore, we flew to Dublin where we picked up the cars. We were later joined by my Uncle Eddie, on leave from the Far East where he was serving with the Coldstream Guards in the Malayan jungle.

From Dublin we headed west to the Atlantic coast, to Belmullet in the northwesternmost corner of Ireland, where my grandfather had a stretch of salmon fishing and a hunting lodge on the Glenamoy River.

Because of all the rationing and privations of life in England at the time, Grandpa was taking no chances and stocked up with hams, tins of biscuits and other provisions before leaving Dublin, imagining that there might be a shortage of food in this remote corner of Ireland. He need not have worried. The local hostelry in Belmullet produced, as a matter of course, dinners consisting of a home-made soup, followed by freshly caught river trout, grouse from the nearby moors and an elaborate pudding. I had never seen so much food in my life, nor had my grandparents since the Thirties.

On the Glenamoy, Grandpa taught me to fly-fish and there I caught my first trout and salmon. He was well pleased with his stratagem just before the war of appointing the most notorious local poacher, known as Michael, as his keeper to guard the river, and remarked that he had never seen the river so full of fish.

One day, when the others had gone to shoot a few grouse, I went with my grandmother to see the dramatic and rocky cliffs that face across the Atlantic towards the United States and which are constantly lashed by giant rollers and gale-force winds. On our way, in the grand old Buick, we reached a stretch of road which, though wide enough for only a single vehicle, was perfectly straight and utterly deserted. My grandmother drew the car to a halt and, placing me on her lap, proceeded to give me my first driving lesson. Though not yet nine years of age, I was not making too bad a job of steering the car when, on the horizon ahead of us, we spied a black and white figure approaching. Believing it to be a policeman, we pulled up smartly and I resumed the passenger seat, only to discover, when we got closer, that the object we took for a distant policeman proved to be nothing more threatening than a black and white cow!

From Belmullet we went on to spend a few days with the Earl and Countess of Rosse at Birr Castle, with its lovely lakes and gardens. But my principal recollection of our brief stay with the Rosses was of the fun I had jumping about in a haystack, and the price I had to pay for it. I already suffered slightly from hayfever and asthma, although I did not, at the time, know the cause. Within minutes my eyes were streaming and, before long, I had the greatest difficulty breathing. That night, as I fought painfully for each breath, Grandma sat up with me all through the night, preparing boiling kettles of Friar's Balsam which I inhaled under a towel and which afforded some relief. I have made a point ever since of giving haystacks a wide berth. It was because of my asthma that my parents, on medical advice, had earlier in the year sent me to school in Switzerland where it was believed that the altitude and clear mountain air would be the best cure.

On the next leg of our journey towards Killarney we had a most unfortunate accident. My Uncle Charlie was driving and, as we came round the corner, we were confronted by an old lady on her bicycle coming towards us completely on the wrong side of the road. Hanging over the handle-bars she had a kettle as well as a large shopping bag. Although we had come to an almost complete stop, the old lady collided with us and was thrown off her bicycle on to the roadway where she lay concussed in a pool of blood. It was a long time before we could summon the *Garda* and an ambulance. Evidently the *Garda* officer had not had much experience of such incidents (cars were few and far between in Ireland in those days) and he had to telephone us the next day at our hotel at Parknasilla on the Kenmare River, our last port of call, because he had forgotten to take down the registration number of our car!

On our return to Cerne, Grandpa Digby decided that the time had come to teach me to shoot. He found an old Four-Ten gun and took me out to a field near the house where I potted some rabbits. Under his guidance I soon became proficient with the gun and most evenings we would go out together to a field known as Belvoir which had numerous mounds in it, marking where the former Benedictine Abbey had stood in the Middle Ages. There were rabbits galore, so many that they had become a plague to farmers' crops. From there we would head up Pilgrim's Way toward the Giant, a pre-historic fertility symbol carved in the chalk of the hillside, which dominates the Cerne valley. At one stage in the early post-war years some interfering busybodies from the Victorian Society decided that the Giant was not 'proper' and should be given a turf loin-cloth so as not to affront the sensibilities of local maidens. But the locals would have none of it, preferring to keep the Giant unadorned and in all his glory as he had been for over 3000 years. It would take us little more than half an hour to shoot as many rabbits as we could carry in our game bags and we would return heavily laden as dusk was falling.

About this time my grandparents gave me a Welsh Arabian pony called Snowdon which had previously belonged to my Aunt Jacquetta. Snowdon was a small but very beautiful grey mare. She was wonderfully swift and had terrific spirit. I loved riding her up on the Giant and on the high, rolling hills surrounding Minterne and the Cerne valley. Most of all I enjoyed being taken hunting by my grandmother. Grandma, although already sixty and conscientious in her work as a Magistrate, County Councillor and Chairman of the Children's Committee, would nonetheless ride to hounds at least two days of the week. Mounted on one of her fine hunters Huw, Dan or Transportation, she would ride side-saddle wearing a navy blue habit, together with a bowler hat with a veil across her face. She cut a splendid figure in the hunting field and there were few who could match her stamina and courage when it came to jumping the huge hedges of the Blackmoor Vale. When hunting with the Cattistock, where the jumps were less awesome, she would often take me with her, initially on a leading rein but very soon without.

I particularly enjoyed cubbing at the very start of the hunting season in early September. In those days it was still an adventure to get up early. But there can be few grandmothers who are happy to rise at 4.30 am to take their grandchildren hunting. We would be in the saddle by 5 am, hack for two hours to the meet, hunt for several hours, often at breakneck speed, before returning home late in the afternoon exhausted, covered in mud but wonderfully exhilarated by the chase.

One spectacular hunt I will never forget was a day we had with the South Dorset. We met at Hardy's Monument, named in memory, not of the Dorset poet and novelist Thomas Hardy, but of Admiral Hardy in whose arms Nelson died at Trafalgar. It was a brilliant crisp morning of early autumn with the Dorset hills rolling down to a shimmering sea. Unlike the Blackmoor Vale with its vast hedges or the Cattistock with its less daunting fences, this was stonewall country, the flintstones having been collected from the fields over the centuries and stacked to make walls, some of which were quite formidable. The hounds quickly picked up a strong scent and we were off. We hadn't been going more than twenty minutes before we arrived at a huge wall. The Master, hunt servants and half-a-dozen of the best mounted, including naturally Grandma, sailed across the wall, leaving the rest of the field, at least fifty strong, together with me, stuck firmly on the other side. I and others tried in vain to find some way round. Meanwhile a huge ruddy-faced man on a powerful cob, made another attempt at the wall. His horse ended up straddling it before rearing up backwards on to him and he was most fortunate to escape without injury. At this point someone yelled, 'Can no one give us a lead?' Suddenly Grandma, who was waiting for me with mounting concern and even greater impatience on the far side, yelled: 'Come on, Winston!' I squeezed my knees and gently prodded Snowdon with my heels. She pricked her ears and in a leap, the strength and spirit of which belied her small stature and her twenty years, we flew over the wall with me clutching her mane for all I was worth to stay on. Three-quarters of the field were never to be seen for the rest of the day. Soon thereafter I went to Eton and Grandma promised me that, when there was another meet at the Monument, she would send my housemaster, Tom Brocklebank, a coded telegram reading: 'GRANDMOTHER DEAD. FUNERAL AT MONUMENT.' She knew that nothing less would secure special leave from Eton. Alas, we never did get our second hunt together at the Monument, but the memory of that day remains one of the most treasured and vivid of my childhood.

· V ·

Chartwell

In the summer of 1946, aged five and a half, I went to stay for the first time with my Churchill grandparents at Chartwell. As a necessary economy and because they had no occasion to use it, living as they did at Downing Street during the week and spending weekends at Chequers, which was fully staffed with a complement of ATS, Chartwell had been closed up throughout the war and the furniture put under dustsheets. Unheated for more than five years, the house had become cold and damp and was badly in need of redecoration. We therefore all stayed in one of the cottages below the main house, adjacent to the small stable yard and my grandfather's painting studio. Also staying with us was a delightful cousin of Grandmama's, Miss Maryott Whyte, known to all of us as Cousin Moppet. Moppet cooked for us and was also detailed to keep an eye on me. She would regale me with tales of her time as an ambulance driver in the war and of one night in particular when, in the darkness of the Blitz, she had been called out in her ambulance to the site of an air raid to tend the injured. No sooner had she arrived on the scene than a policeman asked her in the most matter of fact way: 'Would you mind moving back your vehicle, Miss, there is an unexploded bomb immediately below you!' Such dangers had been the commonplace for the wartime generation, even on the home front.

Delighted to have a grandfather who was a milkman, I now discovered I had another who was a bricklayer. Grandpapa Churchill would regularly spend a couple of hours most afternoons when he was at Chartwell, building a wall around his vast kitchen garden where Mr Vincent, the gardener (still fit and well to this day) grew a wonderful variety of flowers, fruit and vegetables. Grandpapa would don his overalls and, if it wasn't too windy, his broad-brimmed 'Ten Gallon' hat. He would then mix up his 'pug', as he called his mixture of sand and cement to which he added some water. He wielded his builder's trowel with dexterity, placing a layer of 'pug' on the top course of bricks, to make a bed for the new bricks which I would hand him. He would bang them into place with the handle of his trowel, scraping off any surplus 'pug', which would be saved for the next course. From time to time he would get out his plumb line to check that he was building true. I thoroughly enjoyed being his 'Brickie's mate' and, ultimately became quite proficient at it myself, especially when Grandpapa gave me as a Christmas present a miniature building set, complete with tiny bricks and real 'pug' which I could mix up myself to build small houses.

Whilst staying with my grandparents I gave account of life at Chartwell in a letter to the Sherwoods with whom I had stayed at Great Enton:

Chartwell
9 August 1946

Dear Bob & Madeleine,

The time is 3.30. I am having a nice time fishing and laying bricks with my grandfather. Grandma reads to me at night. I hope you are well and having a nice time.

> With love
> from
> Winston Churchill

[Picture enclosed of a railway engine and a house with a gun outside it – probably a memory of Chequers.]

We were all rather cramped living with 'Cousin Moppet' in her small cottage, but she made us most welcome and we were certainly very cosy. Meanwhile, in the main house, the dustsheets were being removed and the house was being put in order after five long years of neglect. Gradually the bare rooms with their musty smell and spooky shapes beneath the dustsheets, were transformed back into a bright, welcoming home. But the scheme of things was significantly changed compared to the layout of the house as it had been in the Twenties and Thirties (to which it has since been restored by the National Trust who now look after the property which is open to the public).

The changes were dictated by various considerations, not least of which was that Grandpapa had become addicted to the cinema which he found a great relaxation. Even at the height of the war he would have a couple of films each weekend at Chequers. After dinner and the dispatch of any pressing business, a film would be shown, on a 16 mm projector set up in the Long Library. The showing would run from about 11.30 pm to 1.30 am and all the staff at Chequers, both indoor and outdoor, including any off-duty military engaged in guarding the house, would be invited to join in. A romantic through and through, he delighted in tales of heroism and great deeds and a particular favourite was *Lady Hamilton*, the epic about Nelson, which he had even shown President Roosevelt when they dined together aboard the battleship HMS *Prince of Wales* at Placentia Bay, Newfoundland, on the occasion of the signing of the Atlantic Charter in August 1941.

I suspect that Grandpapa had been impressed by the purpose-built cinema which his friend Max Beaverbrook had created at Cherkley, and determined to have one for himself at Chartwell. To accommodate the cinema, he converted the dining room on the lower ground floor at Chartwell. Two huge 35 mm projectors – the gift of his friend Sir Alexander Korda – were concealed in an adjacent projection room and the windows were blocked up so that a large screen could be installed across the entire wall at one end of the room.

In later years, when the system was installed and running, I used to enjoy being in the projection room with Mr Shaw who would come up from the village to operate the two giant machines with their powerful arc-lights. He and I would watch the film through a small glass panel in the wall and wait for the telltale mark at the top right-hand corner of the screen, which was the signal that the reel was about to run out and it was time to start the second machine to ensure perfect synchronization, so that the reel-change would pass unnoticed. If the film was particularly long like *Gone With The Wind* – another of Grandpapa's favourites – we would have a fifteen minute break while brandy glasses were recharged, cigars relit and anyone who wanted to could, to use one of his naval expressions, 'pump ship'. As at Chequers, all the staff, including the gardeners and their wives, the secretaries and the duty detective would be invited to these happy family occasions.

Among the other major changes made to the layout of Chartwell after the war was the transformation of the drawing room, on the floor immediately above the new cinema, into a painting studio.

With the help of a detective – one of whom was always on duty to protect him – he set up his easels and paints in his new studio.

As one of the signatories to the Irish Treaty of 1921, which brought into being the Irish Free State, while allowing the six counties of Ulster to remain British, he had been accorded police protection following the assassination soon afterwards of one of the other signatories, Field Marshal Sir Henry Wilson, shot outside his London home in Eaton Square. Thereafter the remaining signatories were granted personal bodyguards for life. Soon after the war one of Grandpapa's bodyguards, Inspector Thompson, had launched off on a speaking tour of the United States taking as his theme: 'How I Guarded Churchill'. Unfortunately for him one of my grandfather's former Private Secretaries happened to be in the Mid-West of America at the same time and, seeing the lecture advertised, decided to drop by. The audience listened in awed silence as the Scotland Yard man told his tale. However, when it came to the question period, the Private Secretary intervened from the back of the hall, declaring: 'We have all, I am sure, been most impressed by Mr Thompson's account of how he protected Mr Churchill in the war. Could he tell us on how many occasions, while guarding the Prime Minister, did he discharge his revolver and what precisely did he hit?' There was a long, embarrassed silence, before Inspector Thompson reluctantly admitted: 'Once – my big toe!' Fortunately the skills of the Scotland Yard men never had to be put to the test, but they certainly made admirable companions, whether to me for my fishing, or to Grandpapa in setting up his easel and paints. Indeed Sergeant Murray, who guarded him for the last fifteen years of his life, picked up many a hint from Grandpapa, and became quite an expert painter himself, modelling himself closely on his style.

The paints, which seemed to come in hundreds of different hues, spanning the entire spectrum of the rainbow, were kept in metal tubes laid out in rows in wooden carrying-cases. He would squeeze small quantities of the paints he needed from their tubes on to his palette-board where he would thin them with the addition of turpentine from a tin can. If he did not have readily available the precise shade of colour he needed, he would experiment by mixing two or more different base colours on the palette-board until he had achieved what he wanted. He invariably painted in oils and had a low regard for water colours, the pale tones of which were too insipid for his taste. He liked bold, bright colours and in *Painting As A Pastime* he vouchsafed his plans for the future:

> When I get to heaven I mean to spend a considerable portion of my first million years in painting, and so get to the bottom of the subject. But then I shall require a still gayer palette than I get here below. I expect orange and vermilion will be the darkest, dullest colours upon it, and beyond them there will be a whole range of wonderful new colours which will delight the celestial eye.

I enjoyed being with him and watching the picture – sometimes a still-life, but more often a landscape – develop from the blank canvas. He did his best to interest me in painting and, when I was just six, he made me a present of a small painting set of my own. In a letter of 5 January 1947 which accompanied the paints he gave me advice on how to use them:

Darling Winston,

Thank you so much for your charming card.

I now send you a box of very lovely paints, and some brushes. These paints must only be squeezed out a drop at a time, not more than the size of a pea. You can mix them with water freely, using plenty of water, but they dry and become no good any more in about half an hour. You may use about three times as much of the white tubes; that is to say a blob about equal to three peas, each time you paint a picture.

Do not waste these paints for they are very hard to get and come from abroad.

After you have tried them by yourself I hope you will come down here one afternoon so that I can show you myself how to use them.

> With much love,
> Your affectionate grandfather
> WSC

PS You do not need to squeeze out all the colours at once, only two or three at a time as you need them.

Though he tried giving me a couple of lessons, his efforts to interest me in the art of painting were, I am sorry to say, to no avail. I showed little talent in that direction and, when I painted him a steamship on a rough sea for *his* birthday, I fear that rather more of the paint ended up on my face, clothes and nursery floor, than on the canvas. This did not prove very popular with my mother.

Grandpapa having appropriated the dining room for his cinema and the drawing room for his paints, almost every other room in the house had to be moved around too. On the first floor Grandmama's bedroom became the drawing room and a bedroom (now a museum room) known as the Henry VIII room was turned into the dining room. This in turn involved Grandmama moving her bedroom up to the Tower Room at the very top of the house. As an economy measure, to save on the eight or nine indoor staff required pre-War, the old kitchens in the basement were abandoned, a smaller one being created on the second floor. Later when Grandmama decided that she was no longer able to climb the steep staircase to the Tower bedroom and she moved instead into her sitting room at ground-floor level adjacent to the front hall.

I loved my visits to Chartwell and spent many holidays there over the years. There was so much to do, there was never a spare minute in the day.

These were the years during which Grandpapa was out of office having been summarily dismissed from his post as Prime Minister by the British people in the hour of victory. Though shouldering the not inconsiderable burden that rested upon him as Leader of the Opposition and, at the same time, writing his mammoth six-volume history of *The Second World War* to keep the home fires burning, he always seemed to find plenty of time to spend with me. Each morning I would visit Grandmama in her Tower bedroom at the top of the house and then, rather later, pay a call on Grandpapa in his room, one floor below. I would pass through his large study with its high vaulted ceiling and its superb view over the Weald of Kent. Above the fireplace surmounted by a splendid oil painting of his birthplace, Blenheim Palace, hung the Union Flag which was raised by British Forces over Rome when that city had been liberated in 1944. On his large flat-top desk were framed miniatures of his father, Lord Randolph, and his American mother, Jennie Jerome. Also on his desk there stood a small but fine bust (which even now stands on my desk before me as I write) in white marble of Napoleon as a young man, aged twenty-six, when he commanded the Army of Italy. My grandfather had a profound admiration for him and the way, in the wake of the chaos of the French Revolution, he had mobilized the French nation to heroic deeds.

Beyond the study was his small bedroom where he would work at his papers and correspondence for two or three hours each morning. I would find him tucked up in bed with a mountain of pillows behind him and a bedtable, cut out to accommodate the shape of his belly, piled high with papers in front of him. He wore a white silk vest – he never wore pyjamas – and a red silk dressing gown. To his right, along the wall, was a shelf on which he kept two or three books, photographs of his parents and a small red-brick wall made out of cardboard over which was climbing a black cat. This did not seem to concern his pet budgerigar, Toby, who, resplendent in his emerald green and yellow outfit, would hop around on the bed, scattering cigar ash over the bedclothes with the fluttering of his wings. The venerable Grandpapa would peer at me over his gold-rimmed spectacles, remove a soggy cigar from his mouth and greet me with a broad smile. He would thereupon dismiss the secretary to whom he was dictating a letter or speech and we would make a plan for the day.

We would make our daily rounds of the property together. The first stop would be a visit to the golden orfe – huge golden red carp – that moved in silent state beneath the waters of a series of fish ponds which he had constructed and which were linked in cascading waterfalls by a stream that made its way down the valley to two large lakes which he had created in the Thirties by damming the stream. He had different calls for the various animals in his menagerie. The golden orfe would answer to a call of: 'Hike! Hike! Hike!' The alacrity of their response was doubtless not unconnected with the fact that, from a green-painted box beside the water's edge, he would cast a couple of scoops of food on to the surface of the water. Instantly the placid surface would turn to turmoil with the large fish fighting among themselves over the food.

Next we would make our way down past the vast swimming pool which he had also built and which had beneath it two massive coke-burning furnaces large enough to drive a battleship, to the upper lake where we would pay a call on the black swans, the gift of the Australian government. There used to be at least two pairs of these magnificent birds with their jet-black plumage and brilliant red bills. They spoke a different language to the orfe and would be hailed with cries of: 'Wow! Wow!' They too would be fed from a strategically placed food bin. Sadly, in spite of wire netting being placed round the lake for their protection, the fox from time to time, to Grandpapa's great dismay, managed to make successful raiding forays, carrying off the swans or their young. He thereupon caused to be erected a miniature lighthouse which flashed through the night, in the hope that the sweeping beam would deter the marauders – a device that, in fact, proved quite effective.

From there we would skirt around the main lake, where I used to spend many a happy hour fishing for roach with Grandpapa's detective, Sergeant Williams.

For me, aged five, the high point of our daily rounds would be our visit to the pigsties at the Home Farm, where Grandpapa kept two or three dozen Landrace pigs, which were highly regarded at the time for their long backs and productivity. Grandpapa loved his pigs and, on arrival at the sties, would reach over the wall to scratch their backs with his walking-stick – a process which the pigs clearly enjoyed. He and they would grunt at each other contentedly across the wall for several minutes. Grandpapa had a high regard for pigs and once remarked to me: 'A dog looks up to man, a cat looks down on man, but a pig will look you in the eye and see his equal!'

During my visits Grandpapa would arrange ponies for me to ride in the glorious beech woods adorning the hills that surrounded the Chartwell valley in a horseshoe framing, at its open end, the spectacular view which extends southwards 20–30 miles over the Weald of Kent. Once he insisted that he and Father were mounted too, so that the three generations could be photographed together on horseback. The view from Chartwell is one of the loveliest in England and it was above all for this that he bought the property in 1921. The valley would be at its most spectacular in the autumn sunlight when the beeches would turn through brilliant shades of yellow and red to gold. Sadly these woods that Grandpapa loved so dearly were to bear the brunt of the hurricane which struck Southern England in the early hours of 16 October 1987. Almost ninety per cent of those once proud trees, some of which had stood for two or three hundred years, were reduced to matchwood in the space of a couple of hours. Surveying the devastation, I was glad that my grandparents were no longer alive to see the fate that befell these fine old trees that were the glory of the Chartwell valley.

I was amused recently to come across an envelope on which my grandmother had written: 'Copied by Winston Churchill (Jr) September 1949'. Inside was a sheet of Chartwell notepaper on which, shortly before my ninth birthday, Grandmama had made me transcribe lines from Grandpapa's *My Early Life* to practise my handwriting:

When does one first begin to remember? When do the waving lights and shadows of dawning consciousness cast their print upon the mind of a child? My earliest memories are Ireland. I can recall scenes and events in Ireland quite well, and sometimes dimly, even people. Yet I was born on November 30, 1874, and I left Ireland early in the year 1879. My father had gone to Ireland as secretary to his father, the Duke of Marlborough, appointed Lord Lieutenant by Mr Disraeli in 1876. We lived in a house called 'The Little Lodge', about a stone's throw from the Viceregal.

With my father and June I spent Christmas of that year at Chartwell. Also there for the festivities were my godfather, Brendan Bracken, and Field Marshal Montgomery with his son David. Less than three weeks later my grandfather was to be plunged into a General Election campaign, in which the Conservatives slashed the Labour majority from 168 to a mere 6.

Chartwell, as may be imagined, holds so many happy memories. Well do I remember the tremendous splash when Grandpapa, already seventy-six years of age, plunged into the swimming pool from the diving board, also the great pleasure which Grandmama and I took in defeating Field Marshal Montgomery on the croquet lawn – about the only field of battle on which he could be defeated. But there were alarming moments too. I loved helping on the farm and at no time more than at haymaking. Grandpapa, in addition to the Home Farm which was quite small, bought another nearby called Bardogs. Much of Bardogs was on a hillside and when I was only twelve years old somebody made the mistake of allowing me to drive the tractor as the bales of hay were being loaded into the hay cart behind. All was well so long as we were on the level but, when I turned to head downhill, disaster struck. I was very small and slight for my age, indeed Father chided me for having 'the appetite of a bird'. Even standing with all my strength on the brake pedal, I did not have the weight to hold the heavy load of the hay cart behind and we rapidly began gathering speed. Bringing into play the skills developed in my long hours of practice on the (brakeless) milk trolley at Cerne, I swung the tractor broadside on to the hill effectively bringing it to a halt, but at the expense of an upset hay cart! I was rather shaken by this experience and was much relieved that nobody dared tell my grandparents what had happened.

When Grandpapa returned to Chartwell at the end of the war, he found himself very hard up, having for more than five years had no opportunity to earn anything with his pen. Indeed it was to be several years before he could complete his *Second World War* memoirs and nearly ten years before he was to finish *The History of the English-Speaking Peoples*, upon which he had embarked before the outbreak of war. He was thus faced with the prospect of having to sell his beloved Chartwell – a sorry contrast to the munificence heaped upon his ancestor, John Churchill, by Queen Anne and a grateful nation following the victory of Blenheim. Fortunately Lord Camrose and a small group of wealthy well-wishers intervened – appalled that the man who had saved his nation, indeed the world, from Hitler should be in financial straits. They purchased Chartwell from him for the sum of £43,800 on 29 November 1946, the day before his seventy-second birthday, on the understanding that he and my grandmother should live there for their lifetime and that, on their death, it would be presented to the nation to be preserved by the National Trust for the enjoyment of the public for posterity.

As a great dynast, Grandpapa was evidently sad at the prospect of Chartwell being alienated from the family, but he no doubt realized that the house and estate were far too large for succeeding generations to manage. However he was keen to ensure that family links with the property were maintained in the years ahead and, in a letter to my father, he expressed his hopes for the future:

House of Commons
29 January 1947

Dearest Randolph,

In my old age I am toiling night & day to provide for those I leave behind me & events have significantly increased my power ... I propose to leave you in my will the farmhouse & its gardens & woodlands which I have bought from Major Marnham (Keeping the farm in my hands for the present). This will come to you after my death and yr mother's entailed for Winston, so that you will have a small but comfortable home close to the Chartwell museum under the National Trust, & so the family name & associations will be preserved by living representatives on the spot.

I have other hopes & plans for yr advantage & for that of Winston. Though my span cannot be long, I build for the future ...

Your loving father,
Winston S. Churchill

In fact his 'span' was to be longer than he imagined. He was to become Prime Minister for a second term of four years and to live for another ten years after that. Meanwhile, inevitably, plans changed. Later that same year my Aunt Mary married Captain Christopher Soames, later Lord Soames, and they moved into the Chartwell farmhouse. It was a comfort to my grandparents to have Christopher and Mary living nearby. His new son-in-law swiftly secured Grandpapa's confidence and respect, coming to manage his farms and race horses. Before long, on his entry to the House of Commons, Christopher was appointed his Parliamentary Private Secretary, becoming the trusted ally and lieutenant to my grandfather that my father would so dearly have wished to be. Eventually the Soames' growing brood of children dictated a move to a larger house and the farmhouse came, like Chartwell itself, to be lost to the family. However, in recent years, my wife Minnie and I, together with our four children have moved to a house in the nearby village of Westerham and are thus able to continue the family links with Chartwell, which Grandpapa had been so keen to see preserved.

In the sunset years of his life, Grandpapa was due to spend more and more of his time at Chartwell. Of a summer's evening, as the shadows lengthened, he could be found beneath the great cedar that stands on the lawn below the house, wrapped in a rug on a *chaise-longue* bathed in the evening sun, gazing out over the distant view or dozing peacefully with an extinct and soggy cigar still firmly in his mouth.

· VI ·

Return to Chequers

All too soon the dreaded day arrived when, in January 1949, shortly after my eighth birthday, I was required to forsake my home, my toys and my soldiers – of which by now Grandpapa Churchill had given me a fine collection – to be packed off to boarding school. Because of my bad asthma, and the eczema and hay fever which went with it, I was sent to a school in Switzerland called Le Rosey, where it was believed the mountain air would do me good. In the summer and autumn terms the school was at Rolle, on the shores of Lake Geneva, but in the winter it moved up to Gstaad in the mountains of the Bernese Oberland for winter sports. I was the youngest and smallest boy in the school, and one of only six English boys out of the school's one hundred and twenty, made up of a score of different nationalities. It was a shock to find that all lessons – including English – were taught in French! We were even fined ten *centimes* if we spoke English at meals. But being thrown in the deep end in this way, I soon became bilingual.

I lived for the skiing and was delighted to find that we were allowed to ski for two hours each afternoon. However, because I was so light, I had a problem on a mountain called the Windspillen with the T-bar ski-lift which pulled skiers up the mountain in pairs. If, by chance, I had to go alone, there was a particularly steep point at the entrance to a wood, where my puny weight was inadequate to counterbalance the strength of the recoil spring and I would find myself being lifted bodily into the air. I would cling on grimly as the wire spun me round. It was an even money chance that I would end up with my skis pointing backwards up the mountain and fall off. But, in spite of these tribulations, I rejoiced in what I soon came to appreciate as the king of sports.

Soon after my arrival at my new school I sent Grandpapa Churchill a postcard of the school. He replied enthusiastically three weeks later:

9 February, 1949

My dearest Winston,

Thank you so much for your postcard, with its nice picture of your school. I am delighted to hear that you are happy and also from your mama that the high air is doing you so much good. It must be great fun skating and skiing in brilliant sunshine. I hope you find your lessons interesting; you should learn all you can about the history of the past, for how else can one even make a guess at what is going to happen in the future?

We have had not bad weather here, and I am making a new pool in my garden so as to have a better waterfall. I expect you have wonderful waterfalls where you are, with which I cannot compete.

Please write to me again as it always gives me great pleasure to hear from you.

Yr loving Grandpapa,
Winston S. Churchill

My mother had meanwhile been to visit me and reported to Grandmama Churchill:

I cannot tell you how wonderfully well Little Winston is. He has already gained 4 lbs, and his appetite is enormous and his cheeks bright pink. I only wish you could all see him now. He has completely forgotten his home sickness, and has entered fully into the school life. Today I took him and four friends to tea – needless to say they were all English boys.

Later in the year, by which time the school had moved down to the shores of Lake Geneva, remembering that Grandpapa had his birthday soon after mine – I had just celebrated my ninth – I had gone down to the post office in the village of Rolle on 30 October to send him a telegram:

WINSTON CHURCHILL CHARTWELL WESTERHAM KENT
MANY HAPPY RETURNS
LOVE WINSTON

To my great embarrassment, I received the following reply three days later:

WINSTON CHURCHILL
LE ROSEY
ROLLE
SWITZERLAND

THANK YOU SO MUCH DEAREST WINSTON FOR YOUR TELEGRAM BUT YOU ARE A MONTH TOO SOON.

LOVE
GRANDPAPA

A couple of years before, my mother had decided to quit the gloom of post-war Socialist Britain in favour of Paris, which had recovered much more quickly than London from the rigours of war. She acquired a small but beautiful apartment at 4 Avenue de New York, adjacent to the Place de l'Alma and enjoying one of the loveliest views in Paris, looking directly across the Seine towards the Eiffel Tower. This was to be her home for the next twelve years of her life and I often visited her there during the holidays.

While spending a few days with my mother in Paris in the summer of 1950, we were invited to lunch by Ernest Hemingway at the Ritz Hotel, in which he felt he had a proprietorial interest having been the first American to liberate the Ritz Bar from the Nazis in August 1944. Hemingway, a large, powerfully-built man with a full grey beard, met us in the hotel lobby and led us down the long narrow passage that leads from the main entrance on Place Vendôme towards the rear of the hotel where the bar is situated. On either side of the passage were the eyecatching showcases displaying the wares of all the most expensive shops in Paris. I had never seen anything like it before and, as we passed the Hermes window, my small boy's eyes went out on beanstalks at the sight of a huge and magnificent knife with a handle made of ivory. With its blade open, it measured fully ten inches. In vain did I seek to attract my mother's attention but, unsurprisingly, she did not share my enthusiasm for this lethal monster – a weapon wholly unsuitable for a child not yet ten years of age, besides costing a fortune.

On reaching the bar Mr Hemingway ordered us each a drink and abruptly excused himself, saying that he had an important telephone call to make. More than five minutes passed. Finally Hemingway reappeared with a triumphant smile on his face and a mischievous twinkle in his eye. In his hand he was carrying a large, beautifully wrapped parcel which, somewhat to my mother's amazement, he presented to me. It did not take me long to discover that it was the knife – the same vast ivory-handled knife – that I had admired a few minutes before in the window. I opened its flashing silver blade and looked in wonder back and forth from the knife to my new-found American friend and benefactor. I could not believe my luck.

My holiday with my mother was at an end and a day or two later I returned to England to spend the remaining ten days of the holidays with my father. In a state of some excitement I told him about my American friend and with pride produced my splendid trophy. Father was full of admiration for my precious knife but, unfortunately for me, too much so. He asked me if I would loan it to him. 'I am just off to Korea,' he explained, 'a place on the far side of the world where there is a war going on. I am going to report the war which we and the Americans are fighting against the Communists. Winston,' he enquired engagingly, 'may I borrow your knife to cut off a hunk of Communist?'

Now I had no idea what a Communist was but, if they were fighting the British and Americans, they were clearly 'not on our side' (to use a favourite phrase of my father's). On that basis 'cutting off a hunk of Communist' seemed a perfectly laudable objective. I was torn between my splendid new present and my duty to my father. Eventually the latter prevailed and, with reluctance and misgivings, I surrendered my precious possession.

That was the last I was to see of my Hemingway knife. Father took it with him, as threatened, to Korea at the end of July 1950 armed with a letter of introduction from his father to General MacArthur. But, contrary to his expectations, it was the Communists who took a hunk off him. He had not been there long before, in the early hours of 23 August, he was wounded while taking part in a night patrol with the US Marines across the Naktong River. As the patrol sought to recross the river, having made no contact with the enemy, they were spotted in the water and attacked with mortars. Several of the patrol were killed and others wounded, among them my father who got a shrapnel wound in his knee, requiring him to be evacuated to hospital in Tokyo. By the time he returned to the front line several weeks later, the Communists had advanced and overrun the hut where he had been billeted and where he had left my knife. Though the Communists had been pushed back once again to the far side of the Naktong, Father reported that there was no sign of the knife. I never quite forgave him for losing it.

Father, who had planned to join us with June and baby Arabella for ten days at the beginning of September, cabled Grandmama from his hospital bed in Tokyo:

SO HAPPY WINSTON IS AT CHARTWELL STOP PLEASE TELL HIM HOW SORRY EYEM NOT TO BE WITH HIM FONDEST LOVE TO YOU ALL = RANDOLPH

Soon after my return to school in January 1951, by now aged ten, I wrote to Grandpapa Churchill to thank him for the portable wind-up gramophone and records he and Grandmama had given me for Christmas and to tell him how much I was enjoying Le Rosey and especially the skiing and skating. He replied the following week:

5 February 1951

My dearest Winston,

I was so glad to get your letter of January 27 in which you tell me so much of your news. I was so sorry not to be at Chartwell when you were there, for it is always a great pleasure to me to see you, and I hope we shall get to know each other better as we both grow older.

I showed your letter to Grandmama and she was delighted you were pleased with the stamps she sent you from Marrakesh. I did not know you were collecting stamps and I will see if I can find a few as they come in on my large correspondence.

I hope you will not lose your early interest in painting because that is a great amusement in after-life, and you seem to me to have a real liking for it.

Please write me other letters and you will always get an answer from your loving Grandpapa

Winston S. Churchill

A fortnight later I told him that I had been selected for the Le Rosey school 'Under Ten-and-a-half' ice hockey team. Rigged up with padding and wearing the school's smart royal blue and white colours, we would take on other schools in a game where, all too often, the objective seemed less to hit the puck into the opposing goal than to trip up the other side by inserting one's hockey stick through the runners of one's opponents' skates! We all had great fun sliding about on the ice. However, unbeknown to me, my time at the school was about to come to an abrupt end.

In the same letter I reported: 'Montgomery invited me out to tea, I enjoyed myself a lot.' Field Marshal Montgomery, the victor of Alamein and close friend of Grandpapa Churchill, was in the habit of renting a chalet in Gstaad for a few weeks each winter and had invited David Verney, one of the few other English boys at the school, and me to have tea with him at his chalet. The Field Marshal had evidently formed a dim view of the behaviour of some of the older boys in the school, some of whom were eighteen years of age and had become too much of a handful for the school authorities. On seeing my grandfather a few days later Monty reported: 'Winston! I feel you should know that your grandson is at a school for snobs!' This prompted Grandpapa to write to both my father and my mother:

24 February 1951

My dear Randolph,

Yesterday Field Marshal Montgomery came to dinner here. He has just spent several weeks in Gstaad. This is the second winter he has done this. On both occasions he saw Winston, and he remarked what a nice little boy he was, and how he had improved. He also told us that having seen him on the slopes he thinks he is a promising skier.

But from personal observation of the conduct of the senior boys in the town and in the neighbourhood of Gstaad, and also from local opinion, he has formed a poor view of the school. He has met the Head, and has not a good opinion of the Direction [Management] and he fears that if Winston is left there much longer he might deteriorate both in character, and what is less important, his work ...

I would urge upon you both that you give this matter serious thought. I have sent a similar letter to Pamela.

Your loving father
WSC

I had no knowledge of what was being discussed behind my back and certainly Grandpapa gave no hint of his concern in his letter to me a week later:

3 March 1951

My dear Winston,

I have received your letter of 18 February. Thank you so much for writing to me and telling me your news.

Field Marshal Montgomery came to lunch at Chartwell the other day and told me all about his visit. It was very kind of him to entertain you. He said you were quite promising as a skier, and gave a good account of you.

> Your loving grandfather,
> Winston S. Churchill

Grandpapa's letter to my parents had decided matters, for my mother was already anxious as to whether – in spite of the attentive coaching of the kindly English master, Mr Hughes – my Latin (taught, like all lessons, in French) would be up to the standard required to pass the entrance examination into Eton. Thus, without further ceremony or even the chance to bid my friends farewell, I was – at the instigation of the Field Marshal – removed from the school at the end of term, never to return. In spite of the opinion that he had formed which, in respect of the older boys, was not mistaken, I owe it to Le Rosey that I became bilingual in French, a competent skier and was disabused of the chauvinism so readily inculcated by an English public school education.

I was next sent to Ludgrove, a preparatory school near Wokingham in Berkshire. Grandpapa was clearly pleased and on 22 March 1951 cabled Grandmama who was holidaying in Southern Spain:

MRS CHURCHILL
HOTEL ALPHONSO XIII
SEVILLE

HOW ARE YOU GETTING ON. MUCH PARTY TURMOIL HERE BUT NOW TEN DAYS' HOLIDAY. WINSTON GOES TO LUDGROVE NEXT TERM.

FONDEST LOVE
W.

The school was run by Alan Barber who had captained Yorkshire at cricket and played for England. He certainly had a powerful drive as those of us who had the misfortune to be punished by him will not soon forget. I no longer recall with what misdemeanour I was charged but, one evening when the whole school had been gathered together, the headmaster, in his broad nasal tone, declared: 'Behaviour in the school is just not good enough and I want the following to put on their pyjamas and dressing gowns and be outside my study door in five minutes time!' To my horror my name was on the list. Those of us who had been named scampered upstairs to undress. Some, who had suffered before, would try stuffing their pyjama bottoms with sheets of blotting paper, but this would invariably be discovered and lead to additional strokes of the cane. I always seemed to draw unlucky with those who chose to beat me and into whose power I had been delivered. In Switzerland, where the law forbids beating children with a cane, the master in charge of the junior school just happened to be one of the champion discus throwers of Switzerland and his bare hand alone had been quite sufficient to transmit a firm and very painful message.

The worst was the waiting as we stood shivering in the dark corridor outside the headmaster's room, having to listen to the shrieks and yells of those who went before us who would emerge with their faces contorted in agony, tears streaming down their cheeks and clutching their behinds. Suddenly it was my turn to step into the headmaster's study. Waving a four-foot cane in his right hand, he declared: 'Churchill! It's just not good enough. Bend down and put your head on the sofa!' With that he threw the bottom of my dressing gown over my head and took a pace backwards before whipping me four times with the cane through my pyjamas. I fled from the room in pain and sought sanctuary in my dormitory. The next morning I remember I had difficulty getting my pyjamas off as the blood from the weals had stuck fast to them. No doubt this was part of the 'character-building' regime which the interfering Field Marshal believed would be so good for me. Fortunately it was to be my only experience of the kind while at Ludgrove.

In contrast to Switzerland, where life had been virtually unaffected by the aftermath of war, the food in English prep schools at the time left much to be desired. Whereas at Le Rosey we had had roast chicken once a week and even, on rare occasions such luxuries as *Pêches flambées,* food at Ludgrove was largely of the 'toad-in-the-hole', 'bubble-and-squeak' variety, followed by stodgy puddings with custard. But, on the credit side, I had a small plot of garden which I could call my own, where I grew flowers, a few vegetables and even two strawberry plants. But, most of all, I enjoyed the scouting. As a scout, I learnt to make a fire without paper, using a single match, some strips of birch-bark and whatever was available in the woods as kindling. I discovered how to signal in Morse-code and to recognize many of the stars and constellations of the night sky. Indeed I became so enthused with these outdoor activities that I wrote to my father to request that if either he or my mother were minded to take me out from school, would they please avoid 'Scouting Sundays'.

That summer, while I was staying with him at Chartwell, Grandpapa Churchill took me to the races at Goodwood to see his horse, Colonist, run. To my huge delight, Colonist, a magnificent grey, did his stuff and won by a nose in a most exciting race. A few days later, in a letter dated 3 August 1951, Grandpapa reported to my grandmother:

> I think Winston enjoyed himself alright riding at Sam Marsh's and swimming and petting Nicko [my cousin Nicholas Soames who was three years old at the

time and is now my colleague in Parliament]. He enjoyed going to the races and spotted a winner which no one else had thought of. The reason was because it belonged to the Aga Khan, whose sons [Karim and Amin, or 'K' and 'A' as they were known] were with him at the school in Switzerland. This is as good a reason as any other.

Holidays with my mother were invariably abroad, either in the South of France or the Swiss Alps. So, with holidays on the farm with my respective grandparents and at the English seaside with my father, I had the best of all worlds. For three or four summers we stayed at a magnificent villa on the French Riviera called the Château de la Garoupe, close to Antibes. It stood on a rocky promontory facing the sea, with superb rock bathing on one side and a lovely, more sheltered sandy bay on the other. It was here that Mrs Martin and I would spend much of our days. I had swimming and diving lessons in the pool at the nearby Eden Roc with an instructor who would come and collect me each morning. As it was a couple of miles each way my mother, at the instructor's suggestion, rented me a motor-scooter, though I was not yet ten years old at the time – something that was perfectly legal in France but which would be unthinkable in the traffic conditions of today. The Velo-Solex was a splendid machine, with a small motor driving the front wheel and propelling it at a good 20 mph. My feet barely reached the pedals and my first stop was headfirst into a prickly hedge but I soon got the hang of it.

In addition to swimming, I learned to water-ski and took to snorkelling. In those days the waters of the Mediterranean had a crystal clarity to them, ranging in colour from a deep indigo blue to a brilliant aquamarine, and I would spend long hours under the water with my mask and flippers. The shafts of sunlight would penetrate deep below the surface, illuminating the myriad shoals of small fish whose coats flashed silver as they manoeuvred in the sunbeams filtering down through the water. On every side the sea was full of plant and marine life, with crabs, star-fish and octopus in abundance. Sadly, today, the Mediterranean, for so long treated as the septic tank of Europe, is fast becoming a 'Dead' Sea. I count myself lucky to have known it when it was truly a Côte d'Azur with a magical brilliance in its sky and sea, which my grandfather captured so well in the paintings he did by its shores.

That autumn a general election was called, just eighteen months after the previous one of February 1950 the results of which, though encouraging, had been inadequate to secure the return either of Grandpapa as Prime Minister or of Father as MP for the naval dockyard constituency of Plymouth, Devonport, where he was trying to dislodge the eloquent and able left-winger, Michael Foot, who had held the seat since 1945. This time around, both Grandpapa and Father hoped for great things, as did I. Not quite eleven years of age I was thrilled to be invited to help my father in his campaign and a plan was made, with the headmaster's approval, that I should travel down with Grandpapa by sleeper train to the West Country where we would join my father who was already engaged in the fray. I wrote in a state of some excitement to Grandpapa:

> Ludgrove
> Wokingham
> Berks
>
> 30 September [1951]

Dear Grandpa,

Thank you very much for having me to stay. I enjoyed it a lot. I am looking forward to go to Plymouth with you. Father took me out to luncheon yesterday. We play football this term. I am reading your book called *My Early Life*. It is very interesting. I hope you win the 'ELECTION'. I hope you are well.

> Lots of love from
> Winston

Ten days later Grandpapa replied by telegram:

WINSTON CHURCHILL.
LUDGROVE.
WOKINGHAM.
BERKS.

THANK YOU SO MUCH DEAREST WINSTON FOR YOUR CHARMING LETTER.

BEST LOVE FROM
GRANDPAPA

I was thrilled to get away from school and travel down with Grandpapa to Devonport. There on 23 October I attended a large and noisy open-air rally of several thousand people, addressed by Father and Grandpapa. It was a very cold evening and, while everyone else was wrapped up warm, I was the only one on the platform without an overcoat. Though it had been planned that I should travel back to London with Grandpapa on the night-sleeper, Father, at my instigation, was able to persuade Alan Barber to let me stay on a couple of days until the election was over.

Polling Day was set for 25 October and that evening, after the polls had closed and the counting staff had finished their task, we all went out on to the balcony of a fine old house, looking down on Plymouth Hoe, where Sir Francis Drake had played his famous game of bowls while waiting for the Spanish Armada to draw near. That night the Hoe was a seething mass of people, jostling with each other in the darkness for a better view. The mayor stepped forward into the arc-lights to announce the verdict of the electorate. To my chagrin, Father had been defeated, albeit by a slim margin. The result was received with wild cheering by Michael Foot's supporters who greeted Father's name with boos and wolf-whistles.

Up to the time of writing, having myself fought seven Parliamentary elections, I cannot recall any where the mob was filled with such bitterness and hatred as that night at Devonport. It was no doubt due to the very considerable poverty that still existed even six years after the war and accentuated by the fact that my father was the son of the Leader of the Opposition whose chances of victory at a national level seemed promising. When, following Michael Foot, Father stepped forward to the microphone to thank the Returning Officer and his staff and to congratulate Michael on his victory, he could not get a hearing. The crowd was howling like a pack of hyenas baying for blood. In the end Michael had to step in to command his supporters to silence before Father could speak.

After the formalities were over, the local Police Superintendent suggested to Father that, in view of the size and temper of the crowd, it would be best if we left by the back door. He clearly did not know my father who exploded: 'I don't go out of back doors!' We therefore went out of the front door where the mob was waiting for us. More than a dozen burly policemen did their best to make a path for us but were powerless to prevent the jeering mob of Plymouth fishwives with hatred in their eyes from pulling my stepmother's hair, kicking our shins and spitting on us before we could reach our car. There are certainly few things more unpleasant than a mob with its blood up as it was that night in Plymouth.

Though Father had failed in his bid to return to the Commons, Grandpapa and the Conservative Party had triumphed and, almost seventy-seven years of age, he embarked upon his second Premiership. Once again – after an interval of eight years – the family was able to celebrate Christmas at Chequers and, for the first time, we were at full strength with my father and all his sisters, Diana, Sarah and Mary, together with their husbands present. Besides Arabella, who was now two, and myself, there was a whole host of Sandys and Soames cousins and we had a wonderful time playing games of hide-and-seek and generally rampaging through the house. The Christmas tree in the Great Hall seemed to reach almost to the ceiling, glowing with dozens of wax candles which had to be painstakingly lit from ladders with long tapers. One of Grandpapa's old bathroom sponges, soused in water and tied on to the end of an especially long bamboo, was kept to hand to douse any candle that threatened to set the tree or the decorations alight. It was one of the happiest Christmases I can remember and we, the grandchildren, were especially thrilled to have Grandpapa back as Prime Minister once again.

That New Year was one of many I spent in St Moritz with my mother, which was a wonderful treat. Skiing was, by far, my favourite sport and I would be on skis all day from dawn, when I would be on the first funicular of the day up the mountain, to dusk. The evenings I spent bowling in the *kegelbahn*. One morning early, I went up to watch the riders on the Cresta run. Like skiing, it was a sport invented by the British who, together with the Swiss and Italians, provided most of the riders for this exciting sport where the rider races down a narrow, twisting ice track lying on his belly on a low toboggan. The toboggan, known as a skeleton, has two metal runners and a sliding top to it so that the rider can shift his weight forward or back to help negotiate the corners which are heavily banked, and often take one beyond the vertical. The track, which from the top is over one and a half miles long, is constructed each December of snow and hosed down every night to make it a completely smooth track of sheet ice. A good rider can attain speeds of 80 to 90 mph and, with his nose just six inches above the ice as he clatters down the run, enjoys a sensation of speed – not to mention fear and exhilaration – greater than I have known in any other sport.

My mother, who was watching the racing from the road-bridge half way down the track, had entrusted me to the care of a jolly White Russian called Sergei Ovsievsky. Suddenly, as we watched the riders race – one of them had just flown out at Shuttlecock corner into a heap of snow and hay – Sergei turned to me and enquired: 'Winston, would *you* like to have a go?' I was beside myself with excitement and accepted with alacrity. There was then the problem of getting me suitably kitted up which, in the case of an eleven-year-old, was far from easy as all the protective equipment was made for grown-ups. A helmet was found which more or less fitted and Lorenzo, the Italian who, for nearly forty years after the war, was employed by the St Moritz Tobogganing Club to look after the skeletons, and other equipment, set about strapping me up with knee pads, elbow pads, and steel shields to prevent the backs of my hands being crushed against the side of the track. Boots proved a problem which was only resolved when Lorenzo managed to fix the Crestas – the metal spikes shaped like the crest on a cockerel's head, after which the run was named – to the toe caps of my ski-boots. Thus attired, I was ready to do battle, though I must confess I had a million butterflies in my stomach. With many instructions about what to do and, above all, what not to do, to avoid flying out of the track before I reached the bottom, my Russian friend launched me forth. Fairchild Macarthy, the bluff Canadian known to one and all as 'Mack' who, bear-like in his long fur coat, ruled the Cresta for three decades after the war with his brisk North American bark, sounded his bell from the control-box and yelled, 'Rider in the run: Churchill!'

Although digging the spikes of my Cresta for all I was worth into the ice, my skeleton and I rapidly gathered speed as I set out on what is unquestionably the most exciting ride in the world. The first my mother knew of what was afoot was when she saw an object – half the size of any of the other riders – flying under the bridge where she was standing. As I clattered down the run at what seemed a terrific speed, from time to time crashing into the sheer ice walls of the track, I began to worry about how I would stop the beast when I got to the end. But, almost before I had time to ponder the matter, I was across the finishing line where the track suddenly sweeps uphill in a long left-handed curve, giving one a sensation of deceleration, climbing and turning all at the same time, something that I can only compare to the sensation experienced as a pilot when pulling out of a dive in a jet-fighter following an air strike.

I managed to make a second run before the Club authorities caught up with me. Anxious lest any injury befall the Prime Minister's grandson, the Committee, later that day, put out a stuffy statement to the effect that: 'The Club cannot be responsible for one so young riding the Cresta.' Their concern was perhaps understandable, but the Committee has yet to be known to accept responsibility for *any* rider, whatever his age! Apparently, at the age of eleven, I was the youngest person – with the exception of Moore Brabazon, later Lord Brabazon of Tara, many years before – ever to have ridden the Cresta and it was to be at least eight years before I was to have the chance of riding it again.

Early in 1952, King George VI died. He and Queen Elizabeth, now the Queen Mother, had seen us through the long years of war and especially strong bonds had been forged between the sovereign and his people as a result. The whole nation mourned his passing but, at the same time, there was much excitement and joy at the prospect of their daughter, Princess Elizabeth, becoming Queen. Towards the end of the year, with preparations in train for the Coronation which was to take place the following summer, I received a most exciting invitation. Marshal of the Royal Air Force, Lord Portal of Hungerford, who had commanded the RAF for much of the war as Chief of the Air Staff, invited me to be his page at the Coronation. In a letter to my mother he wrote:

I have been appointed by the Queen to 'bear the Sceptre with the Cross' and must have a page (12–15 yrs & under 5 ft 5 in tall) to carry my coronet. I think the pages are bound to get a close-up view of the actual crowning, but don't yet know exactly where they stand.

He made mention of the fact that it would involve some rehearsals and that the clothes would cost £200!

As may be imagined I was thrilled at the prospect of being a page at the Coronation, not least for the fact that it would mean getting away from school on at least three occasions, including twice for rehearsals. The most immediate requirement was to be measured up for my uniform which was very splendid and consisted of white breeches worn with white silk stockings and black patent leather buckle-shoes, a white satin waistcoat surmounted by a black and silver frock coat with azure blue cuffs. At my neck I wore a lace ruff and, at my left side, a sword.

For the first rehearsal in May all those with specific parts to play in this splendid and ancient ceremony, excepting only the sovereign, were assembled in Westminster Abbey. We were directed to our places, under the eagle eye of the Duke of Norfolk, the hereditary Earl Marshal of England, and told precisely what was required of us at each point in the ceremony, from the highest functionaries of Church and State down to the smallest pageboy. It is a strange quirk, in a land where the Protestant succession to the throne is ordained by law, that the premier Catholic in the land should be charged with the high responsibility of organizing the Coronation, thereby ensuring the Protestant succession to the throne. Though short of stature and ruddy of face and, viewed from across the great expanse of the Abbey, looking like nothing so much as Mr McGoo, the Duke of Norfolk, trailing a long microphone lead behind him, instantly asserted his authority over the proceedings by the brusqueness of his commands but, above all, by his precise knowledge of every detail of the ceremony.

There was a splendid moment when the Earl Marshal commanded the Archbishop of Canterbury: 'Archbishop! Pray bring the crown!' The Archbishop shuffled off into a corner and reappeared a few moments later bearing a crown in his hands. The Earl Marshal took one look at it from a distance and instantly proffered the stinging rebuke: 'Archbishop! That is the wrong crown! Pray bring St Edward's Crown!' It had an electric effect on the assembled company and, thereafter, each one of us, from the Chiefs of Staff downwards, determined not to give the Earl Marshal any ground for offering us so stinging a public rebuke. For the dress rehearsal, just a few days before the great occasion, my mother supervised my turnout in minute detail, arranging for my hair to be cut and giving the barber precise instructions as to how it was to be done. No sooner had we arrived at the Abbey than I was accosted by Field Marshal Montgomery who could never readily restrain his instinct to be a busybody: 'Boy! Tell your mother to get your hair cut before the day!'

Finally the great day arrived. Though my principal concern was not to trip over my sword or drop Lord Portal's coronet, at the point in the ceremony where I approached closest to the Throne I could not restrain a sideways glance at the mesmeric beauty and radiance of our young Queen. I was amazed that one so slight could bear the great weight of the crown – over $4\frac{1}{2}$ lbs – with such apparent ease. Grandpapa, as Prime Minister, wearing the robes of a Knight of the Garter, had a prominent place and Father who, for the occasion, had been appointed a Gold Staff Officer, was also present. Afterwards my grandparents gave a luncheon at Number 10, whither we made our way through the streets still packed with wildly cheering crowds, many of whom had camped on the pavement for three or four nights to secure positions of vantage. At Downing Street Grand-mama had arranged for all three generations of participating Churchills, Grandpapa, Father and me, to be photographed together in our finery and regalia. It was a proud and memorable day.

About this time Father, who had just produced two books, *They Serve*

the Queen and *The Story of the Coronation*, to coincide with that year's
great events, contracted to write another book entitled *Fifteen Famous
English Homes*. Besides the perennial motivation of shortage of cash, I
suspect that an ancillary motive may have been that, with my school
holidays looming, he was at a loss to know what to do with me. His choice
of subject provided the perfect excuse – had he felt in need of one – to
descend, self-invited, upon his wealthiest friends and the owners of the
stateliest homes in the land. He forewarned our prospective hosts that I
would be with him and that the provision of some shooting or other such
diversion would not go amiss. Thus we sallied forth in Father's battered
station-wagon for our Grand Tour. First stop was Chatsworth where the
Duke of Devonshire was having some major restoration work done, so we
put up in a nearby pub in the village of Bakewell. Father was most
apprehensive to discover that the hotel recommended to us called itself a
'Trust House', fearing that it might have something to do with the tem-
perance movement and that he would be unable to obtain a drink. Fortunately for him his fears proved groundless.

From Chatsworth we went on to spend two or three days with John and
Isabel (Earl and Countess of) Derby at Knowsley in Lancashire. It was as
a result of this visit that my father was asked by John to write the life of
his father, the 17th Earl of Derby, known in the North-west of England
because of his power and prestige as 'The King of Lancashire', the title
my father was to give his book. It was this work which, in turn, established
my father's reputation as a biographer, and led Grandpapa to entrust to
him the task of writing his official biography.

Next we descended upon the Earl of Carlisle, who lived in Naworth
Castle close to the Scottish borders where some most enjoyable rough
shooting was provided. We concluded that particular part of my father's
researches at the magnificent castle of Alnwick in Northumberland which,
within its medieval fortress walls, contains a Renaissance Palace. Alnwick
was the scene of many bloody sieges and battles; indeed in the bailey of
the castle 3000 Scottish prisoners, captured by Cromwell at the Battle of
Dunbar, died in the space of eight days from hunger and exhaustion.

When news of my father's latest literary ventures reached the ears of his
friend Evelyn Waugh, the latter sought to discourage him, pronouncing
that: 'History and Culture are for gentler creatures!' – a view which he
followed up in a letter:

12 July 1953

My Dear Randolph,
    If you have engaged yourself to deliver those articles for publication there is
of course no alternative to their completion. I hope your next work will be
topical. There lies your proper field.

Laura, alas, will be busy with farm & children all the summer, sends her love & regretfully declines your kind invitation. The boy Auberon Alexander is available for little Winston's entertainment. His chief interest is shooting sitting birds with an airgun & making awful smells with chemicals. He is devoid of culture but cheerful & greedy for highly peppered foods. If not closely watched he smokes & drinks.

Shall I bring him for the first weekend of August? I look forward greatly to seeing you.

> Yours ever affec.
> E.

That autumn, at Chartwell, I had the first political discussion of which I have a clear recollection. There had recently been speculation in the press about the possibility of building a tunnel beneath the English Channel – an idea first mooted one hundred and fifty years before by Napoleon when he had designs on Britain but was anxious to avoid doing battle with the Royal Navy. Following lunch and a game of croquet, in which Grandmama and I soundly trounced Field Marshal Montgomery, I asked the Field Marshal his opinion. Replying in his very clipped way of speaking he pronounced: 'Dead against, boy! Dead against! The Huns would be marching through the tunnel in no time flat – we can't have that!' I suggested that, if they ever did, it would no doubt be an easy matter to flood the tunnel and drown any invaders, but he remained adamant.

For Christmas that year my mother and I were invited to stay with some friends, Paul and Peggy Munster, who had a chalet in the small village of Kitzbuhel in the Austrian Tyrol, renowned for its skiing. While there I met and fell in love with a beautiful young English girl with a French name called Minnie d'Erlanger, who happened to be holidaying there with her mother. Alas for me, she only had eyes for the handsome and bronzed Austrian ski instructors. Thereafter, over the years, if my mother was organizing a circus or theatre party in the Christmas holidays, Minnie would always be invited. Little could we know, aged just thirteen at the time, that within barely ten years we would embark together upon a long and wonderfully happy marriage.

· VII ·

Eton

In January of 1954 I was sent to Eton. Though my grandfather had gone to Harrow he was very much the exception within the family, both his father, Lord Randolph, and mine having gone to Eton. It seems that, in his case, the doctors had diagnosed that he suffered from weak lungs – a disability that, fortunately, did not manifest itself in later life – and had judged that 'Harrow-on-the-Hill' would be better for his health than 'Eton-in-the-Marshes'. Grandpapa had taken my father to visit both establishments and had given him the choice. He had plumped for Eton, having concluded that the boys, besides each having a room of their own, had greater freedom there than at Harrow. No such choice was vouchsafed to me, however. Indeed, my parents had been at pains to get me in at all, since they had failed to put me down for the school at birth – their minds being on more pressing matters at the time that I came into the world during those critical days of 1940. Father even had to enlist the support of his old history tutor, Robert Birley, who had by then become headmaster.

I was placed in the house of Tom Brocklebank, a keen mountaineer who had taken part in one of the early expeditions to conquer Mount Everest. His house was called the Timbralls and looked out upon the school's main football ground known as 'Sixpenny'. To a new boy, it was all very strange and rather awesome to be in so large a school with more than 1100 boys. Whereas almost all the other boys wore black tailcoats, I, being among the smallest boys in the school, was required to wear a short Eton jacket, colloquially known as 'bum freezers', together with a broad and most uncomfortable starched collar. I had to suffer this indignity for at least two years for, even at fifteen, I was still one of the smallest in the school. I bitterly resented being marked out from most of my contemporaries in this way and whereas, in later life, one is only too eager to stake out a distinct and individual position for oneself, as a small boy I craved to conform and become lost in the crowd. I was mortified when, ever solicitous for my welfare, my godfather Lord Beaverbrook, having consulted my mother as to what I needed most, gave me a handsome overcoat for my birthday, only to discover that it was made of a brown herringbone material while every other boy in the school had a navy blue overcoat. In retrospect it seems a foolish and trivial matter but I remember being deeply upset by it at the time.

I soon discovered that, at Eton, it was no advantage to be the grandson of the Prime Minister. Possibly because of the much more ready resort in those days to the cane by the Head and Lower Masters and the fact that the half dozen most senior boys in each house, known as the 'Library', were also allowed to administer a thrashing to their juniors, there was significantly more bullying then than is the case today. As one of the smallest in my house and bearing a name that set me apart from the others, I received perhaps more than my fair share. One moment I would be in a room with half a dozen other boys, chatting happily together; the next, for no obvious reason, one would suddenly say: 'Well, Churchill, how about it?' (Surnames were *de rigueur*.) My escape would be blocked by two of the boys putting their weight firmly against the door. I would thereupon be seized and, following a vain struggle my trousers would unceremoniously be removed. They would then take it in turns to beat me with rubber-soled slippers, yelling: 'Take this for being a shit! Take this for being a bastard! And take this for being Winston-bloody-Churchill!'

It was a cross I had to bear, but the great thing about an English public school education is the admirable way in which it prepares one for future life. One can go out into the world confident in the knowledge that life can contain few greater discomforts, humiliations or terrors than those to which one has already been subjected.

On going to Eton, my parents gave me an allowance of ten shillings (50 pence) per week and, later that year, I opened my first bank account. The ten shillings was to cover the cost of newspapers and all incidental expenses but was principally appreciated for the fact that it enabled me once, or sometimes twice a week, to buy a snack, known in Eton jargon as 'sock' at Rowlands, the school shop, where soggy chips with vinegar could be purchased for sixpence.

My first summer, instead of becoming a 'Dry Bob' and playing cricket which I found a dull and tedious game, I joined the 'Wet Bobs' on the river and took up rowing. I rented a Whiff, a narrow, clinker-built rowing boat from Alf, the boatman, who was in charge of the school's huge fleet of rowing boats, which included the swift thin shelled racing eights, which were all kept in a boathouse just upstream of Windsor Bridge under the shadow of the Castle. I spent many a happy hour on the river, though sometimes I would be off rowing for two or three weeks at a stretch as a result of having eczema on my hands which I had to soak in a purple solution of permanganate of potash. The Dame, as the matron was called, in my tutor's house, Miss Eileen Gorman, was a kindly lady and would bandage each of my fingers individually to stop them bleeding.

At the beginning of the summer 'Half', as terms were known at Eton, I wrote to my father about arrangements for the Fourth of June, the most important day of the year in the Eton calendar when the birthday of the founder, King George III, is celebrated and parents are expected to attend. I had a horror that my father would show up, as he had threatened, in his frock coat, which evidently had been the correct dress for parents on the Fourth of June when he was a boy and, in my letter, told him most earnestly that 'parents wear ordinary suits, not frock coats as you said . . .'

On 30 November 1954 Grandpapa celebrated his eightieth birthday with a party at 10 Downing Street. Happily his birthday coincided with that of St Andrew – an anniversary celebrated with a school holiday – and, exceptionally, I was granted leave to go to London for the occasion and was thus in Westminster Hall for the presentation of an Address by both Houses of Parliament to Grandpapa, who was still Prime Minister. At the same time he was given a portrait of himself specially commissioned by Parliament. Grandpapa had agreed to several sittings for the artist, Graham Sutherland, who was among the most highly regarded of English portrait painters of the day. However, when the moment came for the portrait to be unveiled, there was an audible gasp of shock from the assembled company. The artist had portrayed him in shades of sickly green and yellow and it appeared that he might even have a fly-button undone on his trousers. Grandpapa, who had not been allowed to see the portrait in advance, put a brave face on the matter and in his speech of thanks provoked much hilarity by describing it as 'A most remarkable example of modern art!'

The secretaries in the 'garden room' at Number 10 were in floods of tears when they saw it and Grandmama was mortified, regarding it as a personal and calculated insult by the artist – something which those who knew him assure me could not have been the case. However that may be, my grandmother some time later caused it to be destroyed as she could not bear to see Grandpapa remembered in this way. This did not become public knowledge until after her death when a statement was made by her executors.

In the spring of the following year, on 5 April 1955, Grandpapa retired as Prime Minister, to make way for his long-standing heir apparent, Anthony Eden. The evening before he quit Number 10 for the last time, the Queen and the Duke of Edinburgh paid him and my grandmother the great compliment of dining with them there. In advance of his resignation the question had been mooted among the Royal Family as to what further honour or distinction might be conferred upon the greatest Englishman of all time. It was agreed that there could be no higher compliment than to offer him a Dukedom, as was conferred on his great forebear John Churchill, by Queen Anne. However, it has long been recognized in Royal circles that poor Dukes are 'bad for business' and that it is useless to create a Duke who lacks the estates and appurtenances to accompany the style. With this in mind, a carefully laid plot was conceived, in which both Grandmama and my grandfather's former private secretary Jock (later Sir John) Colville were complicitous. Soundings were to be taken to establish whether, in the event of a Dukedom being offered, there was any danger it would be accepted.

When the matter was raised around the dinner table in a completely informal and hypothetical way, it brought a definitively negative response from the old warrior who declared: 'I would not wish to place such a blight on Randolph and Winston's political prospects.' At that time a member of the peerage was unable to disclaim his title and was thereby disbarred from pursuing a political career in the Commons – a situation which was subsequently changed by Act of Parliament to enable Viscount Stansgate to renounce his title and to sit in the Commons as Anthony Wedgwood-Benn, or Tony Benn as he now prefers to style himself. When my grand-father's reaction was reported back, it was judged safe formally to convey the offer of the Dukedom of London. On this being done, however, Grandpapa, to my grandmother's horror and Jock's consternation, made as if to change his mind: 'It is a most remarkable honour,' he mused, 'I would not wish to give offence to my Sovereign by refusing.' It looked for an awkward moment as if he would change his mind and accept; however, it soon became clear that he was teasing them, having had a shrewd suspicion as to what had been going on behind his back. But the offer nonetheless had been made and he had been greatly complimented by it.

By my second summer at Eton I had become sufficiently proficient at rowing to abandon my single-man whiff in favour of a Perfect, crewed by two oarsmen. On 1 March 1955 I reported in a letter to my father: 'Next half I am sharing a Perfect with a boy called Jones, who is quite mad, but very nice. (He thinks of nothing but guns and battleships) . . .'

This turned out to be the same 'H' Jones who, nearly thirty years on, as Colonel commanding the Second Parachute Regiment, was to die in a blaze of glory at Goose Green during Britain's campaign to regain the Falkland Islands in 1982. For this he was posthumously awarded the Victoria Cross.

Apart from this one reference to him in my letter to my father I, in common with many of his contemporaries at school, have no recollection of him whatever, other than as a quiet reserved boy who would keep very much to himself. I must confess that on reading of 'H's' death in a report which made mention of the fact that, like myself, he had been born in 1940, and done his schooling at Eton, I racked my memory in an attempt to recall if our paths had ever crossed, but in vain. Thus I was surprised to receive a call a day or so later from my former housemaster, Tom Brocklebank, to say that he had been asked to write an obituary of 'Jones, *major*' but could remember nothing about him. Since we had both arrived in his house the same year, he wondered if I could help with any memories. Even with my memory prodded in this way I still could remember nothing of him whatever and I was therefore intrigued when I recently came across the above letter among my father's papers. By all accounts, it was not until half way through Sandhurst that he emerged from his shell and began to show signs of being the strong, determined character he was to become. But it is of such stuff that heroes are made.

My father, who claimed to be a Cockney by the fact that he had been born within the sound of Bow Bells, had been a Londoner all his life. However, by now he had reached a point in his life where he felt the need to sink his roots in country soil and turn his back on city life with its idle distractions of gambling and drinking with his friends at White's Club which neither he, nor his constitution, could any more afford. It also marked the moment in his life when, recognizing that the burning ambitions of his youth were not to be fulfilled, he turned his back on the prospect of a political career and determined to devote his remaining years to journalism, in which he excelled, and to the writing of history and biography. Thus, in July of 1953, he rented a lovely house called Oving which enjoyed a distant view across the Vale of Aylesbury in Buckinghamshire. He took to country life with all the relish of a convert, proclaiming himself to be no longer a 'City Slicker' but a confirmed 'Country Bumpkin'. I spent two or three holidays with him there, together with June and Arabella, who had become the most entrancing child with brilliant blue eyes and long blond hair. One of our very first guests at Oving was my father's friend Adlai Stevenson, a man of calibre and distinction who had won the Democratic nomination for the US Presidency but had been defeated by Eisenhower. Father had hopes of buying Oving but it proved too expensive. It is today the home of his friend Michael Berry, now Lord Hartwell.

Finally, in the spring of 1955, he purchased a property on the edge of the Suffolk village of East Bergholt. The house, standing high on a hillside, enjoys a commanding view over the Vale of Dedham towards the River Stour, after which he was to name it. The view was pure Constable; indeed, John Constable lived in East Bergholt and painted some of his finest pictures of nearby Flatford Mill and Dedham Church, which is framed in the view from the terrace. It is an idyllic spot and one where my father was to spend the rest of his days. Brought up in the arid desert of the big city, he plunged himself with a will, as only a townee can, into his new garden, planting a host of specimen trees, including walnuts, tulip trees and other exotic species. He established a fine avenue of pleached limes where, on a hot summer's day, he could stroll in the shade with his pair of beautiful black pug dogs prancing at his heel. But, though an avid enthusiast, his enthusiasm did not extend to getting his hands dirty. On the contrary, he conceived his role in the garden to be that of the Constitutional Monarch, as defined by Bagehot, namely 'to be consulted, to encourage and to warn'.

He came to develop a deep love of the countryside and especially of his beloved Stour which was to become the centre of his universe. He was at one with Constable about the delights of East Bergholt and placed on the terrace a plaque inscribed with a quotation from one of Constable's letters: 'I am come to a determination to make no idle visits this summer nor give up any time to commonplace people. I shall return to Bergholt.' When he first bought the house, much needed doing to it and the garden was a hayfield. But, shortly before Christmas, we had things sufficiently in order to be able to hold an official house-warming party at which Grandpapa and Grandmama Churchill were the guests of honour. I think my grandmother in particular found it difficult to believe that her only son, who had for so long rejoiced in city life, could indeed settle down in the country.

Meanwhile, at school, I had learned the disturbing news that my mother, who had been on a visit to America, had been taken seriously ill and had to undergo a major operation in the New York Hospital. By amazing good fortune an American friend, Charles Wrightsman, had suggested that while she was in the United States she would do well to have a 'check-up' at the New York Hospital. In those days such things as medical check-ups were unknown among Europeans, who conceived them to be typical of the hypochondriac propensities of Americans. There is no doubt that in my mother's case, it saved her life. After the operation she was in low spirits and cabled my father to ask if I could spend the Christmas holidays with her in New York. The plan had originally been for me, together with Father, June and Arabella, to spend Christmas at Chartwell. In the circumstances, my father proposed that I fly to New York to join her after Christmas. But my mother pleaded from her hospital bed by telegram:

GRATEFUL YOUR UNDERSTANDING CABLE LEAVING HOSPITAL 14TH AM SO LONELY AND ALONE WOULD MAKE ALL DIFFERENCE IF WINSTON COULD ARRIVE 20TH DECEMBER PLEASE REPEAT PLEASE CABLE YOUR AGREEMENT LOVE = PAMELA

It was with feelings of great concern for my mother, whom I loved dearly, as well as of excitement at visiting the United States for the first time, that I took the plane for New York. In those days the International terminal at Heathrow consisted of a handful of Nissen huts on the north side of the airport where there was a small waiting-room furnished with basket-weave chairs. From there I boarded a British Overseas Airways Stratocruiser, a wonderful aircraft built by the Boeing Corporation which dominated the trans-Atlantic route at the time, though it did not have the range to reach New York non-stop but flew by way of barren, icy

Newfoundland – a flight that took sixteen hours. By the time I arrived my mother was out of hospital and was installed in the St Regis Hotel, although still too weak to go out and about.

To a fifteen-year-old brought up in wartime and post-war London, New York with its skyscrapers and bright lights was, without doubt, the most exciting city in the world. I was especially fortunate that my Aunt Sarah Churchill, an accomplished actress, was playing in a show on Broadway at the time. One day, when she did not have a matinée, she devoted the whole day to showing me the sights of New York. She was radiantly beautiful with her brilliant green eyes and flowing red hair and there could be few more enchanting companions. Together we went to the top of the Empire State Building on one of those crystal-clear winter days when one can see 50 or 60 miles. We took the Staten Island ferry and visited the Statue of Liberty which, with its torch of freedom held high, has greeted successive generations of refugees fleeing from religious or political persecution in Europe, who have made America what she is today. I was amazed by New York with its bold and magnificent architecture, the height of its buildings, the number and brightness of its lights, especially the magical sight of the lighted Christmas trees stretching up Park Avenue as far as the eye could see. Above all, I enjoyed the instinctive warmth and friendliness of New Yorkers.

My mother was being looked after by a wonderful English nurse called Nurse Matthews. On New Year's Eve, she volunteered to take me out on the town and we went down to Times Square to see the New Year in. We made our way through the jostling, merrymaking crowds and, at my suggestion, headed towards an amusement arcade called Playland, crammed with slot machines and shooting galleries. Seeing that I was doing quite an efficient job with an air rifle against his moving metal duck targets, the proprietor, a 280-pounder from Brooklyn with a fat cigar stuffed in his mouth, greeted me in a friendly way: 'Say, son! You're doing mighty fine! What's your name?' In a perfectly matter-of-fact way I told him. To my surprise, he suddenly became very angry and shouted in a broad Brooklyn accent: 'If you're Winston Churchill [pronounced 'Choi-chell'] – I'm Marilyn Monroe!' I was completely taken aback by his response for, up to then, nobody had ever questioned my name, indeed in Europe it is unheard of for strangers ever to ask one's name.

We spent Christmas at the Greentree estate of Jock and Betsey Whitney near Manhasset on Long Island. Besides an indoor Real Tennis court, Jock, who was proprietor of the *New York Herald Tribune* and later to serve as a most distinguished Ambassador to the Court of St James, kept a pet alligator called Oscar who lived in a shallow pool in the greenhouse. Outside the house was a fleet of more than half a dozen cars and station wagons, each double the size of anything seen in England at the time and, to my amazement and delight, I was allowed to use them to practise my driving on the roads all over the estate. The Whitneys were enormously hospitable and invited us to join them early in the New Year for a week's quail and turkey hunting in their southern home at Thomasville in Georgia. Among their many Christmas presents to me, was a snakebite kit which they said I might need for Georgia where, at that time of year, a warm sunny day can bring the 'rattlers' out of their holes. On arrival there I kept an anxious look-out, but never saw one.

At Thomasville we stayed in the Whitneys' beautiful old colonial plantation house, white-painted, with tall pillars supporting the roof over the veranda. Each morning we would set out in the warm winter sunshine of the South in two mule-drawn wagons laden with iced drinks and a picnic lunch, and with dog kennels at the rear. Those of us who chose, as I did, to ride, were provided with lovely Tennessee 'walking horses' (on which one does not need to rise to trot, they merely walk at double speed). My saddle was equipped with a leather sling for my shotgun that hung inside my leg beneath the saddle. The two 'huntsmen' Spot and Gordon would work the dogs – pointers – in pairs as we made our way through the dry scrub grass of the rolling Georgia countryside. Suddenly both dogs would freeze. This would be the signal for us to dismount and for one gun to walk up on either side of the huntsman. All at once there would be an explosion with up to forty or fifty quail taking flight simultaneously, weaving in every direction. One had no more than a second or two to take aim before they were gone. Occasionally we would come across a vast and incredibly noisy wild turkey which, in spite of its bulk, would fly off at high speed squawking loudly.

Some mornings we would be up before dawn for duck-flighting, making our way by moonlight in a punt through a forest of spooky dead trees standing in a swamp-lake. We would be in position in our 'blinds', a form of hide built on platforms over the water, in time to see the first rays of the sun tinge the white bellies of the duck a pinkish hue as they flew in from a night in the cornfields. Greenwood, as the Whitney estate was called, provided a wonderful glimpse of America's fast vanishing 'Old South'. One evening as I walked back from the clay-pigeon traps with Kate, Betsey Whitney's daughter by her earlier marriage to Jimmy Roosevelt, son of President Franklin Roosevelt, a car drew up alongside us. The occupants enquired if this was the Payne Whitney estate. I replied that it was Jock Whitney's estate. Whereupon the couple in the car asked if we were the children. Without thinking what I was saying I replied: 'No. This is Kate Roosevelt and I'm Winston Churchill.' The couple looked at each other, tapped their heads in disbelief and drove off.

Soon after my fifteenth birthday I decided to be confirmed in the Church of England, though later I was to have a crisis of faith and, for several years, count myself an agnostic. The date was set for the spring when the Bishop of Oxford would be present at Eton College Chapel to perform the ceremony. Of my four godparents, all of whom my father had invited, only Virginia Cowles, who was married to the Labour (later Conservative) Member of Parliament, Aidan Crawley, accepted. Brendan Bracken, though not able to be present could not resist taking a swipe at the Bishop of Oxford in a letter to my father:

> Princess House,
> 95 Gresham Street,
> London EC2
> 14th March 1956

My dear Randolph,

Lord, how old we are getting! It is hard to bring oneself to believe that little Winston was baptised more than 15 years ago.

I have been a most excellent spiritual guardian inasmuch as I have never made any attempt to interfere with the sound divinity teaching he had at his private school and, I presume, from a number of gentlemen in Holy Orders who are fed by Eton to unveil the mysteries of religion.

I shall do my best to be there when little Winston is confirmed by the Bishop of Oxford, who was taken out of a musty cave called Keble College to preside over one of the largest dioceses in England; despite the fact that the holy man had never been in a parish. As we know from the Archbishop of Canterbury's record, there is nothing like accepting the highest ecclesiastical responsibilities with the fervour of an amateur untrammelled by experience or knowledge.

> Yrs
> B

That summer, my third at Eton, I was allowed to give up rowing – I was too small to be any good at it – and instead I began to discover and enjoy some of the freedoms available to Eton boys. To my great delight, I found that I could join the Sailing Club and, better still, that the Sailing Club kept its boats at Bourne End, a lovely stretch of the Thames which had the merit of being over ten miles from the school. To get there a bicycle was needed and I wrote off immediately to Grandma Digby to send me from Minterne the bicycle that all four of my grandparents had given me for my birthday the year before. Thus on half-holidays, while others played cricket or sweated their way up the river, I would escape on my bicycle into the countryside, pedalling my way up the hills past Cliveden and through the magnificent Burnham Beeches, to rejoin the river at Bourne End. Sometimes I would go with two or three friends but as often alone. Occasionally if I could get away in time, the lady who ran the club house would have waiting for me a wonderful lunch of roast beef and Yorkshire pudding – all for five shillings (25p). I would then spend a couple of hours tacking my way up the river and back in a small but lively firefly dinghy. It was a wonderful escape from regimentation and communal living.

I wrote to Grandpapa Churchill to tell him all about it:

T A Brocklebank Esq,
Eton College,
Windsor
9th June [1956]

Dear Grandpapa,

I am sorry I have been so long in writing to you. I hope you are well.

I am enjoying myself very much, because I go sailing, on the river, about ten miles from Eton. The Eton College Sailing Club, to which I belong, have three very speedy sailing boats called fireflies, which are great fun. Father says that for the summer holidays we might hire a sailing boat in Suffolk, because June is also very keen on sailing.

Father came down and took me out on the 4th June, which I enjoyed. Mummy has been over in England for a few days, and she flew back to France two days ago. Mummy has rented a small boat in the South of France for three weeks, and I am taking two of my friends. I hope to see you and Grandmama next holidays.

Please do you think you could send me the History of the English-Speaking Peoples and Marlborough, which you promised to give me. Give Grandmama my love, I hope her neuritis is not hurting her any more. I hope Toby and Rufus are well.

Lots of love
Winston

In addition to the sailing, I was to discover another means of escape. For his seventy-fifth birthday in the summer of 1954 Lord Beaverbrook had invited all his godchildren to a celebration lunch at Cherkley, giving each one of us an excellent Kodak Retinex camera. As a result I developed a passion for photography. I joined the Photographic Society, which had its own dark-rooms, and spent many hours of my spare time there developing films and enlarging prints. I must have become quite accomplished for I soon found myself being asked to do 'leaving photographs' for the most senior boys in my house in their last term, when it was the custom for them to give small mounted photographs of themselves to three or four dozen of their closest friends. The local High Street photographers, Hill and Saunders, at the time charged 1/6d (7.5p) a print. I discovered I could sell mine for 1/- (5p) each, making a 100 per cent profit, while undercutting the opposition by a third. This developed into a useful side line and enabled me to make a modest supplement to my allowance, received from my parents.

Sadly my mother had to re-enter the New York Hospital in July 1956 for a second operation and arrangements were made for me to join her at the very start of the summer holidays. At the end of the month I sailed for New York with my father aboard the *Queen Mary*. In the course of the voyage we met two very pretty Texan girls returning home from Paris who happened to have the recently released record of *My Fair Lady* which had just opened on Broadway. The score and the lyrics were superb and we would sit up to a late hour singing all the songs.

That autumn Britain was preoccupied with the disastrously conceived Suez campaign, launched in response to the Egyptian President Nasser's nationalization of the Canal – something about which the British Government was as sensitive as the US Government is to this day over Panama. Anthony Eden, who had taken over as Prime Minister from my grandfather eighteen months before, was already a sick man. He further made the mistake of falling into the hands of his professional advisers – a peril my father was forever warning against, regardless whether those advisers be legal, medical or, as in this case, military. Father would emphasize, to anyone who cared to listen, the importance when consulting professionals for advice, of remaining firmly in control and, at the end of the day, taking all decisions oneself. When, one day, it was reported that President Eisenhower had cancelled his engagements 'on doctor's orders', Father exploded with indignation: 'Presidents don't take orders from doctors!' Eden, ignorant of this advice, fell into the hands of his generals who mounted the operation as if they were fighting Germans rather than Egyptians. On this basis, and because they did not know whether it was Egyptians or Russians who were driving Egypt's T-54 tanks, recently acquired from the Soviet Union, they ruled out doing the operation with airpower and airborne forces alone, insisting instead on a seaborne assault. This involved the assault-force being ten days on the high seas and guaranteed that the whole world – including the Egyptians – knew precisely what was afoot long before anything started. In consequence vital time and every element of surprise was lost.

The United Nations and world opinion – than which there is nothing more volatile – were given time to mobilize. Both the United States and the Soviet Union – the latter, having just invaded Hungary, was engaged in the brutal repression of its people – brought political, diplomatic and economic power to bear against Britain and France to the extent that, with victory just hours away, they were persuaded to abandon the operation. It was all a tragic débâcle which, for two decades or more, was to have grave consequences for Western interests in the Middle East and, more seriously, for the self-confidence of the nations of Western Europe, which allowed themselves to be convinced that never again, in a world dominated by Super Powers, could the nations of Europe, jointly or severally, take decisive action in the military sphere to protect their own interests. It was to take the resolute leadership of Margaret Thatcher who, a quarter of a century later, repossessed the Falkland Islands in the face of Argentinian aggression, to demonstrate not only to Britain but to the nations of Europe, that middle-ranking powers can still take decisive action when necessary.

By this time I was becoming more politically aware and interested in what was going on in the world and the Suez fiasco prompted my first serious political conversation with my grandfather. He had invited me to lunch with him at his London home, 28 Hyde Park Gate. For some reason Grandmama was not there and we lunched alone. When, in the course of the meal, I asked him what he thought of the Suez business, he shook his head gravely, and declared: 'I do not know that I should have had the courage to start it all in the first place – I certainly would never have dared stop half way!' It was a succinct but damning indictment of the way the operation had been handled.

As soon as I was old enough, I joined the Eton Combined Cadet Force, or Corps as it was known. It was rather like the Scouts at Ludgrove but on a much more elaborate and serious footing. Since membership of the Corps had recently become voluntary, enthusiasm for it had increased markedly. After our first term of basic training which involved hours of square-bashing and arms drill, we were able to pursue a wonderful variety of courses. We were taught about nuclear warfare and the effects of radiation. We went to Bisley to practise rifle shooting and engaged in 36-hour exercises on Salisbury Plain against the Parachute Regiment and the Gurkhas who fired live ammunition over our heads so we might know what to expect. We were able to 'live-fire' most of the current range of British Army weaponry, including machine guns, sub-machine guns and the newly introduced Belgian FN rifle.

But, much as I enjoyed the Corps and attracted as I had been to joining the Fleet Air Arm, I set my sights on going to University and following in my father's steps to Christ Church, Oxford, now that it was evident, following a government announcement in April 1957, that National Service was at an end. Grandpapa, who himself never had the opportunity of a University education, was very keen that I should succeed in this endeavour and while sending me an advance copy of Volume III of *The English-Speaking Peoples*, wrote to encourage me in my efforts:

> Chartwell,
> Westerham,
> Kent
> 11 May, 1957

My dear Winston,

I believe that next year you are hoping to go to Christ Church. I am glad about this, because it is one of the finest colleges in Oxford.

I have been making enquiries, and I hear that the competition is keen and the examination stiff. It will therefore mean *sustained work* if you are to be successful. I do hope you will be, my dear Winston.

> Ever your loving grandfather,
> Winston S. Churchill

P.S. You will see by the nibbled edges that Toby [his pet budgerigar], who is watching, wishes to be remembered too. I am sure that he shares my view. Don't let over-confidence lead to neglect. This might compromise your entry into the serious aspects of life now opening before you.   WSC

Four years earlier the Queen had created Grandpapa a Knight of the Garter and it had been my hope to watch Grandpapa take part in the annual Garter ceremony at St George's Chapel, Windsor. Unfortunately I was unable to escape my studies but I wrote to him immediately afterwards, to tell him of the riding course I was undertaking with the Life Guards:

> Eton College
> Windsor
> 19 June [1957]

Dear Grandpapa,

I am sorry I did not come and watch you at the Garter ceremony on Monday, it must have been awfully hot in all your robes.

I go riding every Tuesday and Thursday at the Life Guards barracks in Windsor; it is great fun, about fifteen of us go. We ride inside a large riding school and we are instructed by an army officer, with a large moustache and a long whip. The horse which I chose was a huge black charger called 'Colonist'! He jumped very well and I just managed to hold on and keep him between my legs.

I was very sorry to read in the newspapers that you auctioned your herd yesterday and that Bardogs will be going too, soon.

I hope you and Grandmama are well; please give her my love.

> Your loving grandson,
> Winston

Grandpapa replied:

> 23 June 1957

My dear Winston,

Thank you so much for your letter. I am glad to hear that you are getting some riding, and enjoying it. I went to Ascot yesterday to see Le Pretendant run, but he did not do quite as well as I had hoped.

We miss the Jersey herd, but we still have the Belted Galloways. I am not parting with them.

> Your loving grandfather
> Winston S. Churchill

I reported to my father that 'Colonist ... jumps well and is well behaved.' However, that was written before the final day of the course when Captain Thomson, a keen show-jumper and one of the finest instructors in England at the time, made the mistake of letting us out of the riding school where we had regularly been schooled in the art of jumping bareback and other equestrian skills. It was a lovely sunny day and he decided to take all fifteen of us on our massive black chargers into Windsor Great Park for the afternoon. Suddenly one boy lost control of his horse and was run away with. The others bolted and the charge was on. Try as we would there was no holding these magnificent but enormously powerful beasts which ended up some with, and others without, their riders in different corners of the Park. Fortunately, so far as we were aware, Her Majesty was oblivious to the mayhem we caused that day in the Great Park with her horses.

Next I did a driving course in which, aged just seventeen, I was let loose in a three-ton Army truck to terrorize the local citizenry around the quiet byways of Datchet and Old Windsor as an instructor introduced me to the mysteries of toe-and-heel gearchanging and double de-clutching with the vehicle's crash gearbox. Finally, my last summer, a small number of us were allowed, without instructors, to drive armoured cars with which we charged on to the Parade ground firing smoke grenades and thunder flashes before parading past Field Marshal Sir John Harding who came to review us at our Annual Inspection.

No matter the wet, the cold or the lack of sleep on the night exercises, we thoroughly enjoyed ourselves and amassed a wonderfully wide and varied training – experience which was to prove invaluable when, in later years, I became a journalist and war correspondent and found myself on patrol with the Royal Marines in the jungles of Borneo, in the field with US and Australian forces in Vietnam and under fire with Biafran forces in the Nigerian Civil War.

At the beginning of 1957 Eden had resigned as Premier on grounds of poor health, leading to intense speculation in the press as to who might succeed him. My father was undoubtedly the best connected and best informed political journalist of his day and, while two days later on 10 January, every daily newspaper in Britain was unanimous that the successor would be Butler, the *Evening Standard* was on sale by 10 am with a banner-lead story by my father forthrightly declaring: 'By 2.30 pm this afternoon Mr Harold Macmillan will have been called to the Palace ...' It was the greatest journalistic scoop of his lifetime, though sadly the editor hedged his bet by putting it beneath a headline reading: IS IT MACMILLAN? It was an object lesson to see him as he worked throughout the night gradually piecing the picture together, by the ruthless use of the telephone with which, one by one, he tracked down and woke from their slumbers all his friends and contacts in the Government and anyone else who might have a nose for what was afoot. Thus by dawn he had succeeded in unravelling a complex and obscure situation. He had been especially delighted to learn about midnight that the Fleet Street pack had, in their early editions, gone nap on Butler. He realized that this gave him the opportunity of a lifetime if he could establish that they were wrong.

Ever at the centre of controversy, Father had, the year before, won a famous libel action against Odhams Press, publishers of the *People* news-paper which had described him as 'A hack, paid to write biased articles.'

In the course of the action he had thoroughly enjoyed himself at the expense of the Counsel for the Defence, a Mr Paul, whose last case it was before retiring to the Judges' Bench. At one point in the proceedings Mr Paul, having shown that my father had himself accused more than one Fleet Street editor of being an 'old hack' – a charge which they had not sought to dispute – turned to my father in the witness box and declared: 'Yet you say it is *criminal* to call you a "Hack"?' Father, swift as lightning, rejoined: 'Mr Paul, this is a civil, not a criminal case!' The jury could not conceal their enjoyment at this discomfiture of Learned Counsel and openly fell about on the bench in laughter.

I stood at my father's side in court at the moment of intense anxiety and excitement when the jury returned their verdict of 'Guilty!' against the defendants and awarded my father the then sizable damages of £5,000 and his legal costs. In the wake of this success, he published a verbatim account of the trial, entitled *What I Said About The Press*. Because it contained some minor disparaging reference to the Smith family, who owned W. H. Smith & Sons, by far the largest chain of newsagents in the country, his book was banned from their shelves. This prompted my father to establish his own company, which he called Country Bumpkins Ltd, to market the book from East Bergholt. He would never miss any opportunity to brandish his wares, especially whenever he could get in front of a television camera, and his book sold like hot cakes. He had some cards printed, announcing 'Banned by W. H. Smith & Sons' giving the address where a copy of the book might be obtained. He sent me a bundle of these cards to Eton and in a letter to him of 8 May 1957 I reported:

I went up to W. H. Smith's at Windsor the other day and slipped some cards into books, and left others in prominent positions on tables stacked with books. Outside the shop (but belonging to W. H. Smith) was a newspaper rack, I placed a card there. However, by far the best way I found was to remove a few picture postcards of Windsor from a rack, thumb through them (although they were all the same) slip in a few Bumpkin cards and replace the whole lot in the rack ...

This prompted the reply a week later:

I was very glad to get your nice letter and to hear of your Bumpkin activities in Windsor ... Mr Colin Duncan who you will remember was my Junior Counsel in the libel action writes as follows: 'Not to be outdone by your son I have thought it a witty idea, when paying my monthly account for papers to W. H. Smith, to write the usual compliments which accompany the cheque on one of your cards!' So you see there are many variants of the Bumpkin teasing ...

Whenever my mother came to take me out from school heads would turn and there would be many a comment. Once when I was still very new to the school my fag-master, Jacob Rothschild, came up to me and demanded: 'Who was that girl you were with yesterday?' I was puzzled and denied I had been out with any girl. 'Oh! Yes,' he countered, 'I saw you with a very beautiful redhead!' I protested that I had only been out with my mother, but he refused to believe me!

By now I no longer had to 'fag' for other boys, but instead had a 'fag' of my own to polish my Corps boots, prepare my tea and run errands – a system of servitude which I am glad to say has now been ended.

I wrote to give Grandpapa the news and to thank him for his cheque for £10 to mark my seventeenth birthday, adding by way of a PS:

I have just been elected to the House Debating Society which involves some responsibilities and some privileges namely a wireless and being able to fag a boy. I had to make my maiden speech at two minutes' notice on Mr Muggeridge's attack on the Queen.

Grandpapa, who had recently returned from a holiday at Max Beaverbrook's villa in the South of France, rejoined:

18 October 1957

My dear Winston

Thank you so much for your letter. I was very sorry to hear you had influenza, and do hope you are quite well again now.

We have had many days of beautiful sunshine both here and at the Capponcina, and the time has passed very pleasantly. I have done some painting in the garden, and also completed two flower studies in my room.

I return to England on October 21, and look forward to seeing you again.

> Yr loving grandfather,
> Winston S. Churchill

My time at Eton was drawing to a close, a prospect I looked forward to without regret. Though my time there had not been happy, I had formed a circle of friends I was sorry to be leaving. Closest among them were the elder of the three Palmer-Tomkinson brothers, Charlie and Chris, who were my contemporaries at Brocklebank's and whose passion for skiing I shared. Tragically their father, Jimmy, had been killed a few years before in Switzerland on the ski slopes of Klosters while training for the British Championships. Whenever my parents were abroad at half-term or unable to take me out from school, the Palmer-Tomkinson boys and their wonderful mother, Doris, would invite me to their Hampshire home or take me with them for picnics in Windsor Great Park with mountains of strawberries and cream. Their friendship provides the happiest memories of my time at Eton. Towards the end of 1958 I sat my examinations for Christ Church, Oxford. But in spite of this, I had been determined to be present at Grandpapa Churchill's eighty-fourth birthday party at Chartwell, for which I managed to get special leave from Tom Brocklebank. To my delight I passed the Oxford examination, securing a place at The House, as Christ Church is known, for the following autumn. However, though I had inclined towards Philosophy, Politics and Economics, the examiners judged that my talents were more suited to the study of Modern History which, at Oxford in those days, began in 55 BC and went up to 1914, when the British Empire, and evidently history, came to an end.

· VIII ·

A Taste of Journalism

With nine months to spare before going up to Oxford in the autumn of 1959, I decided to spend six months polishing up my French language and European history in Switzerland at the University of Lausanne. I must acknowledge that the proximity of the ski slopes was not the consideration furthest from my mind. Thanks to the small Fiat 600 which my mother had given me, I spent most weekends on the ski slopes of Gstaad, barely an hour away, where I discovered a hotel nearby where I could stay for 6 Francs (50 pence) per night, bed and breakfast.

University life was a complete contrast to the years of drudgery and regimentation I had endured at school. It was a wonderful luxury to be able to decide for oneself what to do each day and I savoured my newly found freedom to the full. I had now reached that magical period of life – one that, in an ideal world, should be available to all – that forms the all-too-brief interlude between the oppressive constraints of school life and the treadmill of having to earn a living.

While at Lausanne, I saw a great deal of my friends Patrick and Dolores Guinness, who had a lovely house nearby on Lake Geneva. Patrick was the son of Loel Guinness by his marriage to Joan Yarde-Buller (who subsequently married Prince Aly Khan and is now Viscountess Camrose), and Dolores, who was the greatest beauty of her day, I had known since we had been children together in the South of France. I recall having been shocked at the nonchalant way in which, as we dived underwater together, she would catch octopuses and sea urchins with her bare hands and then chop them up on the rocks. They were wonderfully hospitable and we skied a lot together. Sadly, a few years later, Patrick who, although several years older than me, had been one of my closest friends, was killed in a car crash.

Finding German history uphill work, I wrote to Grandpapa asking him to send me his life of Marlborough and, by way of light relief, his only novel, *Savrola*. As always I received a prompt reply:

> Chartwell,
> Westerham,
> Kent
> 3 May 1959

My dear Winston,
Thank you so much for your letter. I am very glad to send you a set of MARLBOROUGH, and I hope you will enjoy it. SAVROLA is out of print, which I think is a pity. My efforts to get you a copy have not been successful, and so I am sending you my own. Would you send it back to me when you have read it, as it is the only one I have and I would not like to part with it permanently.
I am off to America tomorrow. I look forward to seeing you again soon.

> Your loving grandfather,
> Winston S. Churchill

Meanwhile in the spring of that year my mother had met and fallen in love with Leland Hayward, a Broadway producer. Leland, whom she married a year later, was the producer of a host of Broadway hits such as *South Pacific, Sound of Music* and *Gypsy*. He was at the height of his profession, having started his career in show business as an agent on the West Coast where, among his earliest clients had been Fred and Adele Astaire. Tough and successful in his professional career, all American and with a crewcut to his silver hair to prove it, he had a charm and manner more often associated with the Old World. He had come a long way from Nebraska City, Nebraska, where he had been born and brought up on the banks of the Missouri River. His mother, whom I came to know as Gran Sarah, and whom Minnie and I used to visit at her home outside Los Angeles until her death many years later, aged over ninety, would tell of her journey west by covered wagon before the turn of the century across the great Mississippi to the Missouri River. Every night they formed into a circle around the campfire and several times they were set upon by Red Indians. Leland's father was the local preacher, and would cross the Missouri every Sunday to preach to a black congregation on the other side. On the United States' entry into the First World War, he had raised the first black cavalry regiment of the US Army, leading them over to France where, to his outrage, the British tried to *sell* him the trenches that they were quitting! This was something for which he, and even Leland, were never to forgive the British.

In July I flew to New York to spend a few days with my mother, determined to meet this American whom I rightly judged was my step-father-to-be. To my mother's intense relief – and somewhat to her surprise, as she well remembered my ill-concealed distaste for an earlier suitor –

Leland and I hit it off immediately. I enjoyed his open manner and dry humour, as well as sharing his passion for photography and, later, for flying. There was, however, a note of consternation in my mother's voice when I announced my intention to spend the summer with them, but she gamely agreed, provided I got myself a job.

I was anyway eager to get a summer job and, soon after my arrival, a friend mentioned that there might be a vacancy in Senator John Kennedy's campaign office in Washington, which was in full swing for his bid for the Presidency against Richard Nixon in the election due fifteen months later. I was greatly attracted by the prospect and cabled my father in a state of some excitement on 23 July 1959:

WANT TO GET JOB HERE AUGUST STOP HAVE BEEN OFFERED ONE IN JACK
KENNEDY'S WASHINGTON OFFICE ANXIOUS FOR YOUR APPROVAL STOP PLEASE
REPLY SOONEST THE DRAKE NEW YORK
LOVE = WINSTON

This prompted, by return, the bluntest telegram I ever received from my father who, wrongly, assumed that the offer had come from Jack Kennedy himself:

DONT THINK YOU SHOULD TAKE SIDES IN AMERICAN PARTY POLITICS STOP
SINCE 1776 REVOLTING COLONISTS HAVE RESENTED US LIMEYS INTERFERING
IN THEIR AFFAIRS STOP ASK JACK ABOUT BOSTON TEA PARTY AND WHAT
HAPPENED TO BRITISH AMBASSADOR SACKVILLE WEST IN 1888 STOP SUGGEST
YOU FIND SOMETHING LESS POLITICALLY AND CLIMATICALLY HOT THAN
WASHINGTON STOP LET ME KNOW IF I CAN HELP
LOVE = FATHER

It took me a little while to discover that Ambassador Sackville West had been thrown into the Potomac River for interfering in American politics. But, anyway, the message was clear and I accepted with good grace my father's wise advice. With politics firmly ruled out I turned instinctively towards the field of journalism, of which I had already had a foretaste, having had the chance over many years to see how my father worked. Within a week, I managed to secure a job on the copy desk of the *Wall Street Journal*. The *Journal* even at that time printed simultaneously in seven cities across America and was the first paper in America to have a coast-to-coast circulation, though at 600,000, its print run was small by British standards. I was placed on the news desk where, as a News Assistant, I was given the job of 'rim man', correcting proofs and galleys of stories, cutting them for length and writing the headlines. Since the news desk was short-staffed over the holidays I was given considerable responsibility. This included regular visits to the print room below to discuss details of layout with the printers, each of whom minded one of a large battery of linotype machines where the copy was set in metal 'slugs' of print before being set up in columns on the 'stone', from which it was cast on to drums for loading on the printing presses. Though the *Journal* led in new technology by its ability to print simultaneously in cities across America, it remained in thrall to its heavily unionized printers who insisted there should be one printer for every linotype machine, though it had been demonstrated during a strike that ten such machines could be operated by a single old lady.

The office had no air conditioning and was nearly as oppressively hot and sticky as the Lexington Avenue Subway on which I spent over an hour commuting from 86th Street to Wall Street and back each day. As I wrote to my father, on 4 August: 'At first I was a bit apprehensive, thinking I would be kicked around, being a foreigner, not knowing anything and having continually to ask stupid elementary questions. I could not have been more wrong. It is one of the nicest qualities of an American, that he is easy to make friends with. You resent it, I know I used to – I suppose it is the way we have been brought up. But I certainly found it very nice to walk into that office last Thursday and be called Winston and call the other men there Bob, Sam or whatever it was. I felt I was already one of them – not a stranger, newcomer or foreigner.' Though my father had never put pressure on me or even suggested that I should follow him into the 'family business' of journalism and politics – indeed he had done what he could to encourage me towards a career in engineering or science – he was delighted that I should be doing a stint of journalism. Grandpapa also wrote a letter of encouragement:

> La Pausa, Roquebrune
> Cap Martin, AM,
> France
> 28 August 1959

My dear Winston,

Thank you so much for your letter. I think that you are doing very well to acquire experience of business and journalism in the United States, and it will no doubt prove useful later on. I also entirely agree with your father that you should not get mixed up in any American politics.

I have been having a pleasant stay down here, and the cruise to Greece and Turkey was a great success. We visited Constantinople and met the Turkish Prime Minister and Foreign Minister, and the Greek Prime Minister dined with us near Athens. I go home on Sunday to see the President while he is in London, but will return again here soon afterwards.

I hope to see you when you are back in London.

> Your loving grandfather,
> Winston S. Churchill

That summer went by incredibly quickly. After years of drudgery cooped up in a classroom, it was wonderfully exciting and challenging at last to be doing a job of work in the real world. I thoroughly enjoyed editing copy, writing the headlines, as well as the friendliness of the others in the office with two or three of whom I would nip out for an evening meal at the local Horn & Hardart which was quick and where a very reasonable meal could be had for under a dollar. Another of my allotted tasks was to put into English the garbled version of President Eisenhower's weekly press conference as it came over the newswires. This was always interesting, though I sometimes wondered why it was that the President should make himself answerable each week to the representatives of the press rather than, as in Britain, to the elected representatives of the people. The *Journal's* hours were 2 pm to 10 pm, Sunday to Thursday. Having the morning free was a great bonus and, quite frequently, together with one of my copy desk colleagues, Sam Haines and his Chinese stockbroker wife Abby, I would drive out and spend a couple of hours in the surf at Jones Beach, nearby on Long Island, before heading back, refreshed by the Atlantic breakers, to do a day's work.

At weekends I would rent a huge Buick for just $10 a day and 10 cents a mile, and head out to Long Island to spend my Fridays and Saturdays at the beach resort of Southampton where I stayed with my cousins, Ed and Sarah Russell and their young family. In 1943 when Ed Russell, a young US Navy Officer, had married my cousin Sarah Spencer-Churchill at St Margaret's, Westminster, I had been their page. I had been dressed for the occasion in a white sailor-boy's outfit and, through an oversight, I had been armed with a whistle attached to a lanyard round my neck. At what, aged two-and-a-half, I judged to be a dull, quiet part of the service – no doubt the most solemn moment of all – I had put my whistle in my mouth and blown it. My mother, in horror, had raced up the aisle to grab me and remove the whistle.

My weekends with the Russells were the greatest fun with parties and dances where lots of pretty girls were always to be found. The latest thing at the time were the open-air drive-in movies, colloquially known as 'passion pits'. I was shocked to learn, after taking one young lady to the movies three weekends in succession, that her mother had called mine to ask if my intentions were honourable! An added bonus of weekends at Southampton was that I came to know my cousin, Consuelo Vanderbilt Balsan, Bert Marlborough's mother who, at the age of nineteen, at her parents' behest, had married the 9th Duke of Marlborough. She had been one of the greatest beauties of her day and, still tall and slim even in her eighties, had a wonderful elegance and serenity about her, with her high cheekbones and long, swan-like neck. The Russells, with whom I stayed, had a small cottage immediately adjacent to her magnificent mansion which had a wonderful, old-fashioned, Gatsby air to it. Sometimes we would play croquet together and then have tea on the shady veranda, seemingly a million miles from the crush and bustle of New York City. It was one weekend that I was there that her son, my cousin Bert, was finally cured of calling his mother reverse charge from England. When asked by the American operator who was calling, he had replied: 'The Duke of Marlborough.' 'Say,' rejoined the operator crushingly, 'is that like Duke Ellington and Count Basie?'

My two months working in New York was most exhilarating. It had been a wonderful opportunity to get some work experience before going to university and my appetite for journalism had definitely been whetted. It also gave me the chance of being with my mother, whom I had not seen so radiant and happy in many a year, and of getting to know Leland, of whom I became enormously fond. Since I had no work permit, I had been at the *Journal* officially as an unpaid 'student observer'; however, before I left, the editor gave me instructions to be sure to call in on their London office in Farringdon Street as soon as I got home. This I did and, to my amazement and delight, for I had expected nothing, I was handed an envelope stuffed with more £5 notes than I had ever seen in my life, equivalent in sterling terms to the US minimum wage – then $70 (£20) per week – for all the time I had been with them.

· IX ·

An Oxford Idyll

It was with a sense of great anticipation and eagerness that, in October 1959, I passed through the high arched gateway of Christ Church into Tom Quad and the world of Oxford with its fine cloistered buildings and its skyline of domes and spires. I was fortunate in being allocated rooms in College overlooking Peckwater Quad with its eighteenth-century sandstone façade and the College library. There I shared a 'set' of rooms with a school friend, David Prior-Palmer, with whom I had raced fireflies on the Thames at Bourne End. We each had our own small bedroom and shared a large living-room where we could work or entertain our friends. The bathrooms were in the basement at the bottom of each staircase. Our rooms had a stout outer door known as the 'oak' and, if one was working on an essay and did not wish to be disturbed one would, in Oxford jargon, 'sport' one's 'oak' shutting out the outside world and casual visitors. Each staircase had its own 'Scout' or elderly retainer who was responsible for cleaning and tidying the rooms. We would eat our meals in the vast Hall with its magnificent high vaulted ceiling, surrounded by oil portraits of distinguished alumni, including the College's founder, Cardinal Wolsey, who had risen to power and wealth by doing the bidding of his master King Henry VIII in arranging the disposal of his wife and subsequent remarriages.

For the princely sum of £11 I became a Life Member of the Oxford Union Society which organized lively weekly debates in which all the most distinguished political and public figures of the day would participate. It also boasted a bar, nightclub and library and provided a reasonable meal if one tired of college fare. Although I had no very strong political convictions at the time I allowed myself to be recruited into the Oxford University Conservative Association by its then chairman Philip Whitehead who, ironically, by the time our paths crossed again when we both entered Parliament in the 1970 election, had become Labour Member for Derby North.

To express his satisfaction on my passing into Oxford, Grandpapa gave me for my birthday that year two of his most beautiful paintings: *The Tapestry Room at Blenheim*, a colourful view of the tapestries depicting John Churchill's famous victories, and *The Olive Grove of La Dragoniere*, Lord Rothermere's home in Southern France. These, together with *The Battlements of Rhodes* which he had given me when I first went to Eton, were a wonderful adornment to my rooms in Peckwater Quad, to which, even on a grey day, they brought a wonderful quality of colour and light. Soon afterwards for Christmas he presented me with the pair of 1895 single-trigger Woodward shotguns which he had been given for his twenty-first birthday present by his cousin the Duke of Marlborough and which he had used only infrequently over the years. Nearly thirty years on from the date he gave them to me, they continue to give stalwart service and are finer than any shotgun built today. I was greatly touched that he should have entrusted them to me.

More than anything else while I was at Oxford, I wanted to join the Oxford University Ski Club and win my skiing 'Half-Blue'. The previous Christmas in St Moritz I had met an Austrian by the name of Arnold von Bohlen who was in his first year at Balliol and who was a member of the Oxford Ski Team. I remember admiring his navy blue sweater with its OUSC monogram surmounted by a white crown and decided then and there that, when I went up to Oxford, I would set my sights on winning one. For the sum of £32 – for which my *Wall Street Journal* earnings came in most handy – I signed up for that year's University ski trip to Zürs in the Austrian Arlberg, and at the end of term set out with a large party of undergraduates to participate in a skiing fortnight organized by the some-what anomalous Oxford, Cambridge and Trinity College, Dublin, Ski Club. Some three hundred and fifty strong, including many attractive camp-followers who joined us from as far afield as Paris, Geneva and Vienna, we virtually took over the small mountain village.

As may be imagined, we had a most lively time but the prize for high jinks and practical jokes definitely went to the Irish who had been put all together in one hotel called the Alpenrose, while the rest of us were at the Zürserhof and Lorunser. The only outsiders staying at the Zürserhof at the time were the then world ski champion, a delightful Austrian called Tony Sailer, together with an entire film crew. They had been waiting, through several days of blizzard, for the weather to clear so that they could shoot a movie. When, at last, the first brilliant, cloudless day arrived, they were up at dawn all set to take to the slopes. However, on opening their bedroom doors to fetch their ski boots from the corridor outside, they discovered to their dismay and outrage that their left boots had all disappeared, having been replaced by others that were not theirs and did not fit. The same fate had befallen occupants of all the other hotels with the exception, intriguingly, of the Alpenrose upon whose occupants, inevitably, suspicion fell. It transpired that, in the night, our Irish friends had gone round all the other hotels removing all the left-footed boots and taking them on to the next hotel. The day was well advanced before the boots were sorted out and the Irish were not the most popular members of the party.

But the Irish were not alone in their high-spirited behaviour. On sunny days, as it was getting dark, about a dozen of us would meet up in the mountain hut at the top of the Zürser-See chairlift to drink a few *glühweins* (mulled claret). After an hour or so, by which time we were all very merry and the moon had taken the place of the sun in the sky, we would don our skis and head down the mountain. Perhaps not surprisingly I managed to break *two* pairs of metal skis on successive evenings. I consoled myself with the knowledge that, but for the *glühwein*, it would have been my legs. On another occasion after rather too much Yugoslav *slivovic* had been consumed at the bar, I made the mistake of playfully pushing away a diminutive American, called Al Stepan, who I judged was definitely smaller than me. Nobody had bothered to warn me that he was in fact the Light-Weight Boxing Champion of the US Marine Corps. The next thing I knew I was sailing backwards through a large and very expensive plate glass window for which the manager, Claus Gagern, presented me with the bill with a broad smile on his face. Claus, a jovial old rogue, had left a leg behind at Stalingrad and took our pranks with great good humour. He even allowed us, when nothing else could get about the village as there was so much snow, to make use of his Volkswagen Beetle. On one occasion we somehow managed to fit *thirteen* people, boys and girls together, into it. What it was to be young!

I was fortunate enough to secure my objective of winning a place in the Oxford team and earn my 'Half-Blue' for skiing. In fact I was the only British member of the six-man team which was otherwise composed of Canadians, Americans and Austrians, some of whom had competed both in the World Championships and the recent Olympics. By my third and final year, by which time I had become team Captain, this situation had been reversed and there was only one foreigner left in the team. I was lucky in being the first of the post-war generation of Britons to have had the chance of learning to ski at an early age, after the gap of almost ten years caused by the war.

Having, in the spring of 1960, successfully put behind me my preliminary exams, and with my finals still two years away, I was able to start savouring to the full the joys and freedom of Oxford life. In retrospect I naturally regret that I did not address my studies with the same determination as I did my skiing and, later, my flying, but the serious part of life would be upon me soon enough. I did however make a point of taking in the History lectures of Hugh Trevor-Roper and A. J. P. Taylor. In addition, although it was not strictly my field, I enjoyed attending Roy Harrod's lectures on Economics and, most of all, those of Isaiah Berlin on the subjects of Philosophy, Karl Marx and the Soviet Union. Berlin had the most extraordinary way of speaking and would deliver his lectures at very high speed so that one had to be specially attentive to catch the brilliant flow of words and subtle train of argument. From these weighty, though nonetheless most interesting subjects, I would either return to the House for a meal in College or go off, especially in summertime, with friends – for the most part English and American though including a few Canadians, an Indian, a Nepalese and a Palestinian – to one of the many excellent pubs in Oxford and the surrounding countryside. Particular favourites were the Trout on a stretch of the River Cherwell just outside Oxford where I would often lunch, and for the evenings, the Lamb and Flag at Kingston Bagpuize, a village some ten miles out of town on the road towards Faringdon where Dudley, the large and jovial publican, who had a semicircle cut out of the inside of the bar to accommodate his ample belly, would serve us the freshest and finest game from all the great estates nearby, including Blenheim, though we were too discreet to enquire how he came by it.

In the course of the summer term I found myself invited to many wonderful dances and balls in London and would get back to Oxford with its misty spires only at five or six in the morning when the sun was already up. I was fortunate in having a small 2.4 litre Jaguar which my mother, remembering how she had been given one at the age of nineteen by her father, had most generously given me when I went up to Oxford. When my baby Fiat had expired, my mother had asked me what car I would like and I had suggested an inexpensive 1.5 litre Riley saloon. It was typical of her generosity that she took one look at the brochure and pronounced: 'I don't think much of that,' adding, almost as an afterthought, 'I would like to give you a Jaguar!' Though, at the time, there was no motorway as there is today, the 50-mile journey back from London to Oxford never took more than fifty minutes. There was a requirement, enforced by the Proctors, who were responsible for University discipline, for all cars belonging to undergraduates to display a green light on their front as a means of identification; however, the mechanic who fitted mine, knowing the form, thoughtfully provided a switch beneath the steering column so that it could be switched off if one was out after hours.

In those days there was still a strict curfew imposed on undergraduates, with the college gates being locked from midnight – by which time any member of the opposite sex was required to be out of the college – until 7 am. But these constraints did little to curb our high spirits, indeed they only served to heighten the sense of adventure. The standard way into college at night was to climb from the Oxford Meadows over a six-foot wall into the Dean's Garden. From there we would scale a much higher wall, of some twelve feet or more, and drop down on to the roof of the bicycle shed. Unfortunately, the bicycle shed roof was made of corrugated iron and, try as one might, it was impossible to avoid making a resounding crash as one dropped on to it from the wall above. This would alert Mitch, the benign red-nosed college porter, to one's return and he would rush out from the shadows. If one did not wish to be reported to the authorities it was judged prudent to invite Mitch for a whiskey or two; if, as was so often the case, one was working to a 9 am deadline to write and hand in an essay and had no time for a chat, the promise of an entire bottle was the safest bet.

I spent much of my holidays that summer in America with my mother who had married Leland Hayward in April that year. I wrote to Grandpapa to give him my news and received the following reply on his return from a cruise of the Aegean aboard Onassis's yacht *Christina*:

> Chartwell,
> Westerham,
> Kent
> 13 August 1960
>
> My dear Winston,
>   Thank you so much for your letter which I have greatly enjoyed. I am glad you have had such excellent travels throughout Europe, and I hope you are having an agreeable time in America.
>   We had a very good cruise, and it was most interesting to meet Marshal Tito again. We are now spending some weeks at Chartwell where it is very pleasant, especially when it is not raining.
>   Do not fail to let us know in good time when you will be back in England, as we much look forward to seeing you down here.
>   Our love to your mother,
>
> > Your loving grandfather,
> > Winston S. Churchill

Early in the New Year of 1961 I competed in the British Ski Championships in Murren, Switzerland, where, to the evident surprise of the *Times* skiing correspondent, I came fourth. Sir Arnold Lunn, the father of skiing who, in the last century, had shown the Swiss what to do with their mountains, generously described me as a skier of '*élan* and promise ... up and coming in the over 20 class'.

Before returning to Oxford I went to Stour to stay with my father, who told me that Grandpapa had made a settlement in my favour of the foreign rights of the *History of the English-Speaking Peoples*. On my marriage three years later this was to enable me to buy our first home. I hastened to thank him for his generosity:

Stour,
East Bergholt,
Suffolk
14 January 1961

Dear Grandpapa,

I returned from Switzerland today, and I am spending the night at Stour with Father before returning to Oxford tomorrow.

Father has told me of the handsome financial provision which you have made for me. It greatly exceeds any expectation I ever had and I am at a loss to find the right words to thank you. I am as grateful for the mark of your trust which you have shown in giving me absolute control at the age of twenty-five of the money which you have settled on me, as for the money itself, and I shall endeavour to be worthy of your trust.

More than anything else I am proud to bear your name and I will do my best to maintain its honour.

Your loving grandson,
Winston

While staying at Stour, Father also told me of his wonderfully exciting plan for an expedition that spring across the Sahara and invited me to join him. Shortly before, in the course of a visit to New York, Alan Collins, his American literary agent, had made mention of his plans to drive by Land-Rover from Benghazi on the Mediterranean coast, through the Libyan desert to the Tibesti Mountains in Chad. Alan, jokingly, suggested to my father acquiring a Land-Rover of his own and joining the expedition. To Father, the very mention of the North African desert conjured up memories of Monty, Rommel and his own exploits behind enemy lines with David Stirling and the Long Range Desert Group twenty years before. To the surprise of Alan, who was already beginning to regret having mentioned it, Father found the suggestion irresistible. As soon as he returned to England he telephoned the manufacturers and arranged for a brand new Land-Rover to be shipped out forthwith by sea to Benghazi at an export price of £800. As soon as I could get away from Oxford for the Easter vacation, we flew out to Benghazi.

Libya at the time was ruled by King Idris, a loyal ally of the West, nobody having then heard of Ghadaffi. The United States still had the Wheelus air base in Tripoli and the British maintained a battalion at Benghazi together with an RAF detachment at the nearby air base of El Adem. In Benghazi we met up with the rest of the expedition which included, besides Alan Collins and his wife, Catherine, his brother-in-law Livingstone Pomeroy – appropriately named for the leader of an expedition through Africa – and his English wife, Miggs. Liv, as he was known, was a US Foreign Service officer working for the United States Information Service in Benghazi. At the local golf club he happened to make mention of the expedition to Colonel O'Lone of the Royal Scots Greys who, concerned that his American friends might get lost in the desert and eager to test the British Army's newly delivered 'long wheel-base' Land-Rovers in desert conditions, offered to provide an officer and five men, together with two Land-Rovers to join us. Thus, with two American Land-Rovers and our own, the expedition consisted of five vehicles in all.

Father and I arrived in Benghazi to discover that it was the middle of the holy festival of Ramadan which, as we discovered, is guaranteed to bring any strictly Moslem country to a grinding halt for a whole month of the year. Despite repeated visits and long hours at the port – the same that my father had tried unsuccessfully to blow up with David Stirling in the war – our efforts to extricate our Land-Rover from the hands of the Libyan Customs officials proved vain and it was clear that we were getting – and going – nowhere until, that is, Father produced a wad of local bank notes. In an instant the customs officials' eyes lit up and they were suddenly galvanized into action, just like the Llanaba Silver Band, invited to play at a school Sports Day in Wales, as described in Evelyn Waugh's inimitable *Decline and Fall*, in which the bandmaster declares: 'No music can we play, whatever, on Sunday but Holy music – except you pay us double!'

Meanwhile Father discovered that the Army had in mind to send us off into the Sahara without a radio and promptly chided the kindly colonel with charges of recklessness and irresponsibility in allowing a dozen souls to head off through thousands of miles of desert without any means of communication. The colonel submitted and ordered another Land-Rover, specially fitted out with a long-range radio to accompany us.

Finally, with the return of Livingstone Pomeroy, from Tripoli, where he had been taking some examinations connected with his Foreign Service work, the expedition was all set to get under way. Father, convinced or at least feigning to believe that Liv was a CIA man, teased him with having gone to take examinations to secure promotion from 'Spy, Third Class' to 'Spy, Second Class'. With such raucous banter being exchanged, our convoy headed down the flat coastal road to Agedabia where we set up camp for the night before striking southwards at dawn next day into the Sahara proper. Soon we had troubles with the radio vehicle which, since it was an afterthought, had not been properly serviced and kept breaking down. After forty-eight hours it had become so troublesome the decision was taken to send it back. Instead, a massive 'portable' radio, together with an even heavier generator, was delivered to us by air, courtesy of the RAF.

With the coast road once behind us, the signs of civilization were now few and far between. There was no road, only a rough track with occasional markers to lead us through the sand dunes. The conditions were not easy. For an hour or two we would make excellent progress then, suddenly, we would reach a patch of soft sand where the vehicles, one after another, would sink in up to their axles and become stuck. We were prepared for this and had pierced steel sand tracks which could be used to coax the vehicles forward, but they had to be dug out with shovels before the sand tracks could be slipped under the wheels. This in midday temperatures which already reached 110 degrees Fahrenheit and which, as we headed deeper into the Sahara, were to exceed 130 degrees, was hard and hot work. I tried using a technique which I had previously found effective in snow, of rocking the vehicle out by alternately engaging reverse and first gears. The result proved disastrous. Not only did the rear wheels of the heavily-laden Land-Rover sink even deeper into the sand until the rear axle and differential casing were completely buried but, as I was to discover within three days, there is no surer way of burning out a clutch plate.

As may be imagined this did not make me the most popular man on the expedition for, by then, we were more than 500 miles and three days' driving from the nearest garage and the whole convoy was brought to a halt. Fortunately we had with us a mechanic from the Royal Electrical and Mechanical Engineers who, like all Welshmen in the British Army, was called Taffy. Taffy was slight in build with sandy hair and a ready smile and what he did not know about Land-Rovers was not worth knowing. He immediately set about dismantling the gearbox where the vehicle had come to a halt in mid-desert. In the absence of any lifting-gear John, an immensely strong and stocky Scotsman, straddled the gearbox with his legs, like tree trunks, spread on either side. By means of a heavy steel chain around his neck, he supported the gearbox for an hour or more while Taffy worked expertly to change the clutch plate. The sweat was streaming off them in the intense heat but, within two or three hours, the job was complete and we were able to leave at dawn next day for the oases of Djalo and Kufra. Though the curses of the army had, I thought, been remarkably restrained in the circumstances, I admit to a sense of relief when, the very next day, one of the Army Land-Rovers broke down with precisely the same complaint and I was no longer alone in the club. Again the convoy had to halt while Taffy and John repeated their skilful but utterly exhausting double-act. However, we had, by now, used up our only two spare clutch plates and, with some 5000 miles of desert still ahead of us, we had no choice but to radio back for more spares which were parachuted in to us by an RAF plane from El Adem at dawn the next day. At that point even the Americans, who had regarded it as an unnecessary encumbrance, acknowledged Father's good sense in insisting that we had a radio with us.

By then, Libyan oil was just beginning to flow in significant quantities and, in the course of the first four or five days of our journey, we came across several oil camps with their tall drilling-rigs among the sand-dunes. Occasionally we called in on the rigs, where we were always greeted most hospitably, to secure supplies of ice for what Father called his 'magic box' – an icebox which he had packed full of such delicacies from Fortnum and Mason's as *lobster bisque* soup and *pâté de foie gras*. The Americans who, it is well known, cannot survive without ice even in a cold climate, thought that my father's idea of ice in the Sahara was the most ridiculous thing they had ever heard of and had firmly told him before we left that it all would be melted within twenty-four hours, including the *foie gras*. For the first week at least Father, to his satisfaction, had been able to prove them wrong and our ice and cold drinks were much in demand by the rest of the expedition. However, as we headed ever deeper into the Sahara, the oil camps became fewer in number. It was at this point that Father decided to seize the opportunity afforded by the Southernmost of the oil camps of quitting the expedition, taking the once-weekly plane that serviced each of the camps, and flying home to England in time to see his newly-planted bulbs blooming in his garden at Stour. It had taken him less than a week to conclude that, without Monty and Rommel, the desert was not such a fun place as he had remembered it to be. He departed, declaring that the Americans had 'no conversation', by which he meant that they refused to listen to his, nor were they minded to pay much heed to the endless stream of instructions and advice from 'an old desert hand'.

We left my father and Alan Collins, who had not been well, at the oil rig where a plane was due the next day which would take them back to Benghazi. Father entrusted to me his Land-Rover and what little was left of the supplies in the 'magic box'. With two of the original fourteen members of the expedition gone, there was significantly more room for us all. However, life was definitely quieter and less fun without Father. I invited one of the soldiers, a young Corporal from Glasgow by the name of Pollock, to share my Land-Rover which, like the others, was very heavily laden.

The back of each vehicle was loaded with 25 five-gallon jerry cans of petrol, together with a further 5 plastic jerry cans of equal size containing water. Since there were no more than three points in the course of the 5000-mile expedition where we could refuel – having made arrangements with Shell to drop off some fifty-gallon drums for us at strategic points on our itinerary – we had to carry sufficient fuel for at least two weeks of motoring. Supplies of drinking water were almost as scarce and, in spite of the 25 gallons carried by each vehicle, we had to practise strict water rationing, limiting ourselves to one gallon each per day. This was not as much as it might sound given the searing temperatures which, by midday, would regularly exceed 120 or even 130 degrees Fahrenheit, especially when the vehicles became stuck in the sand, compelling us to great exertions and causing us to sweat profusely and develop a fierce thirst. On top of the jerry cans we had 8 or 10 cases of British Army Compo rations containing such delicacies as steak and kidney pudding, treacle pudding and other items ideal for survival in the Arctic. On top of all these we had all our personal kit including camp beds and sleeping bags. As if this was not enough, we had allocated to our Land-Rover the bulky generator, weighing some 200 pounds, that was required to power the radio.

At night we would sleep under the stars with the whole firmament of heaven revolving above us. Once we had left the coastal strip behind us there was virtually no humidity in the air and, in consequence, the galaxies, nebulas and planets sparkled with a brilliance not seen in other climes and could be seen right down to the horizon. In the cold night air, where the temperature would drop almost to freezing by dawn, I would lie awake under this celestial panoply, contemplating the infinite and wondering if our own existence is a mere accident of evolution or part of the grand design of some unseen being; whether indeed our planet is unique in having life and, if not, what form of beings might occupy other planets of our own or more distant galaxies of the universe. It was certainly humbling to reflect what a tiny part of creation is constituted by the planet Earth and the affairs of man, which readily can appear to be so important.

From Kufra, with its lush green groves of date palms and its life-giving wells that transform the desert there into a garden where a wonderful variety of fruit and vegetables flourish, we headed south towards the black hills of Jebel Sherif where, during the Second World War, a patrol of the Long Range Desert Group – with which my father had served – had been attacked by the Italian Air Force. With nowhere to take cover they had been badly shot up, all their vehicles set ablaze and many had been killed. Others were to die of thirst before they could reach water. But a handful miraculously survived a 180-mile march across the desert with only a single can of water between them and that with a bullet hole just a quarter of the way from the bottom. We had read details of the engagement and came to these dark, forbidding hills shortly before dusk, to see what traces we could find twenty years on.

At dawn the next morning, just a few yards from where we had made our camp for the night, I stubbed my toe against something in the sand. I dug down with my hand and found a tin which, to my amazement, still had its label intact reading 'Lipton's Finest English Sausages'. The tin was dated 1939. This find spurred our efforts and, in the space of the next couple of hours, we found the remains of the LRDG vehicles lying between the hills where they could find no hiding place. Though burnt out, because of the lack of humidity and the sand blasting effect of the relentless desert wind there was not a trace of rust to be found.

A sense of timelessness pervades the desert and I had an eerie feeling that the action might have taken place only days before. We could in places even make out the tracks made by the vehicles where they had been covered over by the sand, which had then been swept away again. Nearby there stood in silent vigil a small cross made out of the wood of an ammunition box. That night as I lay in the warmth of my sleeping bag I felt very close in my thoughts to the four survivors who, knowing they were several hundred miles from any known water supply or friendly forces, had pondered their fate in this very spot before deciding to march South to Tekro, a French outpost over 200 miles away held by the Allies, rather than to Kufra which, though only half the distance, was in enemy hands. It was ten days before the French patrol, following their footprints in the sand, found all four. Three were delirious and one died soon after being found.

From this desolate spot our route took us south-east to Jebel Aweinat, a mountain which marks the meeting point of the borders of Libya, Egypt and the Sudan. Here we found pre-historic cave drawings of animals long since extinct in the Sahara such as buffalo and elephant, confirming the belief that, a few thousand years ago, the Sahara was a fertile region supporting a wide variety of vegetation and wild life. Nestled against the foot of the mountain we found a collection of friendly nomadic tribesmen, whose homes were igloo-like structures consisting of a rough wooden framework covered by palm matting. They scratched out their harsh existence hunting gazelle with spears and minding their small herds of goats. We had with us a scientist from the Smithsonian Institute in Washington, Dr 'Call-me-Hank' Setzer who, each night, would set his traps to catch different species of desert animals, which are nowhere to be seen in the heat of the day. By far the most numerous were the mouse-like gerbils which scurry busily about at night. Occasionally he caught one of the silver desert foxes that prey on the gerbils and later, once we reached the high mountains of the Tibesti, to his delight he found green monkeys and baboons.

The journey from Aweinat to Faya-Largeau in Chad, took us over some of the most inhospitable terrain to be found on this planet. Some days we would be driving across flat, sandy desert at high speed, with the vehicles stretched over several miles in line abreast when, without warning, we would find ourselves in the most treacherous terrain where all the vehicles would sink deep into the sand and it would take us an hour or more even to make one mile. There were other times when we found our path blocked by sand dunes 100–200 feet high forming a barrier that stretched like a mountain range as far as the eye could see and which would require a detour of many miles before we could find our way round or through. But, even rougher on the vehicles than the light sand known to the nomad tribesmen as *fech-fech*, which would explode into clouds of dust as we drove into it, invading every part of the vehicle and making it difficult to breathe even with makeshift face masks, was the rock desert. For several days, as we headed down into Chad on a route that no expedition had taken since General Leclerc's amazing and victorious march with the Free French from Chad, to join up with the Allies in North Africa, nearly twenty years before, we had to contend with terrain resembling a moonscape with craters and boulders on all sides. Occasionally one of the vehicles would become struck with its axle or crank case suspended on a rock and we would laboriously have to jack it up with its one ton of stores, and remove the rock before we could make progress.

By day we navigated with the aid of sun compasses mounted on the wings of the vehicles, checking our direction periodically against hand-held magnetic compasses. At night we would use a bubble-sextant to 'fix' our position by reference to the stars – an art in which Lt. Gibbs, the British Army Officer accompanying us, was expert, having been sent on a celestial navigation course with the Royal Air Force before we left. However, a major difficulty arose from the fact that, quite often, the three different sets of maps which we had brought with us – British, French and US Air Force – would show a vital point, such as a mountain pass or a water hole, twenty miles or more apart.

More than ten days after we had quit Kufra, leaving behind us all greenery and evidence of civilization, we suddenly came upon a large lake, stretched out before us, fringed with palm-trees where, dominating the scene from a rocky promontory, stood a magnificent white fortress. We rubbed our eyes, wondering if it was not just another mirage of the desert but, as we drew closer, a French *Tricoleur* was run up a flagpole. This was Ounianga Kebir, a fabulous and most welcome oasis in a vast and inhospitable desert.

The commander of the French Army garrison, Sergeant-Chef Thierey, greeted us most warmly and insisted that we stay with him in the fortress, where he was one of the only two Europeans among two dozen ebony-black Chad soldiers. Although it was impossible to swim in the lake as its high salt content would burn the skin, our host showed us to a superb natural pool, fed from below by freshwater springs and lying in the shade of a palm grove at the very edge of the lake, where we were able to wallow to our hearts' content. After two and a half weeks without a bath, and no prospect of one for a further three, we could not believe our luck to find a natural swimming pool in the heart of the Sahara. At Ounianga we were able to obtain a variety of fresh vegetables and fruit, as well as an abundance of small local pigeons to supplement our Army rations, for which our enthusiasm was rapidly waning. One evening, for our benefit, the Sergeant-Chef marshalled all the local girls together to dance the *Tam-tam*, the slow, soporific dance of the tribes-people of the Sahara, to the beat of native drums. They turned out in all their brightly coloured finery and were adorned with the most elaborate jewellery – something which they prize very highly – and with gold bangles and rings through their noses and ears.

From the much larger, dusty oasis of Faya-Largeau, where we were able to replenish our stocks of fuel and water, we headed North into the heart of the Tibesti Mountains but, less than two days on our way, we found ourselves caught for three days in a *Ghibli*, as sandstorms are known locally. The sky became completely obscured and, at times, we could see only forty or fifty yards as the swirling sand invaded every part of our anatomy and equipment. We had no choice but to call a halt for two days until the storm blew over but, meanwhile, we were using up precious supplies of water. When, at last, the storm abated and we were once again able to continue on our way we found ourselves in the spectacular landscape of the Tibesti with its high, barren mountains, rugged rock formations and extinct volcanoes, some of which have craters a mile or more across. As we approached the mountains, in what we knew to be one of the most deserted parts of Africa, we were amazed to see half a dozen vehicles coming towards us at speed from the opposite direction, churning up clouds of dust behind them. It turned out to be a French Army patrol for, although Chad had recently become officially independent, the French had an agreement whereby they retained control of security. Colonel Baylon, the senior French officer in Northern Chad at the time, greeted us most warmly and, though it was only shortly after dawn, insisted on plying us liberally with whiskey as more than twenty large, jet-black *Goumiers*, as the Chad soldiers were known, stood in front of their Dodge Power Wagons, looking formidable in their desert-goggles and with scarves wrapped round their faces to keep out the desert sand.

Once among the mountains we came across the occasional Tebou tribesman. These natives of Tebesti are, for the most part, hunters and were armed with steel-tipped spears which they had fashioned themselves and with which they were expert at stalking gazelle. In among the mountains, water was more plentiful and we found several small oases where we were able to replenish our water supplies. We also bartered beads and other trinkets we had brought with us for vegetables and dates.

From the Tibesti we headed North on the final leg of our journey towards Sebha and Tripoli. On the way we met a camel train of fierce-looking Touareg warriors, making their annual journey north with their herd of nearly one hundred young camels which they would sell to the more prosperous Libyans, before returning later in the year with their camels laden down with the summer date-crop. But, by now, my studies were pressing and I was already a few days late for the start of the summer term at Oxford. On arrival at Sebha, by which time we had covered some 5000 miles of desert in the space of five weeks, I was able to catch a flight from the local desert strip to Tripoli and fly home to England, having completed a most exciting and memorable journey. To this day I have a yearning to return to the desert with its vastness, its solitude and the translucence of its night sky where one feels closer to the myriad stars than to the bustle of city life.

Following my return to Oxford I wrote a couple of articles which, to my surprise, were published by the *Sunday Express* prompting my grandfather, on 5 May 1961, to send me a telegram:

AN OXFORD IDYLL

WINSTON S CHURCHILL
CHRIST CHURCH
OXFORD

I WAS SO PLEASED TO GET YOUR LETTER AND I THINK YOUR ARTICLE IS
GOOD. GRANDMAMA AND I WOULD SO MUCH LIKE YOU TO COME TO
CHARTWELL. DO PROPOSE YOURSELF FOR A WEEKEND.

LOVE
GRANDPAPA

At the end of the summer term, Grandpapa invited me to lunch with
him at Hyde Park Gate twice in a week. On each occasion, when lunch
was over, he took me with him to the House of Commons. Not until the
hands on the dining room clock reached five-to-three would he get up from
the dining table. Bullock, his driver would be waiting outside with the
black Humber. At the top of Hyde Park Gate we would swing right,
towards Knightsbridge. If, as they usually were, the lights at the top of
Exhibition Road were red and Bullock showed signs of stopping, Grandpapa would tap with impatience on the glass divider, exhorting Bullock:
'Do not delay a Member of Parliament going about his business – pray,
proceed!' On arrival at the House I would be installed on the bench under
the gallery where I was at the same level as the MPs and had a ringside
view of the proceedings. We would both be in our seats by 3.15 pm when
the Prime Minister, Harold Macmillan, would rise from the Treasury
Bench to answer Questions. It was an unequalled and unforgettable introduction to the House of Commons.

That summer Grandpapa invited me to spend a few days with him as
his guest at the Hôtel de Paris in Monte Carlo. One evening we dined with
his friend, the Greek shipping tycoon, Aristotle Onassis, at a superb
restaurant called the Château de Madrid, perched high on the mountainside
just off the Haute Corniche road between Monte Carlo and Nice. Among
the guests at the dinner were Greta Garbo and her friend and confidant
George Schlay. There is no doubt that my grandfather enjoyed the company
of beautiful women. He had been an ardent fan of Miss Garbo since her
early screen successes and had seen all her movies many times, *Queen
Christina* and *Ninotchka* being special favourites. Though the years had
taken their toll and she had become something of a recluse, she was still a
wonderful-looking woman. Grandpapa remained in thrall to her as well as,
no doubt, to the memory of what she had been.

We were sitting at the table closest to the window which commanded a
spectacular view down the rocky cliff face to the Mediterranean, sparkling
in the moonlight. All at once, in the middle of dinner, Miss Garbo, seated
on Grandpapa's right, announced that she had a problem. Towards the
end of his life my grandfather had difficulty hearing highpitched female
voices (not that Garbo's could in any way be so described) and Onassis,

whenever he was with him, would stand ready to relay the conversation.

'What did Miss Garbo say?' enquired my grandfather solicitously. Onassis, replying in excellent English, but laced with a heavy Greek accent, answered in a loud voice so that he should be heard: 'Miss Garbo, she say, she is too hot in her long English lambswool underpants, so she proposes to take them off.' This announcement caused quite a stir among diners at the immediately adjacent tables. Grandpapa, not sure if he had heard quite right, asked in a tone of some surprise: '*What* did Miss Garbo say?' Onassis, ever eager to be helpful, repeated once again what he had already said but with even greater deliberation. By now the eyes of the whole restaurant were rivetted on our table as Miss Garbo proceeded to execute a most discreet striptease beneath the tablecloth while Grandpapa patted her gently on the knee, intoning: 'Poor lamb, poor lamb!' as the offending garment was removed.

While in the South of France Grandpapa would invariably go for a drive in the afternoon. He particularly enjoyed taking the steep, scenic route up the mountainside overlooking Monte Carlo to the golf course of Montagel on the high plateau above. On reaching the golf course, we would get out of the car and stretch our legs. On one occasion, seeing that I had fallen into conversation with his bodyguard, Sgt Edmund Murray, late of the Metropolitan Police and, before that, of the French Foreign Legion, Grandpapa demanded to know: 'What did Murray say?' Repeating faithfully Sgt Murray's words, I replied: 'Sgt Murray says it's very dry up here.' Grandpapa, well aware how tinder-dry was the parched grass of late summer and the fire hazard this presented (though this did not stop him sucking at his half-extinct cigar), chose deliberately to ignore this and, knowing all too well the lines on which Sgt Murray's mind was liable to run, exclaimed with an impish smile: 'Yes! There isn't a pub for miles around!'

Grandpapa, though he could in no way be described as a serious gambler, thoroughly enjoyed spending an hour or two of an evening in the Casino at Monte Carlo, where he could never resist a flutter on the roulette tables. Though I was not yet quite twenty-one, he would take me with him and, for once, no one questioned my age. We passed by the expensive chemin de fer tables where the really wealthy – in those days mostly Greek shipowners, or the likes of King Farouk of Egypt (it was before the Arab oil had started flowing in serious quantities) – would make or lose fortunes in an evening's play. Beneath the elegant chandeliers men in evening dress would place their bets for very high stakes while many beautiful ladies, clad in the most exotic Paris creations and dripping with diamonds, stood at their elbow. It was a glamorous, glittering if shallow *demi-monde* with which it amused Grandpapa on occasion to mingle. Grandmama, however, at an early stage in their marriage let it be known in no uncertain terms that she disapproved of gambling, which offended the financial proprieties of her Scottish upbringing, as well as of the social riff-raff which inhabits casinos. Though I never saw Grandpapa take more than £100 with him to the casino and his gambling could not in any way be termed reckless, Grandmama left him in no doubt that she regarded it as a foolish extravagance, indeed a folly, though she had long since given up telling him so.

I recall her once telling me how, in the Thirties, they had been spending a few days together at a hotel in Beaulieu called La Réserve when, after dinner, Grandpapa had announced that he was off to the casino. Grandmama begged him not to go and, certainly, she would never have considered aiding and abetting such an expedition by her presence. But, despite her entreaties, he had gone. Meanwhile Grandmama retired early to bed with a book. 'In the early hours,' she recounted, 'I rolled over in bed and heard a strange noise. Reaching out with my hand in the darkness I sensed that the blanket was covered in pieces of paper. I turned on the bedside light and to my amazement saw that it had been transformed into a patchwork quilt of 10,000 Franc notes!' Though relieved that he had not lost, this gesture did nothing to assuage her firm disapproval of casinos, let alone secure her blessing for such sorties in the future.

Whenever I visited the South of France I always made a point of visiting my godfather, Lord Beaverbrook, at his beautiful villa, La Capponcina, at Cap d'Ail, where from the terrace Grandpapa painted many of his most lovely paintings of the pine trees overhanging the sparkling, aquamarine waters of the Mediterranean and of the view along the coast towards Monte Carlo. Although, like my grandfather, my father adored Max and enjoyed his company hugely, he also regarded him as one of the most mischievous of human beings, at times bordering on the wicked. One of my father's favourite stories to illustrate the point occurred in the late Fifties when Beaverbrook was taken ill while in the South of France. He telephoned his doctor in London, Sir Daniel Davies. Dan Davies, a delightful Welshman who hailed from the valleys of Aberystwyth, was physician to the Queen and, as it happened, to my mother and me. That very day Sir Dan's elder daughter was getting married and he was somewhat preoccupied with the hectic last-minute arrangements of a family wedding, when the summons came through from Beaverbrook: 'Dan, is that you?' demanded the gruff, instantly recognizable voice with its broad Canadian accent that forty years living in England had done nothing to tame.

'Yes, Lord Beaverbrook,' replied the doctor in his gentle Welsh lilt.

'Dan, I'm sick and I need you out here right away.'

'Well, Lord Beaverbrook,' protested the doctor, 'I'm afraid that will be difficult as it is my daughter's wedding day.'

This excuse served only to produce a roar of protest from the cantankerous old Canadian who thundered in peremptory tones not usually associated with those about to expire: 'Dan, I'm a dying man. You cannot abandon me when I need you. Now, listen carefully. There is a Viscount airliner waiting for you at Northolt airport. It will be ready to leave in one hour's time and you're to be on it. A car will be outside your home in 15 minutes.'

The saintly, mild-mannered doctor succumbed to these hectoring blandishments, abandoned his daughter's wedding and dutifully flew to his dying patient's side. However, by the time he arrived at La Capponcina some four hours later, Lord Beaverbrook was sitting up in bed feeling somewhat better. The local English doctor from Monte Carlo, Dr Roberts, had meanwhile dropped by, prescribed some tablets and pronounced that there was nothing seriously wrong with the old man, a diagnosis in which Dr Davies concurred.

My father, arriving at La Capponcina a day or so later, to visit Beaverbrook, found him already out of bed and clearly on the mend. It has to be said that Max, the son of a Presbyterian Minister, disapproved of my father's fondness for whiskey and would invariably and ostentatiously draw attention to this vice by summoning his butler Albert and, in a loud voice, commanding: 'Albert, bring Mr Churchill some Scotch whiskey!' To which the elderly retainer would reply in a mournful tone: 'Yes, Lawd!'

After three or four minutes Albert reappeared bearing a silver salver on which was set a bottle of whiskey, a soda water syphon, a tumbler and some ice. Beaverbrook, instantly spotting that the whiskey bottle was new, bellowed: 'Albert! That's a new bottle of whiskey! What happened to the old bottle?'

'Well, Lawd,' lamented the butler, 'there was not much left in the other bottle and the Doctor from London drank it.'

'That god-damn doctor!' growled the crotchety old Beaver, clearly well back on form.

While in the South of France, Grandpapa gave my grandmother a report of our holiday in his own hand:

My dearest Clemmie,
Here is a letter in my own paw. All is vy pleasant and the days slip by. We are steadily wiping off old friendship's debts with lunches and dinners. I find it vy hard to write a good letter and wonder at the rate with which my friends accomplish their daily tasks. It is amazing they can succeed so well.
But now here I have written what is at least the expression of my love, Darling. When I was young I wrote fairly well, but now at last I am played out. You have my fondest love.

Your devoted
Winston

P.S.: I am daily astonished by the development I see in my namesake. He is a wonderful boy. I am so glad to have got to know him.

When our holiday was at an end the Monaco police and the French *gendarmerie* insisted on providing us with a motorcycle escort to Nice

Airport. Grandpapa expected, indeed required, to be driven fast but, being driven round the sharp bends of the coastal *corniche*, which was only wide enough for two or, at a pinch three vehicles in any direction, at a speed which never dropped below 50 mph and was more often 75 was a remarkable experience. Two of the French motorcycle *gendarmes* went before us in line ahead and, taking up position half way across the approaching lane and with whistles clenched firmly between their teeth, would blow furiously and use expansive gestures with their left arms to sweep into the gutter any oncoming traffic. The lady driver of a tiny Citroën Deux Chevaux, confronted by this awesome spectacle and with a precipitous drop to the sea on her near side, slammed on her brakes in panic, almost causing the two vehicles behind to crash into her.

I returned to Oxford that autumn, at the start of what was to be my final year at university, a whole month early, with every intention of buckling down to some hard work for my degree. Due to shortage of space in college, those of us in our final year were required to find accommodation out of college. Through Mitch, the Christ Church porter, I managed to find 'digs', consisting of a bedroom, bathroom and small sitting room in the home of a British Leyland car worker and his wife who lived at 4 Newton Road. I had not been back long before my solitude was rudely invaded by a couple of friends who kicked the book I was reading from my hands and insisted that I join them for lunch at the Bear Inn in Woodstock, renowned for its good food. Against my better judgment I agreed. A couple of hours later, on my way back to Oxford, I noticed, through something of a haze, a sign which read: 'Learn to fly with the Oxford Aeroplane Club' – an invitation to which I also succumbed.

A few months earlier, possibly on the strength of the fact that I had done a few laps of the Nurburgring in Germany in my 2.4 litre Jaguar, my mother had got it into her head that I was determined to motor-race and had charged my stepfather, Leland, with the task of dissuading me. Leland, though his career was in the theatre, had always had a passion for flying and was, himself, an expert pilot. It was his love of aviation that had led him and a friend in the Second World War to set up a flight training establishment field at Thunderbird Field, Phoenix, Arizona, to which thousands of British and American pilots came to do their pilot training. He was to kick himself in later years for the fact that, soon after the war, he had sold the airfield which stood on the edge of what was to become the fastest-growing city in the United States. Even while bringing a succession of hit musicals to Broadway, he had kept alive his interest in aviation as part owner of a small commuter airline in California called Pacific Airways and, shortly before his sixty-fifth birthday, he fulfilled his ambition of becoming a qualified helicopter pilot. He spoke to me earnestly about the dangers of motor-racing, insisting that if I wanted to go fast it was safer to do it in an aeroplane. He thereupon offered me, as a twenty-first birthday present, the cost of getting my pilot's licence. Having flown all my life as a passenger in the back seats of aeroplanes, I fear I did not, at first, show too much enthusiasm for his wonderfully generous offer.

However, that afternoon, on the spur of the moment and after too good a lunch, I decided to give it a try. I swung my car into the entrance of Kidlington Airport and drove up to the control-tower, below which were drawn several small single-engine aeroplanes. I enquired about flying lessons from a wiry young man who sported a red, bushy, unmistakably RAF moustache. By way of answer, he took my upper arm in a vice-like grip and led me out, without a word, to a small two-seater Piper Colt aeroplane with the wings on its roof and proceeded to give me my first taste of flying a light aircraft. Before we were even back on the ground I had fallen victim to the flying bug and, for the next three weeks, could think of little else. Within four days I had made my first solo and, thereafter, there was no stopping me. I wrote to Grandpapa of my adventures:

4 Newton Road
Oxford
10 September 1961

Dear Grandpapa,

Thank you so much for the wonderful time in the South of France, I greatly enjoyed my stay with you. It was a pity that we did not have better luck at the Casino.

Since I have been back in Oxford I have been taking flying lessons, which are tremendously exciting. Today I did take offs and landings – we came down with quite a bump! After that I learned how to recover from a spin and a stall.

I leave for South America in about a fortnight and I hope before then I have an opportunity of having luncheon with you and Grandmama. Please give her my fondest love.

Your loving grandson,
Winston

Grandpapa replied by telegram four days later:

WINSTON CHURCHILL ESQ
4 NEWTON ROAD
OXFORD

SO THRILLED AT YOUR FLYING LESSONS. WE HOPE NO MORE BUMPS STOP
PLEASE COME AND SEE US BEFORE YOU LEAVE FOR SOUTH AMERICA

LOVE GRANDMAMA AND GRANDPAPA

In the space of three and a half weeks and at a cost of just under £300, I managed to clock up the thirty hours then required to take the test and acquire my pilot's licence.

My father, who had just been invited by Grandpapa to write his official biography, was at the time negotiating the sale of the foreign rights. A publishing house in Argentina, interested in acquiring the Latin American rights, had sent him two first-class return tickets to Buenos Aires to discuss a contract. In the absence of anyone he might sooner take, Father asked me, at very short notice, if I would care to join him – a proposition which I accepted with alacrity. However, he was insistent that we flew in separate aeroplanes – not such an easy matter at a time when there was only a fraction of the flights there are today. Like Grandpapa, he was a great dynast. Conscious of the fact that we were both only sons and recalling that none of Marlborough's male heirs had survived to marriageable age, he had long since made it a rule that we should never fly in the same aeroplane. For some strange reason the logic of this argument did not extend to travel by motor-car which, with him at the wheel, was infinitely more hazardous, since he was not even capable of driving even the sixty miles from London to East Bergholt without stopping at least once at a pub to fill up.

In the circumstances I decided to fly out ahead of my father to spend three days with friends in Rio de Janeiro, before joining him in Argentina where, in addition to a few days in Buenos Aires, we spent a weekend at a magnificent cattle ranch known as La Concepción. But the high point of the trip was, undoubtedly, our visit to Peru. After being lavishly fêted by our ambassador in Lima, Sir Berkeley Gage, we flew to Cuzco, the ancient Inca capital in the heart of the Andes – for once breaking our rule of not flying together, as there was no alternative flight and our time was strictly limited. The flight in an unpressurized DC-4 aircraft of Fawcett Airlines left at dawn and, though we flew at 20,000 ft sucking oxygen from individual plastic tubes, the snow-covered peaks of the Andes still towered above us to 22,000 ft or more. On landing at Cuzco which stands nearly 12,000 feet above sea level we discovered that the departure of the daily train to Machu Picchu, the Lost City of the Incas, was craftily synchronized by the locals so as to ensure that it left shortly before the once-daily flight from Lima landed, requiring visitors to night stop in Cuzco whether they liked it or not. Father, after judicious enquiries, was able to establish that, for a not too exorbitant sum, we could charter a small self-propelled railcar to ourselves. However, before we could leave, the rarity of the atmosphere at that altitude got the better of him. The fact that he was in the habit at the time of smoking 80–100 cigarettes a day did not help and we had to find a hotel room where he could lie down for a couple of hours to catch his breath before we could set forth.

From Cuzco, where the ancient Incas had had their Sun Temple at which human sacrifices had, on occasion, been performed, we embarked on quite the most exciting rail journey I have ever made. Our private British-made railcar, powered by its own diesel engine, climbed laboriously for the first few miles up to a 13,000 ft pass which stands on the Grand Divide of the Andes. Behind us every stream and river flowed west to the

Pacific: ahead of us lay the headwaters of the mighty Amazon, winding its way some 4000 miles to the Atlantic. On reaching the summit of the pass, the driver switched off the engine and we proceeded to coast downhill at a steady 30–35 mph, in complete silence apart from the rhythmic 'clickety-clack' of the wheels on the rail joints. At first the country before us was a wide open plain of fertile grasslands comparable to the Basque country around Pamplona in northern Spain. But, soon, the track plunged more steeply, requiring the driver to apply the brake as we entered the narrow valley of the Urubamba River which had carved its path out of the rock over the centuries. The dry savannah of the plain rapidly gave way to a lusher, greener and ever more tropical scenery as we found ourselves hemmed in on all sides by towering mountains.

Eventually, after a journey of some five or six hours, we reached our destination, a tiny station deep in the valley beside an already wide and swiftly flowing river. High on the hillside above us stood the amazingly well-preserved ruins of Machu Picchu to which the Incas had retreated in the face of the fifteenth-century Spanish Conquistadors. These remarkable and extensive ruins made out of carefully carved stone and fitted together without the use of any mortar, went undiscovered until the beginning of this century, surrounded as they were by the high, forbidding rock faces of the Andes which, for centuries, had kept sacred the secret of the Incas.

From Peru Father travelled to Mexico, while I hurried on to New York where my mother and Leland had arranged a party in their beautiful Fifth Avenue apartment to celebrate my twenty-first birthday before I returned the next day to Oxford for the start of term. Among those at the party was my grandfather's friend, the distinguished American financier, Bernard Baruch, who generously gave me a gold tie-clip. A few days later, when I lunched with Grandpapa Churchill, he gave me a most handsome black crocodile cigar case with my initials in gold, together with two large boxes of cigars.

From New York I hastened back to Oxford to resume my studies and my flying though, I must admit, it was the latter that had captured my imagination. I soon discovered that I had no shortage of intrepid friends willing to risk their lives in my hands and, best of all, pay for the privilege. I established I could rent a four-seater Piper Tripacer from Oxford for £14 an hour. Split four ways it brought my flying down to £3.50 an hour and I didn't mind where I flew to at that rate. Sometimes it would be to Brighton for a fine dinner and if, on our return overhead Oxford, we discovered that the flare path would be lit for an hour or so longer, we would pop up to Birmingham for a coffee and brandy before returning to land at Oxford. As winter gave way to spring we became more adventurous, hopping across the Channel for lunch or to Monte Carlo for the weekend of the motor-racing *Grand Prix*, all of which proved the greatest fun though I cannot pretend it enhanced the quality of my degree. Had the examiners invigilated me on my flying – that would have been another matter! But at least, when the time came for me to leave Oxford that summer, I took with me, besides an Honours Degree in Modern History, many happy memories and left behind a broad spectrum of friends, in sharp contrast to my time at Eton. My horizons had been greatly expanded, not solely in the direction my professors had in mind.

· X ·

African Adventure

The previous winter Arnold von Bohlen – whose place I had by then taken as Captain of the Oxford Ski Team – and I were riding together on a chairlift high above the Zürs valley in the Austrian Arlberg, when our conversation turned to Africa. He, too, had recently been on a trip to Africa which, as in my case, had only served to whet his appetite for further adventures in that exciting and mysterious continent. We also had in common the fact that we had each recently learnt to fly and had become wildly enthusiastic aviators. There and then we decided to rent a small aeroplane from Oxford Airport and fly around the entire continent of Africa.

As soon as I had obtained my degree from Oxford in June 1962 I flew to America to stay with my mother and Leland who, by then, had bought a house in a wonderful situation overlooking the Croton Lakes near Mt Kisco in New York State. While there I undertook an intensive six weeks' Commercial Pilot's and Instrument Rating course with the top flight-training organization in America called Flight Safety at La Guardia Airport. Though I was not to have sufficient hours in my log book until the following year to obtain my Commercial Pilot's Licence and Instrument Rating, I was determined to learn all I could about the art of navigation, especially over inhospitable terrain where many of the conventional aids which are taken for granted in Europe or America just did not exist. It would clearly also be important to be able to fly and navigate the aircraft by reference to instruments alone, given the virtual certainty that at some point in our journey we would find ourselves in a tropical thunderstorm. Since, for our flight around Africa, we would have to rely primarily on dead reckoning and map reading I decided to fly out to Los Angeles and spend a few days with Leland's friend, Bud Gurney, flying across the Nevada, Arizona and California deserts.

Bud had started his career in aviation flying the air mail coast-to-coast from California to the eastern seaboard in competition with the Pony Express and the railroad. Thereafter he and Lindbergh had flown the 'Flying Circus' together, never starting any aerobatic manoeuvre more than 50 ft above the ground otherwise, as he explained to me, people could see the show from all around and would not pay their entrance fee. When Leland had made the movie of Lindbergh's epic solo flight across the Atlantic, called after his plane *The Spirit of St Louis*, Lindbergh had insisted that his friend, Bud, be employed as technical adviser. For the making of the film a wonderful collection of vintage biplanes were assembled and restored. On completion of the shooting, Leland had given Bud one of the planes they had been using, a 1929 Gypsy Moth, on condition that he kept it in good flying order for them both near his home in California.

Bud, at the time, was Chief Pilot of United Airlines. He had recently completed flight trials on the DC-8, which was on the point of entering service with the airline. He mentioned that one part of the test involved placing the aircraft in a steep nose-down attitude while applying full reverse-thrust to all four engines – a remarkable manoeuvre in a large commercial jet. At the same time, between regular flights to Honolulu, he was, as a brilliant self-taught mathematician who had worked out his own form of calculus, doing a project for North American Rockwell on the cruise control problems of an aircraft which, twenty years later, was to become the B-1 bomber. What I learned from Bud, in the course of the few days I spent with him, was to prove invaluable on our African adventure. We rented a single-engine plane from a small airfield near Los Angeles and headed out across the California desert on a two-day navigational flight which took us over the spectacularly beautiful Painted Desert, Bryce Canyon and Death Valley as well as the gaping gorge of the Grand Canyon.

On my return to England I negotiated to rent a beautiful blue and white single-engine Piper Comanche for just £7.75 per flying hour, on the understanding that we would be responsible for the fuel, oil and insurance. Lloyd's of London were prepared to lay the remarkably favourable odds of 22 to 1 against the aircraft being a total write-off! To the many friends and relations who chided us for our decision to fly round Africa on only a single engine, across thousands of miles of desert and jungle, we pointed out, quite truthfully, that with two engines we would be twice as likely to have an engine failure – a somewhat fallacious argument, albeit factually accurate. The fact was that our budget did not extend to a second engine. Nevertheless we did take seriously the possibility of our one and only engine – a brand new 250 hp Lycoming – quitting on us and assembled a comprehensive survival kit. Besides food and water for a week, we took with us everything from matches and a ball of string to morphine tablets and a .38 Smith & Wesson Police Special revolver, the latter as we had heard tales of the peculiarly unpleasant ways in which certain Ethiopian tribes were in the habit of dealing with uninvited guests. Others, more pointedly, remarked that with our experience – which amounted to less than 250 hours between the two of us – we had no business being allowed even to fly across the English Channel, let alone make a 20,000-mile flight around Africa. But we only took such discouragement as a challenge.

My flying was causing both my Churchill grandparents some anxiety and, earlier that year my grandmother had written to express her concern:

10 March 1962

Dearest Winston,

Since your visit to us the other day, I have been thinking about something that is giving your grandfather and me a good deal of anxiety: that is your flying.
We are both so pleased that you should have learnt to fly and to enjoy piloting yourself, but we are disturbed that you may undertake flights in weather that is not adequately good for your present standard of experience and for the relatively simple aircraft you are flying.

This is not casting any doubt on your skill, but I have been told by several people with first-hand experience how easy it is in bad visibility to get lost and to be in peril through icing or radio failure, particularly in a single engined aircraft. So I do hope that you will set our minds at rest by assuring us that you won't undertake your trips about the country unless the weather is really reliable.

Your loving grandmama
Clementine S. Churchill

I hoped I had managed to allay their fears but, before setting out on our journey, I went to tell Grandpapa Churchill of my plans. We lunched alone together with my grandmother at 28 Hyde Park Gate and Grandpapa did not conceal his anxiety. 'It is a very hazardous enterprise,' he declared, 'I am not at all sure that I approve.' I had long since learned by experience that the only way to deal with Churchills – whether my grandfather or my father – was to stand up to them. It was the only language they understood and respected. To hesitate or show weakness was fatal and guaranteed one would lose the argument. 'How dare you, Grandpapa!' I rejoined. 'When *you* were my age, you had already come under fire in Cuba, fought on the North-West frontier of India and were on the point of charging with the 21st Lancers at Omdurman!' He paused for a moment's reflection before replying: 'I think you have a point,' adding, as I took my leave of him, 'You have my blessing!'

The final preparations were made, but for three days our departure was delayed by thick fog blanketing all of Southern England. Though frustrating this proved to be no hardship as my cousin, Sunny Blandford (now

Duke of Marlborough) and his then wife, Tina, invited us to stay with them at their lovely home nearby at Charlbury. Tina, who was Greek and had previously been married to Ari Onassis – with whom I had first met her – was a wonderfully gay, warm-hearted person of great beauty and endowed with a bubbling sense of humour. When, later, I married, she was to become godmother to our elder son, Randolph, but tragically died not long after.

Finally there was a change in the weather and we were able to leave the November mists of England behind us, and head East across the Mediterranean by way of Italy and Greece to the Lebanon, which in those days enjoyed the reputation of being the most stable and democratic country in the Arab world. For this reason it was known as the 'Switzerland' of the Middle East. From Beirut we continued eastwards to Damascus and the magnificent Roman ruins of Palmyra which stand in the Syrian desert astride the old Silk Route from China and the East. Thanks to my Palestinian friend from Oxford days, Farouk Toukan, who had met us in Beirut and travelled on with us from there, we were received most hospitably in Jordan at the Ragadan Palace in Amman by a then very young King Hussein. Who would have imagined that, in spite of repeated threats to his life by President Nasser of Egypt and, more recently, by the PLO, Al Fatah and the PFLP, Hussein would prove to be the longest-surviving head of State in all the Middle East? Amid all the turmoil of Middle East politics, he has remained in power for more than a quarter of a century – an amazing feat in that part of the world. He made clear in his conversation with us that, though every Arab hoped for unity, this could never be imposed by the domination of 'a demagogue like Nasser', whose expansionist programmes he was determined to resist. He further expressed his strong opposition to Nasser's military intervention in the Yemen, though it was clear, given the massive scale of the Egyptian Army's modern Russian equipment, that his protests could only be verbal. What stood out most of Hussein's characteristics – and this has been reinforced by meetings I have had with him over the years, both in Amman and in London – were his courage, his astuteness and most noticeable of all his good manners, though I confess I have always found it disconcerting to be addressed as 'Sir' by a monarch.

Our flight from Amman which took us across the Dead Sea – at which point our altimeter was indicating 1250 ft *below* sea level – and over the Gulf of Aqaba, Sinai and the Suez Canal to the lush, green Nile delta was spectacular. Though modern Cairo with its poverty and squalor – exacerbated by President Nasser's vast military expenditure and foreign adventures – proved a disappointment, ancient Cairo came fully up to expectations. The Pyramids of Giza and the treasures of Tutankhamen's tomb, displayed in the Cairo Museum made us eager to visit the Valley of the Kings amid the barren hills near Luxor where they were found. I recorded the following account of our visit in my diary at the time:

By far the least impressive of all the tombs was that of Tutankhamen. It is small and near the surface. When one considers the wealth of treasures that came out of even this small tomb, it is impossible to hazard a guess at the wonders and wealth that the larger of these magnificent morgues, consisting of numerous chambers hollowed out of the rock deep in the bowels of the earth, must have contained. The extensive and detailed paintings on the walls of the burial chambers and passages leading to them must have taken innumerable hours – even years – of labour by an army of artists working in the hot and humid, air-starved rooms with little or no light to illuminate their lives' labour which was condemned, so they must have supposed, to remain in the deep, dark caverns for eternity, unseen by human eye. It is curious to reflect on the power of these Pharaohs who were able to keep whole masses of their people employed during their life-span on a project solely destined to help them on their way to an afterlife. Their preoccupation with Death must have been paramount, for as soon as they ascended the throne of Egypt, at no matter how tender an age, work was set on foot, not to build palaces that might make their earthly lives more comfortable and pleasant, but in preparation for Death.

At Aswan we found work on the massive High Dam going on round the clock, with dozens of Swedish rock drills boring into the granite and Russian trucks with tyres five feet high transporting loads of boulders to build the coffer or foundation dam. With more than 1700 Russian technicians and 25,000 Egyptian workmen engaged in the construction of the High Dam, there had been no project in Egypt on a comparable scale since the days of the Pharaohs themselves. To escape from this hubbub of activity, we took one of the feluccas that were tied up along the river bank and sailed downstream to Kitchener's Island, with its superb garden, containing an incredible variety of tropical trees and shrubs. Later, we sailed slowly upstream as the sun was setting in fiery splendour behind the Aga Khan's mausoleum, perched on top of the sand dunes to the West. I took the helm as the boatman knelt at the bow and turned to pay his evening devotions towards Mecca. It was a peaceful and serene moment.

From Aswan we followed the course of the Nile South towards the Sudan. While on the short flight from Luxor to Aswan we had skimmed along the surface of the river no higher than the mast-tops of the feluccas and the palm trees on the banks, we now climbed to 12,000 ft as the flight to Khartoum was the longest we had so far made and all of it across desert. At that altitude the air was much cooler and, even more important, our radios had a much greater range; thus, in the event of our only engine quitting we would at least have the chance to put out a distress signal before crash-landing. On arrival at Khartoum a pair of British pilots, working for a crop-spraying firm employed by the Sudanese Government in locust control, kindly offered us a couple of spare rooms at their house for the three nights we were to be there.

It was impossible for me to visit Khartoum without going out to the barren rock-strewn plain on the banks of the Nile where my grandfather, some sixty-five years before, had charged with the 21st Lancers at Omdurman, in what was to be one of the last cavalry charges of history. A small obelisk, protected by iron railings from desecration, stands as the only evidence of the great battle in which more than 10,000 Sudanese perished. From the crest of Jebel Surgham, Arnold and I surveyed the desolate plain around us trying to recreate in our minds' eye the scene that had greeted my grandfather at dawn on the day of the battle when it was submerged under a teeming mass of humanity over 80,000 strong, with 8200 British and 17,600 Egyptian soldiers standing in the path of the 55,000 man Dervish army as it advanced in battle order with its banners streaming bravely. How different the scene must have looked just five hours later with this proud and gallant army cut to ribbons. In the words of Hilaire Belloc: 'Whatever happens we have got, the Maxim gun – and they have not!' The fire-power of the machine gun, which the Sudanese did not possess, combined with disciplined volley rifle-fire had been the decisive factors. The scale of the slaughter was terrible, 25,000 casualties were strewn about the field, 10,000 of them corpses, their blood staining even the red rock a darker hue. We lingered at this spot, deep in contemplation, as the lengthening shadows overtook the plain, the sun set with a brilliance not seen in more temperate climes and the battlefield was plunged into darkness.

It was from that very spot that my grandfather had surveyed the scene at dawn on the morning of 2 September 1898, and in *The River War* he gave a wonderfully vivid account of the charge in which he had taken part, of 400 Lancers against 2700 of the enemy in one small corner of the battlefield:

The trumpet jerked out a shrill note, heard faintly above the trampling of the horses and the noise of the rifles. On the instant all the sixteen troops swung round and locked up into a long galloping line, and the 21st Lancers were committed to their first charge in war. Two hundred and fifty yards away the dark-blue men were firing madly in a thin film of light-blue smoke. Their bullets struck the hard gravel into the air, and the troopers, to shield their faces from the stinging dust, bowed their helmets forward, like the *Cuirassiers* at Waterloo. The pace was fast and the distance short. Yet, before it was half covered, the whole aspect of the affair changed. A deep crease in the ground – a dry watercourse, a *khor* – appeared where all seemed smooth, level plain; and from it there sprang, with the suddenness of a pantomime effect and a high-pitched yell, a dense white mass of men nearly as long as our front and about twelve deep. A score of horsemen and a dozen bright flags rose as if by magic from the earth. Eager warriors sprang forward to anticipate the shock. The rest stood firm to meet it. The Lancers acknowledged the apparition only by an increase of pace. Each man wanted sufficient momentum to drive through such a solid line. . . . The riflemen, firing bravely to the last, were swept head over heels into the *khor*, and jumping down with them, at full gallop and in closest order, the British squadrons struck the fierce brigade with one long furious shout. The collision was prodigious. Nearly thirty Lancers, men and horses, and at least two hundred Arabs were overthrown. The shock was stunning to both sides, and for perhaps ten wonderful seconds no man heeded his enemy. Terrified horses wedged in the crowd, bruised and shaken men, sprawling in heaps, struggled, dazed and stupid, to their feet, panted, and looked about them. Several fallen Lancers had even time to remount. Meanwhile the impetus of the cavalry carried them on ... Then, and not until then, the killing began; and thereafter each man saw the world along his lance, under his guard, or through the backsight of his pistol; and each had his own strange tale to tell ... We were alone together – the cavalry regiment and the Dervish brigade. The ridge hung like a curtain between us and the army. The general battle was forgotten, as it was unseen. This was a private quarrel. The other might have been a massacre; but here the fight was fair, for we too fought with sword and spear. Indeed the advantage of ground and numbers lay with them. All prepared to settle the debate at once and for ever. But some realization of the cost of our wild ride began to come to those who were responsible ... In 120 seconds 5 officers, 65 men and 119 horses out of fewer than 400 had been killed or wounded.

Thus Kitchener's army avenged the death of General Gordon, who had perished in 1885 at the hands of the Dervishes following the revolt stirred up by their formidable religious leader, the Mahdi. In the course of our stay in the Sudanese capital I contrived to meet Abdullah al Ameen, the grandson of the Mahdi and a young man of my own age. Though most friendly, he could not conceal his abiding anger with Lord Kitchener for having gratuitously slaughtered so many of his people in battle – a sentiment which my grandfather had also shared.

Khartoum stands at the confluence of the White and Blue Niles. The former has its source in Lake Victoria, nearly 1500 miles to the South in Uganda, while the latter originates at Lake Tana high in the Ethiopian mountains. From Khartoum we followed the course of the Blue Nile eastwards towards its source, being forced to climb to over 15,000 ft to clear the rocky peaks shrouded in dark thunderclouds that towered up ahead of us. We carried no oxygen – a requirement for commercial pilots above 10,000 ft. At this altitude the mathematical calculations needed to work out our position or to compute the amount of fuel remaining were noticeably harder work. There were no towns, roads or railways to serve as landmarks by which we could fix our position, only numerous small rivers and mountains, which were indistinguishable one from the other. To add to our difficulties we later discovered that the radio beacon at Gondar, near the shores of Lake Tana, and another which lay on our route, were out of service, only being switched on for scheduled flights by Ethiopian Airlines. We therefore had no choice but to navigate solely by dead reckoning, flying a predetermined course though we had no accurate forecast of the winds on our route. Our task was made no easier by the fact that we had frequently to alter course to avoid the giant cumulus clouds, which blocked our path and near which we encountered violent turbulence. Meanwhile, our long-range high-frequency radio had become unusable as the lead weights had fallen off the aerial which we trailed behind us from a fishing-reel. However, 100 miles short of Addis Ababa the needle of our radio compass swung round to show that at least the beacon there was working.

Ethiopia, at the time, had a longer tradition as an independent nation than any other in Africa and was also unique in having been nominally a Christian land since the fourth century, with the Coptic Church retaining a powerful influence right up to modern times. It seems likely that Ethiopia was the Realm of Prester John, the Christian kingdom with which the medieval monarchies of Europe hoped to join in a grand crusade against Islam, and which the early European explorers of Africa were so anxious to reach.

This remote Kingdom remained essentially a feudal land where the authority of the Emperor, who by legend traced his descent from Menelik, the son of King Solomon and the Queen of Sheba, went virtually unchallenged. We had the good fortune, in the course of our stay in the Ethiopian capital to be received by Emperor Haile Selassie, known as the Lion of Judah. Outside the entrance to the Imperial Palace, a fully grown lion lay on the grass verge of the driveway, chained to a tree. As we walked by he stretched himself, got to his feet and wandered lazily over to sniff us. Fortunately I declined Arnold's offer to take a photograph of me patting the lion on its nose, for we subsequently discovered that a member of a BBC television crew had lost the seat of his pants to the animal in this very way. The Emperor received us in a long wood-panelled room furnished with finely worked carpets. As we entered, he got up from his desk at the far end of the room. We had been briefed on the correct protocol by the British Ambassador, Sir John Russell and, from the door, we both made a bow which the Emperor returned. As we shook hands with him we bowed a second time, unlike his own subjects who were required to prostrate themselves before him. The formalities over, he took his place on a raised throne and motioned us to two seats on his right-hand side. Though tiny in stature he had a commanding presence. Wearing a tan uniform, on which was arrayed a vast number of decorations, he sat ram-rod straight with his hands clasped before him.

Already in his seventies, he had come to power as Regent in 1916, becoming Emperor in 1930. When Mussolini invaded Ethiopia, before the Second World War, the Emperor had in vain pleaded his nation's cause before the League of Nations in Geneva, which proved powerless in the face of such brazen aggression. He had remained in exile in Britain until restored to his throne in 1941 by British forces who liberated Ethiopia from Italian domination. Although he understood English and was fluent in French, our interview was conducted throughout in Amharic through an interpreter. At only one point did he break into English. Knowing that there was a sizeable contingent of the United States Peace Corps engaged in teaching English in the schools and assisting with irrigation projects, I asked him whether such technical assistance was preferable to direct financial aid. The Emperor's eyes lit up and, grinning broadly, he cut across the interpreter to exclaim: 'Cash, of course, is first class!'

With advancing years, the Emperor's absolute authority was on the wane and in 1974 he was overthrown by a military coup leading to a Marxist dictatorship over which the Soviet Union proceeded to establish decisive control and which has proved an unmitigated disaster for the peoples of Ethiopia, most especially for the people of Eritrea and the Somali nomads of the Ogaden, hundreds of thousands of whom have died or been driven out of the country by Cuban and Ethiopian soldiers backed by Soviet-bloc military advisers. The frail and elderly Emperor, eighty-three years of age, is believed to have been murdered in 1975, by suffocation with a pillow.

In the course of our visit to this wild but magnificent land, Arnold and I spent a most wonderful day on horseback charging up En Toto, a 12,000 ft mountain overlooking the capital, on small but remarkably strong mountain ponies in the company of the British Ambassador and his family. John Russell, and his delightful Greek wife, Aliki, were the most generous of hosts and after three hours or more in the saddle, just as we were thinking what a long way it was back to lunch and how we would have done well to bring some sandwiches, we rounded a crest near the top of En Toto to find ourselves confronted by an amazing sight. Persian rugs had been spread out on the ground, tents set up and a lavish banquet laid out on trestle tables with white-gloved footmen in attendance to serve it. Sadly, British ambassadors no longer entertain in such style any more.

From the mountain fastnesses of Ethiopia we flew on to Aden, originally a coaling station on the route to India set on the southern tip of the Arabian peninsula, where it commanded the entrance to the Red Sea and, beyond it, the Suez Canal. It was still, at the time, a British Protectorate and we landed at the RAF base of Khormaksar where Hunter jets and military transports were lined up. When next I had occasion to overfly the airfield, some fifteen years later, it was crammed full of Soviet MiG fighters and Antonov transport aircraft, which were there to secure a dominant position for the Soviet Union astride the sea lanes vital to the security of the West.

Our original plan had been to fly direct to East Africa but, on the spur of the moment, we decided instead to visit the Yemen, a remote mountainous country where, three months before, an Egyptian-inspired coup had taken place against the Imam, the traditional ruler. Civil war had broken out between the Royalists and the new Republican regime which, at the time, was backed by a 12,000-strong force of Egyptian soldiers – a figure which was later to increase to 60,000 – sent on the instructions of President Nasser to intervene in the fighting.

Abandoning our trusty Comanche in Aden, we flew on an Egyptian-operated Dakota of Yemen Airlines to the Republican-held capital of Sana'a. The aircraft was not the best maintained and had many screws and rivets missing from the airframe, while the freight that was loaded aboard consisted almost entirely of cases of vodka and scotch whiskey addressed to the Russian legation in Ta'izz. In the capital, where we surveyed the damage to the Imam's palace caused by artillery bombardment, we aroused the curiosity of the local tribesmen with their rugged bearded faces, turbanned heads and short curved daggers stuffed in the front of their belts. Arnold and I were repeatedly asked if we were Russians. When we replied we were not and I admitted to being British, darkly suspicious glances were cast in my direction, since Britain had refused to recognize the puppet regime installed by Nasser. As we wandered through the marketplace amid blacksmiths fashioning daggers on their anvils, cobblers making shoes on their lasts while yet others sat crosslegged puffing dreamily at their mildly narcotic hubble-bubble pipes, a terrific shout suddenly went up and everyone rushed off to surround two truckloads of captured Royalist tribesmen that had just arrived. A crowd of three or four hundred surged round the trucks eager for a public lynching. When, eventually, the vehicles succeeded in entering the nearby prison compound, several of the crowd, whose blood was up, scaled the prison walls brandishing their daggers. A Yemeni citizen standing beside me, who was surveying the scene with obvious relish, seeing that I was in some doubt as to what might be the fate of the couple of dozen bedraggled tribesmen, grinned broadly and explained with an unmistakable gesture, drawing the fingertips of one hand from ear to ear beneath his throat.

We were accommodated at the government guesthouse where the other guests were, without exception, either Egyptian or Russian. At dinner we sat at a table with several ruddy-faced Russian technicians with whom we exchanged welcoming nods, though we had to leave it at that since we knew no Russian and they evidently had no English, though we were able to discover that the reason for their presence was to construct a military airfield.

We returned to Aden by way of Ta'izz where for twenty *rials* (£6) we were able to secure the two front seats of a Land-Rover which ended up with a total of 18 passengers on board, for the twelve-hour journey on a narrow, unpaved, dusty road which wound through spectacular mountain passes with numerous hairpin bends and precipices. When, in the middle of the night, the driver announced that we had arrived at our destination, and it turned out we were still forty miles from Aden, we were glad that we had refused to pay so much as one *rial* until we reached Aden. A lengthy discussion ensued in the course of which Arnold and I, with only a dozen words of Arabic between us, managed to enlist the support of some bystanders before the driver consented to take us to our hotel in Crater, the Arab quarter of Aden.

Having seen something of the Republican side of the conflict, we flew on the next day in our own plane to Wadi Ain, a desert strip on the border of the Aden Protectorate, adjacent to Royalist-held Yemen. The Royalists showed us with pride some of the Russian automatic weapons they had taken from the Egyptians, as well as four Egyptian paratroopers and an infantryman whom they had recently captured. Though Nasser was to increase fivefold the number of Egyptian forces engaged in the conflict, and make use of poison gas against these tough, courageous tribesmen, he never managed to secure the victory he was seeking and was ultimately forced to withdraw in ignominy.

From Somalia, I wrote to Grandpapa Churchill to give him an account of our travels:

Mogadishu, Somalia
21 December 1962

Dear Grandpapa,

I write to wish you a happy Christmas and also to send you a bullet which I found near the top of Surgham Hill on the field of Omdurman. I see no reason to suspect that it was not from the battle, although it is rather odd that the nose should have been bored out.

While I was in Khartoum I met a man whose grandfather (on his mother's side) was the Mahdi. I had a long talk with him and he was a very nice man; he was however still very angry at Lord Kitchener for killing so many Sudanese.

Our expedition is proving most interesting and three days ago I filed a news story for United Press International on the Yemen situation.

I hope the weather in England hasn't been too beastly and that you are in good health. The Emperor of Ethiopia with whom I had a forty-minute interview asked me to convey his best wishes to you and told me that he had received a reply to the telegram he had sent you for your birthday and he was delighted about it.

Your loving grandson,
Winston

Shortly before Christmas we reached Kenya, which was due to become independent a few months later. Just as the Kenyans had fanciful illusions as to what Uhuru – 'freedom' in Swahili – would bring in terms of increased living standards, so too some of the Europeans harboured exaggerated fears of another Congo with a breakdown of law and order leading to tribal massacres. Events were to prove both these hopes and fears to be largely unfounded. We arrived in Nairobi on Christmas Eve, exactly six weeks after leaving England, having flown some 6500 miles. We had planned to stay at the Norfolk Hotel but friends, to whom we bore letters of introduction, would have none of it and insisted that we spend Christmas with them. Thereafter we went our separate ways for a few days, Arnold going off on a big-game safari with the German Consul, while I went to stay in the Rift Valley with friends of my father's, Tom and Diana Delamere. Diana had previously been married to Sir Delves Broughton who was charged and acquitted of the murder in 1941 of her lover, Lord Errol of Happy Valley fame.

The Delamere estate of Soysambu, near Elmenteita, is one of the most lovely in all of Africa. It stands on the floor of the Rift Valley, part of a fault in the earth's surface stretching from the Dead Sea, into which the River Jordan flows, and as far South as Malawi, and has commanding views across a broad plain towards the mountains. Because the valley enjoys a much lower rainfall – 20 inches a year compared to more than 50 in the hills on either side – it is suited only to cattle raising and had, in consequence, become the home of the Masai tribe, while the Kikuyu, who are principally agriculturalists have, like the majority of Europeans, favoured the more fertile uplands.

I had declined Arnold's invitation to join him on safari, explaining that I had no desire to shoot the wonderful variety of creatures that roam the plains of Kenya, except with a camera. When we met up once again in Nairobi, Arnold returned covered in mud, having spent three rather wet days under canvas. Nevertheless he was well satisfied with his safari, having shot an eland, a kongoni and a Grant's gazelle. 'Too bad you don't shoot,' he remarked dismissively. After all my insistence that I had no wish to shoot I scarcely had the heart to tell him that my 'quiet weekend' had not been so quiet after all. Indeed I had not been at Soysambu more than half an hour before a Masai tribesman came to report that there was a buffalo troubling the womenfolk of the local village when they went to draw water from the well and he wanted us to do something about it. My host's son, Hugh Cholmondeley, the present Lord Delamere, grabbed two big-game rifles from the wall and tossed one to me.

With the Masai as our guide, we made our way on foot through thick bush fifteen or twenty feet high. For half an hour we heard and saw nothing. Then, suddenly, the Masai froze. He had heard the shrill cry of the tick-bird that sits on the buffalo's back and warns it of approaching danger. All at once the three dogs we had with us caught the scent of the buffalo and rushed into the dense thicket just ahead. There was a terrific bellowing and baying and the bush shook all around us in violent tremors. It was only then that we realized that we had taken on more than one beast. In fact it turned out that there were *three* buffalo, two fully grown and a young bull. Though they were no more than ten yards from us, we were unable to see them, so dense was the undergrowth. Had the three of them charged together our situation would have been perilous in the extreme, since there was not enough open ground to fell them before they would be upon us. Fortunately, the young bull attempted a flanking movement to get downwind of us before charging and we were able to drop him dead as he crossed the clearing at full gallop. It was some time before we were able to deal with the other two remaining monsters, both large bulls with a good forty-five inch spread between their horns. One took five shots in the head before giving up the struggle. Several Masai soon appeared, attracted by the shots. They rapidly and expertly hacked the meat off the carcasses, returning triumphantly to their village as dusk was falling with a banquet for their New Year's dinner.

There are few countries that can equal Kenya for the grandeur of its scenery or the variety of its wildlife and there can be no better way of seeing it than in a light aircraft. Having the good fortune to have one of our own, we made full use of it. We circled snow-capped Kilimanjaro before landing at its foot to visit the game reserve of Amboseli. There, in the space of a few hours, we were able to see a wonderful array of wildlife, including elephant, rhinoceros, antelope, gazelle, wildebeest, warthog, baboon, zebra and giraffe. Some were gathered in herds of fifty or more on the open plain; others stood in solitary splendour among the fever trees. We then flew down to the coast at Kilifi where we spent a couple of days deep-sea fishing in the Indian Ocean.

We returned to Nairobi to find the capital in a state of great excitement. Independence was due before the end of the year and the politicians had just returned from the Christmas recess to prepare for the elections that would decide which party would form the first post-independence government. Just a few days before, Malcolm MacDonald, Kenya's last British Governor – against whom my father had once fought a by-election in Ross and Cromarty in 1935 – had arrived to take up his post. There followed a succession of garden and cocktail parties to which Arnold and I found ourselves invited. The most noticeable figure at all these functions was Jomo Kenyatta, an imposing figure who surveyed the scene, fly-whisk in hand, with the benign contentment of a grandfather at a children's party. It was difficult to believe that this seemingly kind old gentleman was the same man who had been convicted and gaoled for instigating the Mau Mau terror just a few years before. Ironically it was by then on him and his brilliant right-hand man, Tom Mboya, that the hopes of Kenya's Europeans were pinned.

Khaki wedding: my parents' marriage
St John's Smith Square, 4 October
39

ged 2 (1942)

With my Mother in London, 1942 (aged 2)

Welcoming US troops to London, 1942 (aged

birthday painting for Grandpapa, 1947 (aged 7)

With Grandmama and Grandpapa Churchill on the steps of 28 Hyde Park Gate, 1947 (aged 6)

Clapping Colonist to victory at Windsor Races, 10 September 1950 (aged 9)

With Grandpa and Grandma Digby in the shrubbery at Minterne, 1950 (aged 9)

Helping Father at Plymouth, Devonport general election, 1951 (aged 11)

With Grandpapa in the garden of No. 10, 1952 (aged 11)

ronation Day: with Grandpapa at No. 10, June 1953 (aged 12)

Cresta Run, St Moritz, with Sergei Ovsie
(left) and Gianni Agnelli (right), January
(aged 11)

The Oxford Ski Team at Zurs, Austria, w
Arnold von Bohlen (3rd from left) and sel
(3rd from right), December 1959 (aged 19

trusty Piper Comanche 'Uniform Zulu' near the Congo, January 1962

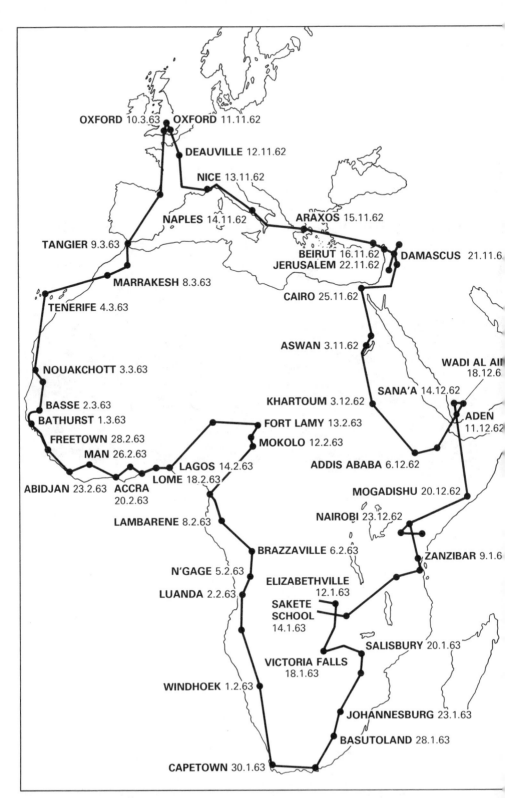

My itinerary for the African journey

fine lunch in Luanda

the White House with Father to accept
US honorary citizenship from
sident Kennedy, April 1963 (aged 22)

Writing an article following President Kennedy's assassination, November 1963 (aged 23)

last photograph of Grandpapa aboard *Christina* on a cruise to the Ionian Islands, June 1963

My engagement to Minnie, May 1964 (age

Waiting for the bride with my best man
(Father), 15 July 1964 (aged 23)

paigning in Bexley with Ted Heath, general election, October 1964 (aged 24)

he US lecture circuit, October 1965 (aged 25)

Jennie's christening at Newick Parish Church, Sussex (l to r Randolph, aged 2, me, Minnie and Jennie, Father, Arabella, Deborah Kerr, godmother to Jennie, the Rev. Diamond, April 1967, aged 26

Correcting proofs of *The Six Day War* with Father on the terrace at Stour, July 1967 (aged 26)

· XI ·

Lost over the Congo

The languorous heat of the Equator and the pungent fragrance of cloves, which hung heavily in the air, gave no hint of the violence and bloodshed that was so soon to overtake the tropical island paradise of Zanzibar, where the Arabs, the descendants of Omani slave-traders, still held sway over the African majority. Then, stopping only briefly in Dar-es-Salaam on the mainland for a meeting with Julius Nyerere, President of what was soon to become Tanzania (following the take-over of Zanzibar), we headed inland towards the heart of Africa and Katanga in the former Belgian Congo, where United Nations forces were fighting to prevent the secession of that province under its remarkable ruler, Moise Tshombe. In Elizabethville the UN commander, an Indian officer by the name of Brigadier Raja, told us that within a week UN forces would be in control of Kolwezi, where the Katangese were making their last stand, and Tshombe would be ousted. Since Elizabethville was overcrowded with journalists and it was impossible to reach Kolwezi overland, as the road and rail bridges had been blasted with dynamite, we decided to fly there the next day. However, that evening at a nightclub appropriately called the Noir et Blanc packed with Africans and Europeans gyrating to a hot rhythm, we met a group of young men whose fair hair and fresh complexion proclaimed them to be Swedes. It turned out that they were Swedish pilots forming part of the UN force and were there with a squadron of Saab J-29 jet-fighters. We asked them if they would be good enough not to shoot down our small Comanche. They assured us they would not but, on hearing that it was painted blue and white – the UN colours – they warned us to expect a warm welcome of machine gun fire from the Katangese *gendarmes* if we attempted to land at Kolwezi. We therefore took the decision to fly to a small airstrip called Mwinilunga in the very north-west corner of what was still Northern Rhodesia, now Zambia. From there we hoped to find road transport to the Katangese capital before the UN attacked.

In Elizabethville we had met a couple of German journalists from *Stern* magazine called Elton and Lebeck, who had kindly driven us around in their car. Now we returned the favour by offering them a lift in our aeroplane since it had two spare seats. We had made it a rule never to fly in the afternoon in this part of the world where the heat of the sun and tropical humidity combine to make a build-up of clouds which, later in the day, develop into violent thunderstorms. But there was no time to be lost if we were to reach Kolwezi before Tshombe surrendered or the United Nations attacked. Thus it was not until 4.49 pm that we got airborne from Ndola, one of the Copper Belt towns where we had to go to clear customs and refuel.

The cumulus clouds of Equatorial Africa are unsurpassed in their majesty. But the gleaming crests which tower serenely to fifty or sixty thousand feet conceal the terrible forces of nature that have engendered them – forces which have been known to rend a large airliner in pieces and scatter the debris over an area of several square miles.

An hour out of Ndola, close to the spot where in 1961 the aircraft carrying Dag Hammarskjold, the United Nations Secretary-General, had crashed killing all on board, we flew into a violent thunderstorm. For a while we had been dodging the squall line of thunderstorms that lay across our path but now the clouds, dark and threatening, closed in on all sides. We could still have turned back but, determined not to miss whatever action there might be in Kolwezi, we decided to press on. The crackling on our high frequency radio, due to electrical interference, became so intense that I was forced to remove my earphones – I had already lost radio contact with Salisbury Air Traffic Control and I had been unable to relay our last position report. Our radio compass swung round aimlessly, pointing first at one storm cloud, then another. All at once we found ourselves in torrential rain and had lost sight of the ground. Neither Arnold nor I was qualified to fly on instruments but, fortunately, I had taken the precaution of doing about forty hours of simulated instrument flying before we set out for Africa.

It became much darker. I switched on the panel lighting and kept my eyes fixed on the instruments, so as not to be blinded by the flashes of lightning all round us. Suddenly we ran into severe turbulence which flung the aircraft about with alarming violence. The pressure on the two control columns became terrific and the wings were flexing under the force of successive updraughts and downdraughts. We cut back the power, reducing our speed from 150 to 100 knots, to lessen the strain on the aircraft. We pulled our seat belts as tight as they would go and, with anxious glances at the wings to make sure they were still there, we headed onwards through the darkness.

Miraculously, after what was no more than twenty minutes of wild pitching and buffeting, but which seemed an eternity, we came out of the storm. The sky ahead was clear, but on the vast expanse of horizon that opened up before us there was no landmark to be seen – not a track, not a village, not even an isolated farmhouse by which we could check our position. To make matters worse our US Air Force maps which had proved so good hitherto, had printed across them in this area 'Relief Data unreliable'. Without a landmark in sight nor any radio beacon within range, it was soon apparent that we were lost.

All the way out from England, the flying had been straightforward. At every stage of the journey thus far we had been able to keep in radio contact and there had almost invariably been prominent landmarks or radio beacons to guide us to our destination. It had all been too easy and we had become over-confident. We now realized that in allowing only half an hour before sunset to find Mwinilunga, a small airstrip set in desolate country, we had made a serious, possibly fatal, mistake. But there was no time for recriminations. Only a few minutes of daylight remained in which to extricate ourselves from imminent catastrophe. By my calculations we were now due to reach Mwinilunga at 6.52 pm – just eight minutes before sunset and, so near the Equator, the light fails fast with virtually no twilight.

Nothing showed up at 6.52. We strained our eyes in every direction but, except for innumerable streams – swollen by the recent cloudburst and glistening in the evening sunlight – nothing interrupted the greenery of bush and jungle that stretched beneath us as far as the eye could see, across the 5,000 ft plateau that forms the watershed of Central Africa. The sun was sinking fast towards the horizon. I quickly computed that if the wind against us was no more than 20 knots we could get back to Ndola, the only airfield with night landing facilities within our range, with fifteen minutes of fuel remaining. But what if the thunderstorms were still in our path or the wind against us was stronger? (We were later to discover that it had been 30 knots.) It was by no means certain that we could reach Ndola and to crash-land after dark would be fatal. We realized we had less than five minutes in which to get the Comanche on the ground, then the sun would dip below the horizon and darkness would steal swiftly across the plain. Beneath us the thick bush now and then gave way to more open terrain, but the ground was uneven and waterlogged. We knew we would be lucky if it was only the plane that was wrecked in attempting a forced landing in this sort of country where there was no sign whatever of human life.

The sun was just settling on the horizon. The light was already failing and, with it, our hopes. Suddenly out of the corner of my right eye I caught sight of a faint light-brown line among some woods about a mile to the north. 'An airfield!' I shouted, grabbing the control-column from Arnold and banking the Comanche steeply to the right. It was not until we were actually over it that I could believe my eyes. There, set among some trees, was a short, extremely narrow grass runway. We made a tight circle, put the wheels and flaps down and, with our landing lights on, slithered to a halt on the rain-sodden grass.

By the time the propeller had swung to a standstill, it was already pitch dark. Within minutes the flash of lanterns could be seen approaching through the jungle. Our original destination had been a small village in the north-westernmost corner of Northern Rhodesia, or Zambia as it was soon to become, immediately adjacent to the borders of the Congo and Angola, in both of which there were conflicts raging. Not knowing in which country we had landed it was with a sense of relief that we realized the voices approaching through the darkness were English and we soon found ourselves surrounded by a dozen or more people who seemed to be under the impression that we must be mercenaries attempting to escape from Katanga.

We discovered that we had landed at Sakeji Mission School in Northern Rhodesia, just ten miles from the border of the Congo and less than fifteen from Angola. We had passed within five miles of Mwinilunga, without ever seeing it, due to the jungle surrounding the airstrip, and had landed twenty miles further north at an isolated mission station that did not even feature on our maps. One of the missionaries, Dr Henry Hoyth, offered us a meal and accommodation for the night. He told us he had come to Sakeji as a missionary before the First World War, but Sakeji School, for teaching the children of missionaries from missions up to 300 miles away in the Congo and Angola, had only recently been established. Indeed the airstrip had been completed less than six weeks before and he told us we could have flown on for several hundred more miles before finding another. After dinner Jim Hess, son of the school's principal, read from the Bible for a minute and, after the Lord's Prayer, thanked the Almighty for having guided us safely to Sakeji – a sentiment with which we were in full-hearted agreement. He then added the cryptic entreaty to 'make the runway dry enough' for us to take off safely the next morning.

It was not until the following morning, when I saw the airstrip by daylight, that I appreciated the full significance of Jim Hess's concluding prayer. As Arnold and I examined the mud-covered runway, Dr Hoyth told us by way of reassurance: 'Of course we've never had an aircraft as big as a Comanche in here before. Only a couple of weeks ago a Cessna – much lighter than your plane – never got off the ground.' So saying, he pointed to a pile of debris among the trees at the far end of the runway.

Each day Arnold and I took it in turns to captain the aircraft and fly from the left-hand seat. That day was my turn. I paced out the runway – 1500 ft. Because of the elevation of the field – 5700 ft above sea level – and the high temperature, the aircraft handbook specified that just over 1500 ft of dry concrete runway was required to get the Comanche airborne. Though there was almost that distance, the runway far from being made of dry concrete, consisted of grass, mud and standing water. We made the aircraft as light as possible, offloading all our baggage and emergency equipment. I decided that the only way I could get airborne was if I left Arnold behind to bring on the baggage and equipment by road to Mwinilunga, together with the two German journalists. Dr Hoyth, wearing shorts and an open-necked shirt, stood in front of the Comanche holding his handkerchief out to see which way the wind was blowing. As I climbed into the aircraft he remarked cheerily: 'Well, there is only one way to see if you can get her off the ground!'

Not over-eager to join the wrecked Cessna among the trees at the top end of the runway, I decided to take off in the direction of a gentle downward slope. Although this meant a light tail-wind for take-off, it had the important advantage that, at the bottom end of the runway, the ground broke away and there were no high trees to be cleared. I fired up the engine and taxied to the top end of the runway; however, the ground was so muddy that the wheels became stuck as I tried to turn the Comanche around. The entire village, black and white alike, had turned out to watch, and in no time dozens of eager hands had swung the aircraft round into position. After an especially thorough check of the aircraft and with the brakes still on, I gently pushed the throttle-control to its forward limit. I waited three or four seconds while the sturdy Lycoming engine developed full power, gave Arnold a 'thumbs up' sign and released the brakes. As the Comanche gathered speed the mass of black and white people waving from the side of the runway became a blur. I kept one eye on the airspeed indicator, the other on a pile of wood towards the end of the runway on the left-hand side. I knew from my reconnaissance on foot that I had to be airborne by the time that I reached the pile of wood for, beyond that, lay a continuous stretch of mud and water, followed by a ditch. The airspeed indicator, which had at first swung round rapidly, seemed stuck at 55 mph (the best speed for a short take-off in a Comanche being 85 mph).

There was a terrible surge and skid each time the aircraft struck patches of mud, and I had the sensation that the brakes were being applied with great violence. By now I was abeam the pile of wood and the airspeed was still only 55 mph – a good 10 mph below the stall speed. I eased back on the stick with no effect. The end of the runway was terrifyingly near. I jerked the stick sharply back. The stall warning hooter was blaring in my ear but, by a miracle, the plane bounced off the ground for a split second, just long enough for the speed to increase and for the Comanche's 250 hp engine to lift it into the air.

On landing at Mwinilunga, just ten minutes later, the pilot of a Central African Airways Dakota which had come in behind me told me: 'Salisbury lost contact with you last night in the storm and they asked me to check if you had got here safely. I've already let them know you're okay. But where have you just flown in from?' When I told him where we had spent the night, he looked at me in disbelief. Though he had been flying in those parts for a dozen years or more he had never heard of Sakeji School and was insistent that I mark the airstrip on his map in case he ever needed to make a forced landing there for, as he admitted, he still sometimes got lost while trying to find Mwinilunga. I counted myself lucky that my guardian angel had watched over me with such vigilance.

At the airfield I met up with Arnold and we were fortunate to find some Belgians working for the Union Minière mining company, who offered us a lift to Kolwezi sitting on carcasses of frozen meat which they had just unloaded from the Dakota. The situation we found in Kolwezi was, in the literal sense of the word, explosive. 110 metric tons of TNT had been removed by Tshombe's Katangese gendarmes from the stocks of the Union Minière and attached in generous quantities to all the major installations in the town including the nearby Delcommune Dam. If these were detonated, as threatened, hundreds of thousands of people living on the river banks below the dam would be killed by the unleashed flood of water that would burst from the reservoir and, some asserted, the surge of water would flood the capitals of Brazzaville and Leopoldville nearly 2000 miles downstream near the mouth of the Congo River.

As UN forces closed in round the city, fear was abroad in the streets. Houses were shuttered and windows boarded up. Kolwezi's 4000 Belgian inhabitants, many of them women and children, remained for the most part indoors. Rumours were rife of atrocities committed by UN soldiers during the capture of Elizabethville a fortnight before and there was general apprehension at the prospect of an attack by an army of Irish, Ethiopians, Indians and Indonesians. Added to this was the fear that Tshombe's gendarmerie might panic and run amok, as the UN forces drew near. Arnold and I made our way to the Presidency, an undistinguished suburban villa which Tshombe had commandeered as his temporary headquarters, where a meeting of his cabinet was just breaking up and we were fortunate in having a brief meeting with him. However, by late evening, it had become clear that Tshombe had decided to surrender and had agreed to fly to Elizabethville the next day to meet one of U Thant's representatives, bringing to an end the Katangese secession. We therefore returned after dark to the Presidency to procure the necessary exit permits, without which we could not get out of the country. We were told that the cabinet was once again in emergency session and that it would be some time before we would get our permits. We decided to wait and sat down on the grass verge of the driveway within fifteen feet of the entrance to the Presidency which was guarded by a stocky Katangese gendarme armed with a sub-machine gun.

As we sat in the darkness we could see through the white muslin curtains into the room where Tshombe was talking with members of his cabinet.

Suddenly above the low murmur of voices in the room we heard the brisk tramp of boots on the driveway. We immediately recognized Bob Denard, the mercenary commander, a solid six-foot six-inch Belgian with an enormous red moustache, together with two of his colleagues, all of whom I had interviewed earlier in the day. Carrying their sub-machine guns at the ready, they marched swiftly to the entrance of the Presidency, pushed aside the dumbfounded Katangese guard and kicked open the door which gave immediately on to the room where Tshombe and his ministers were sitting. In an instant the mercenaries had taken up position in two corners of the room, covering everybody inside with their weapons. All at once half a dozen jeeps carrying the rest of the mercenaries drew up with the squeal of brakes outside. Inside the grounds of the Presidency, Tshombe's Katangese guards, forty strong, became alarmed. In the darkness there was the snap of a rifle being cocked, rapidly followed by others. One of the mercenaries shouted in French from outside in the roadway: 'If they don't let Bob and the others out unharmed, we'll kill every black in the place.' Arnold and I, sitting in the shadows between the mercenaries and the Katangese, began to feel a trifle uncomfortable. This was certainly one way to get ourselves an exit visa from Katanga, but not the one we had in mind. After several long minutes Denard strode out of the Presidency and, seeing us, commented by way of explanation: 'Nothing unusual – just a slight misunderstanding!' Whereupon the mercenaries disappeared into the night as quickly as they had come and an uneasy silence fell on the sleeping town of Kolwezi. It seems that the mercenaries, an ugly bunch of hired killers, were anxious to ensure both their payment and safe conduct from the Congo.

When, the previous summer, in company with my father, I had visited the General Assembly of the United Nations in New York I had allowed myself to be impressed by this supposed temple of peace and palace of justice, on which so many of the hopes of mankind were founded. But my experiences in the space of a few brief weeks, first in the Middle East and then in Africa, swept away my illusions. In the Yemen there had been no sign of UN forces to defend that small and primitive land from brazen Egyptian aggression. By contrast, in the Congo, where the UN were to be found in strength, it was abundantly clear that they were there not to prevent outside aggression, nor even to restore order in those parts of the Congo that, following independence, had descended into chaos and rapine. Rather they were there to end the secession of Katanga, the one province where some semblance of law and order was to be found.

The insignificant stream that babbles by Sakeji school, gently turning the missionaries' small waterwheel and providing sufficient electricity to generate their electric light, soon grows into the mighty Zambezi River and, after a tortuous 700-mile southward journey, affords the most breathtaking spectacle in all of Africa – the Victoria Falls. As we approached by air we were surprised to see a large white cloud resting on the ground ahead of us. The fact that it was a cloudless day made the sight the more remarkable. Only when we got closer did we realize that the cloud was hanging over the Falls and was made of spray thrown up hundreds of feet into the air by the fury of the Zambezi waters plunging headlong into the gorge below. The Victoria Falls, discovered in 1885 by the Scottish missionary David Livingstone, during his transcontinental journey of exploration, are broader than those at Niagara and more than twice the height – 354 feet as against 175 feet. Livingstone, like so many explorers of his day, called his discovery after the British monarch. But the Falls are known to the local Africans by the more descriptive name as 'The Smoke that Thunders'. They have named it well, for the roar of the waters can be heard for miles around and, standing on the edge of the gorge, one feels the very ground trembling beneath one's feet.

· XII ·

Mines, Boers and Crocodiles

Having read my great-grandfather Lord Randolph Churchill's account of his visit to Salisbury – Fort Salisbury as it was then known – in 1891 when it consisted of no more than two rows of tents on either side of a muddy track with a Union Jack flying overhead, I was amazed at what the British pioneers and their descendants had created in the space of just seventy years. The 'huts and tents of the pioneers' which he described had given way to giant skyscrapers and modern office blocks. The 'one regular street' had blossomed into broad tree-lined avenues – Cecil Rhodes had insisted that they be wide enough for an eight-pair team of oxen to be turned around with ease. The Southern Rhodesian capital, since renamed Harare, had become a bustling, prosperous city reminiscent of a boom town of the American Midwest. Lord Randolph, temporarily fed up with politics at home and drawn by the 'attractions of travel, of the chase and specially of seeking gold for oneself', had made an expedition to Mashonaland, as what is today Zimbabwe was then known. The journey from England, which took him seventeen weeks, can today be accomplished in fewer hours. The voyage by sea to Cape Town had taken him three weeks, in the course of which the small steamer in which he travelled passed through the oppressive heat of the tropics, met heavy seas and, shortly before reaching its destination, caught fire.

At that time the railway line from the Cape extended only as far as Vryburg on the edge of the Boer Republic of the Transvaal, 150 miles North of Kimberley, where Lord Randolph broke his journey to visit the diamond mines which had recently been amalgamated by Cecil Rhodes into the De Beers Company and which were already producing some £2 million of diamonds annually. From Vryburg it was a four-day ride by horsedrawn coach to Johannesburg which had grown in only five years, to become a prosperous town of 15,000 inhabitants, following the discovery of gold on the Witwatersrand. The Rand, as it came to be called, was already yielding £2.5 million worth of gold each year and was fast becoming the world's richest goldfield. However, it was only once the Limpopo River was crossed, that the difficult part of the journey began. As in the Wild West of America only a few years before, this was the land of the pioneers: the land of opportunity. Dragging their ox carts through raging torrents, crossing wild, desolate plains, enduring hardship and braving the hostility of tribes in their path, the pioneers pressed resolutely onwards, determined that they should come to a promised land. There were rumours of gold in Mashonaland, reputedly the land of King Solomon's Mines, and these men, turning their backs on the humdrum routine of daily life, came to risk all in the hope of making their fortunes.

It took Lord Randolph's expedition six weeks to cover the 400 miles from Fort Tuli, on the banks of the Limpopo, to Fort Salisbury, their destination. On the way the ox-drawn wagons became stuck in the fast-flowing stream of the Wanetse River and, crossing the dry grassland on their way to the high veldt, the expedition only narrowly escaped destruction by a veldt fire. By the time Fort Salisbury was reached, four out of thirteen horses and thirteen out of twenty mules had died of 'horse sickness' (probably caused by the Tsetse fly); besides this, two of the oxen had broken their necks falling into a gully and another had strayed. In spite of these misadventures Lord Randolph concluded: 'I have been exceptionally fortunate.'

Perhaps because my great-grandfather had trekked with the pioneers who, with their descendants, built that land into the prosperous modern state it had become by the time of my visit in the early Sixties and the fact that, in the course of several visits, I had come to know them well, I have always felt a bond of friendship with these tough, self-reliant, courageous sons of the pioneers, who are the embodiment of many of the finest qualities of the British nation and who, in two world wars, immediately and without hesitation, had rallied to Britain's defence, especially as pilots in the Battle of Britain and in the fighting in North Africa with the Long-Range Desert Group. It was this fellow feeling that prompted me fifteen years later – by which time I was a Member of Parliament myself and had been among the first to be promoted to the Front-Bench by Margaret Thatcher – to vote against the renewal of economic sanctions against Rhodesia. This was at a time when the British of Rhodesia, under attack from a Moscow-backed terrorist campaign, had already accepted the two key demands of successive British governments, namely elections based on universal suffrage and African majority rule.

That vote in October 1978 led to my instant dismissal as Conservative Party Front-Bench Spokesman on Defence and to my exclusion from her ministerial team when, a year later, the Conservatives won the 1979 general election and Mrs Thatcher formed her first administration. As I walked out of the 'No' lobby, defying a *one-line* whip and a request to abstain, I was confronted by the Conservative Party Chief Whip, Humphrey Atkins (now Lord Colnbrook), who was lying in wait for me. Making no attempt to conceal his pleasure, he accosted me with a disingenuous half-smile and the words: 'You're fired!' Bearing aside the Front Bench, over half the Conservative Party in Parliament had defied the Whips to vote, as I had, against the renewal of sanctions. What makes this episode the more ironic and bizarre is the fact that Mrs Thatcher privately agreed with us. Indeed, subsequently, on being informed by a close colleague that he too had been among the rebels and feared he may have 'done the wrong thing', she had replied: 'I am not sure you did at all!' Be that as it may, she had bowed to the earnest entreaties of the Shadow Foreign Secretary, Lord Carrington, who – convinced that he had a better understanding of Africa than she – had warned that, if the Conservative Party voted against Rhodesian sanctions, she would find herself ostracized by the Afro-Asian members at the forthcoming Commonwealth Prime Ministers' Conference in Lusaka in August 1979, less than a year later, by which time she might herself be – and indeed was – Prime Minister. As may be imagined, I have reflected long and hard over the past ten years on my decision to cast my vote as I did on that occasion but what, at the end of the day, is the value of public service – indeed of life – if those involved do not have the courage of their convictions and are not prepared to suffer the consequences?

Salisbury, today renamed Harare, provided our first encounter in Africa with the colour bar, though in a far less extreme form than we were to discover in South Africa. While our hotel would not admit Africans, we nonetheless found restaurants and nightclubs where blacks and whites mingled freely, something unheard of in South Africa at the time.

In a book entitled *First Journey,** which I wrote following my visit to Africa, I recorded my view that: 'If the Europeans in Southern Rhodesia fail to recognize that the only way they will be able to remain in the country is by handing over the greater part of their political power to the Africans, then they (like the Europeans in Kenya in 1960) must be brought to this realization by the British government. There is little time to be lost. Fear that motivates the policies of the South African government, is already creeping into Southern Rhodesia, and fear is the worst enemy of reason.' Because so much time was needlessly lost before embarking on the task of building a multi-racial society, based firmly on democratic principles and respect for minority rights, the opportunity may have gone for ever as Zimbabwe today moves ever closer to authoritarian rule and a one-party state.

On our way south towards the Cape of Good Hope we stayed a few days in Johannesburg as the guest of the prominent industrialist, Harry

* Published by William Heinemann 1964.

Oppenheimer, who arranged for us to visit a gold mine on the East Rand where we descended 7000 ft below ground level. We also visited the State Model School in Pretoria where my grandfather had been imprisoned, following his capture by the Boers in 1899, and from which he had made his dramatic escape, which made him a national hero and launched him on his political career.

After a brief diversion to the mountain kingdom of Basutoland, known today as Lesotho, we reached Cape Town two and a half months after leaving England – hardly a record for the London-to-the-Cape route which had been a challenge to pilots of light aircraft ever since the 1920s. Many made the flight successfully; others were never heard of again. One famous flight was that of Captain Lancaster, whose aircraft and remains were not found until thirty years later in the heart of the Sahara. Today, with more reliable machines and an increasing number of radio and navigational aids, the flight is not as hazardous as it was in days gone by although, as our own experience proved, far from uneventful or unexciting.

On our arrival a telegram, dated 27 January 1963, was waiting for me at the British Embassy:

DEAREST WINSTON WE ARE FOLLOWING YOUR TRAVELS WITH GREAT INTEREST
YOUR FATHER HAS SENT US THE REPORTS YOU HAVE WRITTEN STOP WHEN
YOU GET HOME COME AND SEE US QUICKLY LOVE
GRANDPAPA AND GRANDMAMA

Cape Town, standing on the sea near the point where the Indian Ocean and South Atlantic meet and with Table Mountain rising dramatically behind it, is, without doubt, the most attractive city in Africa. It was founded in 1652 by Dutch settlers and has many lovely old Dutch buildings to recall the fact, while the climate year-round is that of the Mediterranean with vineyards and sub-tropical plants of every kind abounding. But even in the course of a brief visit I came to understand what Lord Randolph meant when he had referred in his book* to the 'stubborn and mulish ignorance of the Boers' and I found it difficult to contain my outrage at the attitude of certain Boers to the Africans and their brutish treatment of them.

One evening we were invited by the parents of some friends to a barbecue party beside the swimming pool of their beautiful old Dutch house in the hills above Cape Town. I soon found myself engaged in a political discussion with one of the other guests – an elderly Boer. In a loud voice he proclaimed: 'It'll be fifty years before these people learn even to pull a lavatory-chain!' I thereupon enquired how long he thought the whites in South Africa could maintain their supremacy. This question seemed to provoke our fellow guest to a paroxysm of rage. 'Before we surrender,' he declared, 'we'll kill every bloody nigger in the place, and you bloody liberals

* *Men, Mines and Animals in South Africa.*

[pointing at Arnold and myself] will be the first to be shot.' At this juncture, Arnold and I, standing with our backs to the pool, were unable to restrain a laugh and, the next minute, we found ourselves sailing backwards through the air into the swimming pool, though we had the compensation of bringing our fellow guest into the water with us.

This incident was swiftly reported in somewhat fanciful terms to Martin Gilbert, a History don from Merton College, Oxford, who was helping with the great biography of my grandfather, and who was to carry the work forward to completion following my father's death. He in turn wasted no time in relaying the report to my father:

PRIORITY RANDOLPH CHURCHILL EAST BERGHOLT SUFFOLK FOLLOWING
LETTER RECEIVED BY SOUTH AFRICAN UNDERGRADUATE DATED JANUARY 31ST
FROM CAPE TOWN QUOTE DAD DISGRACED HIMSELF BY HURLING YOUNG
WINSTON CHURCHILL AND GERMAN FRIEND INTO THE SWIMMING POOL STOP
I DO ADMIT HE WAS PROVOKED BEYOND MEASURE AS THEY TOLD HIM THEY
WERE ALL FOR THE NATIVES AND WOULD HELP TRAIN THEM IN SABOTAGE
AND OTHER UNPLEASANT THINGS STOP POOR OLD REACTIONARY WHITE SOUTH
AFRICAN DAD COULDN'T STAND THAT AND REALLY BLEW HIS TOP STOP HE
GOT A BIT BRUISED IN THE PROCESS AND VERY WET INDEED STOP UNQUOTE
SO THE CHURCHILL TRADITION LIVES ON
= MARTIN GILBERT

In *London to Ladysmith via Pretoria* my grandfather records a conversation he had with a Boer soon after being taken prisoner in 1899. He asked the Boer why his people were so opposed to British rule. The following was the reply:

We know how to treat *Kaffirs* in this country. Fancy letting the black filth walk on the pavement! Educate a *Kaffir!* Ah, that's you English all over. We educate 'em with a stick. Treat 'em with humanity and consideration – I like that. They were put here by the God Almighty to work for us. We'll stand no damned nonsense from them. We'll keep them in their proper places. What do you think? Insist on their proper treatment will you? Ah, that's what we're going to see about now. We'll settle whether you English are to interfere with us before the war is over.

My grandfather concluded:

What is the true and original root of Dutch aversion to British rule? It is not Slagters Nek, nor Broomplatz, nor Majuba, nor the Jameson Raid. It is the abiding fear and hatred of the movement that seeks to place the native on a level with the white man.

This then is the crux of the matter. The Boer regards the African as little better than an animal and dislikes the British for fear of being made to treat the African like a human being. This was the argument between Briton and Boer at the time of the Boer War, and this is the argument that continues to this day. Unfortunately for the Africans and for the more civilized Europeans, 60 per cent of the white (or voting) population is Boer and, from a comparison of the conversation my grandfather had with his Boer and the one I had beside the swimming pool with my Boer, Boer opinion, firmly entrenched behind the dogmatic beliefs of the Dutch Reformed Church, has advanced little since the nineteenth century. I hasten to add that there are of course many civilized and well-informed Afrikaners, whose outlook is more reasonable and rational, and it would be a mistake to suppose that every Briton in South Africa is a lily-white liberal; nothing could be further from the truth. However, it is a plain fact that both the government and the electorate that put it in power are predominantly Boer in complexion and it is they who must bear the ultimate responsibility for South Africa's self-defeating and objectionable racial policies.

From Cape Town we headed north across the Kalahari Desert towards Windhoek, the capital of South-West Africa, nearly 800 miles away. This was to be the longest leg of our entire flight. The Comanche's safe range was only 600 miles at its normal cruising speed of 180 mph. However, by reducing our cruising speed to 160 mph, we were able to cut our fuel consumption from 12 to 8.5 gallons per hour, enabling us to reach Windhoek with half an hour's reserve of fuel. Flying a light aircraft more than two miles high above a burning desert is a most exhilarating feeling. The clarity of the moistureless air is intense. At that altitude the horizon extends more than a hundred miles on all sides and the desert stretches out below as far as the eye can see. The glare of the noonday sun strikes fiercely upwards from the barren waste, yet here the air is cool and fresh. One has the sensation of being on top of the world – provided of course that the engine continues to purr smoothly and you know where you are. After coming so close to disaster over the jungles of Central Africa, we determined to pay particular attention to our navigation whenever we were over featureless country. I therefore made a habit of establishing our position every ten minutes of our journey.

Unlike the great yellow sand-seas of the Sahara, the Kalahari is predominantly red and rocky. Dark conical hills protrude from its flattish surface and in places we found deep canyons reminiscent of parts of Colorado. In spite of the claim of the ranchers that their country is the 'Texas of Africa', the chief wealth of what is now known as Namibia comes, not from its cattle, but from the diamond-fields on the coast of Namaqualand which are the richest in the world.

Immediately to the north, neighbouring Angola, still ruled by Portugal at the time, proved a remarkable contrast to the discrimination so evident in South Africa. Coming from the land of apartheid, we were surprised on our first evening in the capital, Luanda, to find an African man and a European woman dining together at the next table in the best hotel in town. It was no less astonishing the next morning to see children, black, white and coffee-coloured, shouting and playing together as they came out of the schools at midday. This was a far cry from South Africa. Nonetheless the Portuguese found themselves confronted by a nationalist movement in the form of the Angolan Liberation Army, trained and equipped outside the country and financed from Moscow, which was waging a terrorist war against them. We contrived to see something of the country by spending a couple of days in the jungle on patrol with the Portuguese Army.

Our next stop, Lambaréné, set on the banks of the Ogowe River deep in the jungles of Equatorial Africa, was then still one of the more remote places on the African continent. On our three-hour flight from Brazzaville, capital of the former French Congo, we had overflown a seemingly limitless expanse of dense tropical rainforest. Had our engine failed, our best chance of survival would have been to ditch the aircraft in one of the numerous crocodile-infested streams that intersect the jungle. From Lambaréné's small airstrip we walked two miles to the river bank where we crossed by ferry to the island on which stands the village of Lambaréné. There we found someone to take us by pirogue, a dug-out canoe, to Dr Albert Schweitzer's hospital about a mile upstream.

The setting sun, as it sank behind the jungle-covered hills of Lambaréné, momentarily turned the broad waters of the Ogowe River into a shimmering sheet of burnished gold. Then, suddenly, it was night. The elderly African propelled his flimsy craft with an increased vigour. He did not like paddling his canoe after dark for fear of being shipwrecked against the dark motionless mass of a hippopotamus. To avoid the swift current in mid-stream, he hugged the bank under an overhang of branches and trailing creepers which reached almost to the water. On attaining the upstream end of the island he altered course and made for the opposite shore. Soon we were gliding in under the palm trees that line the waterfront below the hospital and the canoe came to rest with a slight lurch on the sandy beach. Numerous small fires were flickering in the darkness; around each was huddled a group of Africans cooking their evening meal. By the light of the flames we were able to make out the long, low shadows of the hospital buildings of Lambaréné.

Before setting out for Africa I had gone to the Tropical Diseases Hospital in North London to be inoculated against cholera, yellow fever, typhoid (A & B), typhus and tetanus. There I ran into Olga Deterding, the Royal Dutch/Shell petroleum heiress, who was a friend and benefactor of Dr Schweitzer and who had gone out on several occasions to Equatorial Africa to work as a volunteer nurse at his hospital. She was leaving for Lambaréné the very next day and had told me that − if our plane ever got as far as Gabon − we should be sure to look in on Dr Schweitzer.

As it was, it had taken Arnold and myself nearly three months to reach Lambaréné and, although I had sent her a cable from Brazzaville three days before, warning her of our arrival, I had no idea if she was still there. A figure clothed in white and surmounted by an enormous white pith-helmet emerged from a hospital-building; it was one of the European nurses. I asked her if Miss Deterding was still at the hospital, only to learn that she had left ten days before to return to Europe. Not wishing to impose ourselves unannounced on the great man just before dinner, we decided to make our way back in the darkness to the village to try to find lodging for the night.

Just then Mlle Silver, a Dutch nurse who was among those who had been longest with Dr Schweitzer, appeared and greeted us most warmly, declaring: 'We received your telegram and when we heard an aeroplane fly over after lunch we thought it was you; the doctor insisted on going to meet you and set out in his pirogue to the airport where we waited for an hour or more. But it was not your plane that had arrived, so we came back to the hospital.' I was much embarrassed, supposing that Schweitzer had assumed from my cable that it was my grandfather who was arriving. Mlle Silver assured me that this had not been the case and led us by the light of a paraffin lamp to a small room, simply furnished with two iron beds, a table, chair and washstand. She brought us a pair of paraffin lamps and told us that dinner was at 7 pm but explained that 'hospital time', determined by the whim of the doctor, was running half an hour behind local time. She said that we had best go by the bell that would be rung when dinner was ready.

When the dinner bell sounded we were shown to two empty places opposite Schweitzer who sat at the middle of a long wooden table. He jumped up from the table and shook us both firmly by the hand. His first question was to ask us whether we had arrived by motorboat or pirogue. When we replied the latter, a beaming smile of approval came over his face. It seems that this was one of the criteria by which the doctor judged his guests. Dinner was attended by the thirty or more members of the hospital staff, all of whom were European with the exception of a Japanese doctor and his wife, who were running the nearby leper village. The two longer sides of the dining hall were made of gauze netting designed to keep out the mosquitoes while at the same time allowing a breeze, should there be one, to pass through the room. But that evening there was not a breath of air. Lambarene lies within fifty miles of the Equator, and the heat and humidity are oppressive. Perspiration was running down the faces of those present, doctors and nurses alike.

As I was enjoying what I had assumed to be a piece of mutton, Schweitzer leant across the table and enquired: '*Eh! Bien, Monsieur Churchill, comment aimez-vous notre crocodile?*' I smiled a knowing smile, confident that I was having my leg pulled. Thereupon the whole table, who rarely joined in the doctor's dinner conversation, roared with laughter at my disbelief. Schweitzer explained that crocodile was quite a delicacy in these parts, where fresh meat was rare. He told us that except for rice, which had to be imported, almost all the food for the hospital was locally grown, including bananas, mangos, papayas and coffee, as well as that strange fruit inevitably found on desert islands by the treasure-hunting castaways of boyhood books – the bread-fruit, which in fact tastes more like potato. This was certainly more practical than the situation we had found prevailing at Brazzaville, our last port of call, where the head waiter of a restaurant had excused the enormity of the bill by explaining that all the food had to be flown in three times a week by Air France from Paris.

Across the dinner table Schweitzer told us with a chortle how he had recently felled a great okoume tree, one of the largest trees to be found in all the rainforests of Equatorial Africa. As he sweated with a crowbar to roll over the fallen giant, he noticed an African in a smart suit standing watching him in the clearing. When the great Doctor appealed to the man to give him a hand, a look of horror came over the African's face. 'No, no,' he replied with poignancy. 'You misunderstand, *I* am an educated person – I don't do manual labour!' Sadly, such a state of mind is not confined solely to Africa but is all too prevalent in Britain and other countries of Europe, above all among those who have enjoyed the privilege of a university education and feel the world owes them a living.

After dinner, the table was cleared and hymn books were brought forward. The doctor announced a hymn in German and strode over to his old upright piano that stood at one side of the room. A dim paraffin lamp lit his tousled grey hair, droopy moustache and ruddy complexion, as he played with a vigour remarkable in a man of eighty-eight. When the hymn was done, the doctor read a passage from the Bible and gave a brief and pointed explanation of the text he had read. Then all retired for the night.

In the early hours of the morning there was a violent thunderstorm, attended by a deluge of rain such as one only experiences in the tropics. All was clearly lit up by the almost continuous flashes of lightning and, looking out through the gauze-covered sides of our room, it was as if we were standing under the lip of a waterfall. However, by the time the reveille bell pealed out at 6.30 am, there was not a cloud in the sky and the sun was rising swiftly above the palm trees.

Schweitzer's hospital stood on the side of a hill overlooking the broad Ogowe River. It was surrounded by the impenetrable primeval forest that encroaches on all sides. Here the visitor finds Africa as he has imagined it should be – a land of steaming, teeming rainforest where massive trees and tumultuous jungle exclude the light of day and thwart the advance of civilization. The hospital at Lambaréné was not out of character with its surroundings.

To those visitors who came to Lambaréné expecting to find a clean, modern hospital, Dr Schweitzer's establishment was, inevitably, a shock. Some 500 Africans were accommodated in the long, low hospital buildings made of wood and corrugated iron. The buildings were divided by partitions into cubicles, each with its own entrance. The cubicles, in which the patients lay side by side on wooden bunks, presented a dismal picture of darkness, dinginess and squalor. Outside, on the doorstep, sat those inmates who were less seriously ill, some of them deep in contemplation. Beside them were the dead embers of the fire on which they had cooked their meal the previous evening; and, on all sides, there was a litter of wash pots, cooking pots, empty bottles and rusting tins. In the open drainage ditches that ran beside the hospital buildings slops, old bandages, banana skins and other refuse lay putrefying and stagnating in the sun. The hospital's only sanitary facilities were two 'long-drop' latrines, kept under lock and key for the exclusive use of the European staff. They consisted of two wooden huts standing side by side on an elevated platform, supported by stilts over a ditch which was a seething mass of maggots and flies. The 500 or so Africans were supposed to do their business on the edge of the jungle, but most were sick and others were lazy, with the result that few got that far. There are certain things one associates with hospitals the world over, even those in the bush, in particular concrete floors, whitewashed rooms, iron beds, electricity, lavatories, running water, covered drains, and the distasteful, all-pervasive smell of disinfectant. But none of these were to be found in the African quarters of the hospital at Lambaréné.

Dr Schweitzer explained to me, when I questioned him on this point, that the African has a horror of European-type hospitals. Many, he told me, would sooner suffer or even die from lack of medical attention, rather than go to a modern hospital with its unfamiliar, unfriendly, antiseptic atmosphere. At Lambaréné they could bring their families with them, wear their own clothes and live the life to which they were accustomed, while at the same time undergoing medical treatment. There could be little doubt that this was why so many came to Lambaréné rather than to the Government-run hospital, not far away. Indeed some came from 200 miles or more upstream by pirogue or river steamer to be treated at Schweitzer's hospital.

Soon after lunch on the day after our arrival we witnessed what was evidently a regular hospital ritual. A dozen or so bedraggled Africans, some of them armed with shovels, lined up before Schweitzer. He called them briskly to attention – an order not so briskly complied with – and thereupon they removed their hats and, with a deep bow and grins on their faces, they intoned: '*Bonjour, Grand Docteur!*' Schweitzer, seeing us watching, blushed slightly and then chuckled in his merry way, explaining that this was his labour force and he had to check that they were all present and correct. Most of the hospital patients brought with them at least one member of their family to act as their guardian and to cook for them. All the able-bodied men, including some of the lepers, were put to work digging or some such activity, which they performed with a singular lack of vigour. At the end of the day they were given a ration of bananas and rice and, at the end of the week, they received a *cadeau* from the Doctor of a few pennies.

One afternoon, a Sunday, we took a pirogue and went with one of the German doctors at the hospital on his rounds to the village of Abangue a couple of miles upstream. The small village, inhabited solely by Africans, was one of the most delightful that we saw in all of Africa. A broad grass path lined on either side by clean, well-constructed huts led up from the landing-place where brightly-coloured butterflies flitted by the water's edge. The first hut had a great fishing net hung up outside to dry in the sun. The owner invited us in and proudly showed us the masks – most sinister in appearance – that he was making for the Saturday night dances that took place in the village. Next door was a man who repaired clocks and radios. Further along a man with a sewing machine was sitting outside his house mending some clothes. The huts, which were built of palm trees, had big windows and were furnished with locally-made tables and chairs. In one of the huts there were two pretty girls reading through a pile of notebooks. They told us that they were both married to the local school-teacher and were correcting some French homework done by the children. The father of one of the girls was sitting outside the house relaxing in the sun. We sat down on the ground beside him and had a long talk which ranged from local politics to the price of a wife which, at the time, was £15. As he explained: 'It's all right for you Europeans to lead a bachelor existence, you have servants to look after you and cook for you. We do not. Instead we have to buy a wife. But it's no use having just one wife. You need at least two, so that if one gets sick there is still one to look after you!'

As I discovered in the course of our stay, there had, for several years, been a battle raging between Schweitzer and those members of the hospital staff who were anxious to see built an air-conditioned operating theatre. They quite justifiably pointed out that the existing one, with its gauze sides, let in the dust from outside and became so hot that two nurses were required constantly to mop the surgeon's brow to prevent the sweat falling into the open wounds of the patient on the operating table. The doctor had, at last, reluctantly accepted the necessity for this and the concrete foundations for the new building had been laid and posts installed to bring mains electricity to the village to provide lighting and air conditioning for the operating theatre. However, Schweitzer, perhaps due to his distaste for the modern world and newfangled equipment, had mischievously postponed the project in favour of an extension to the guest accommodation. But, as one of the staff remarked philosophically to me: 'Everything is relative. There is no point having a modern, air-conditioned operating theatre if the patient, as soon as he returns to his cubicle, is going to pull the dressing aside and poke around with his finger to see what has been done to him. Although we use the latest drugs and the most modern surgical techniques, it is really eighteenth-century medicine that we are practising here.'

The doctors and nurses at Lambaréné were mostly Dutch, Swiss or German, and many were highly qualified. However, except for a couple of the nurses who had been with the doctor for a very long time, most of the staff came for a period of just two or three years. Among those working at the hospital at the time of our visit were a young American couple in their mid-twenties, he a doctor from North Carolina, she a nurse. After reading of the work of the Great Doctor in the tropical forests of Africa, they had decided to devote their lives to assisting him in his work at Lambaréné. They had sold everything they had in America and taken a boat for Africa. Sadly, within a year of their arrival, they were planning to leave, feeling that all initiative towards improving conditions at the hospital was being stifled and they were clearly sadly disillusioned. This couple were perhaps the exception. The majority of the staff found their work deeply fulfilling, not only for the vast amount of practical experience they were able to accumulate but, above all, because they were working among people desperately in need of their skills.

Schweitzer's reputation was so great that at the snap of his fingers untold resources from the great American charitable foundations, no less than from his many admirers throughout the world, could have been made available for the modernization of his hospital. Yet it was evidently his wish to keep Lambaréné as he had originally conceived it. He had built the hospital and the nearby leper village largely with his own hands from such materials as could be obtained locally. He had been thirty-eight years old when he had first arrived in Lambaréné and already he was a doctor four times over, in theology, philosophy, music and medicine. He had written two authoritative works, one on Bach, the other on organ-building, besides a handful of other books on Christ and civilization. An academic career full of promise seemed to lie before him. Yet, as he pointed out in his autobiography, he deliberately turned his back on it: 'in order to devote myself from that time forward to the direct service of humanity'. He was very conscious of this 'act of renunciation' and, later in his book, made the assertion that: 'There are no heroes of action: only heroes of renunciation and suffering. But few of them are known, and even these not to the crowd, but to the few.' Perhaps the most obvious exception to this rule was Schweitzer himself.

When he had first come to Lambaréné there was no other doctor for hundreds of miles around and an epidemic of sleeping sickness was raging. For want of medical attention the local people were dying on all sides from this and other diseases. Founding a hospital in the heart of the jungles of Equatorial Africa was a remarkable achievement and one that required enormous courage and dedication. That had been in 1913.

But half a century had passed since then. Africa had changed immeasurably in those fifty years: Schweitzer and Lambaréné hardly at all. He had weathered well. During all his time in tropical Africa he never contracted any serious disease – a tribute to his remarkable constitution and stamina. Pith helmet on, he would stand for hours beneath the equatorial sun directing some new building project or resolving a dispute in the hospital. And, in the evening, when darkness had fallen on Lambaréné and all was silent, except the sounds of the jungle, the glow of a paraffin lamp could be seen shining out from the tiny room where, amid a rummage of papers, books and tools, he would sit at his table writing late into the night, in the cause of civilization and peace. At least so long as the '*Grand Docteur*' lived, Lambaréné remained a corner of Africa unspoiled by the advance of the modern world – a backwater cut off from the mainstream of the African Revolution.

With only a brief stop at the exotic mountain island of Fernando Po in the Gulf of Guinea, we flew northwards to the French Cameroons, where we landed near the small market town of Mokolo. On landing, there was no sign of a customs officer, instead we found ourselves surrounded by a bevy of bare-breasted maidens carrying water pots on their heads who were most curious to see our aircraft. On walking into town we found that the market was in full swing with animals, wonderfully coloured materials and exotic spices displayed on all sides. But we soon discovered that this was a market with a difference which was only held once a year and was known as the *Marché des Fiancées*. To our amazement we found ourselves being offered young girls, some no more than twelve years of age, though well endowed for all that, who were being put up for sale by their fathers. There seemed to be a general disappointment when we left without making any purchases.

Our next port of call was Fort Lamy, the capital of Chad. Though two years had passed since my overland expedition through the Sahara to the Tibesti mountains, I thought it worth enquiring if my friend from my early morning desert encounter, Colonel Baylon, was still there. It turned out that indeed he was and had, meanwhile, been promoted to be Commander of all French forces in Chad. I telephoned him from the airport and, to my amazement, he appeared within five minutes to collect us in a camouflaged staff car and drove us back to his house on the banks of the Chari River. Although it was already late in the afternoon, he insisted on laying on lunch for the two of us and with a deep military bark ordered his batman, '*Allez vite! Apportez whiskey, champagne, foie gras!*' All of which was miraculously produced. He entertained us royally and insisted that we stay the night as his guest.

From the very heart of Africa we headed west by way of Nigeria and Ghana to the Ivory Coast where, deep in the jungle, near the small town of Man, we saw some of the most remarkable tribal dancing to be found anywhere on the African continent, involving a demonstration of how, at least until the turn of the century, child sacrifice was practised with children being tossed into the air and caught on the point of a knife. What was more serious, because it was for real, was the ceremony of female circumcision which followed and for which a dozen young women, wearing only loin cloths, were being prepared by the elder women of the tribe with the application of a white paint in an intricate design to their naked bodies, as the reverberating jungle rhythm of the tribal drums beat ever more urgently.

Flying by way of Liberia and Sierra Leone, we reached the tiny British colony of Gambia on the westernmost coast of Africa. We were somewhat apprehensive about the final stretch of our journey home across the Western Sahara, not only because it was across the most arid and featureless part of Africa, where an engine failure could prove fatal but, especially, by reason of the fact that the French, through an organization called the ASECNA, which was responsible for air safety in the Western Sahara, laid down the strictest rules governing flights over this most inhospitable of regions. We had been led to believe that this included a bar on flights across the Sahara by single-engine planes. The prospect of being required to retrace our steps by way of Central Africa and the Nile, adding nearly fifty per cent to the time and expense of our journey, appalled us.

We therefore decided not to announce our flight to the French authorities at Dakar, in neighbouring Senegal. Instead, we made a private arrangement with a splendid English air traffic controller called Trembath, at Bathurst Airport, today known as Banjul. We were determined to make one last excursion into the African heartland to visit a tiny outpost in the Mauretanian desert called Boutilimit. Well aware of the perils of crossing the desert without announcing our flight to the authorities, we arranged with Trembath that, before landing at Boutilimit, we would radio him on the high frequency waveband: 'Bathurst Tower, this is Comanche "Uniform Zulu" [our call-sign] – landing point Bravo now.' The agreement was that, provided he received that signal, no search and rescue operation would be launched. Once we had crossed north of the Senegal River we were into the desert proper with scarcely any identifiable landmarks but, with the aid of a single radio beacon more than one hundred miles away on the coast, we had no difficulty in finding the wonderful *Beau Geste* type fortress set among the sand dunes that stretched as far as the eye could see, and we duly radioed our friend Trembath to let him know of our safe arrival.

As the propeller swung to a standstill, I opened the cabin door and was struck by a blast of hot air as if from a furnace. I quickly slammed it closed once more, as the needle on the outside air-temperature gauge rose rapidly to over 130°F. Having landed in Mauretania without visas or permission of any kind, we waited to see what would happen next. After three or four minutes we saw a Land-Rover approaching in a cloud of dust from the direction of the fort. It drew up alongside and two men got out. One, brown-skinned and wearing a revolver on his belt, was evidently a Moorish gendarme; the other was a young Frenchman. We explained we were on our way to Nouakchott, the Mauretanian capital, and had dropped in for a brief visit. They were evidently not accustomed to having tourists but, far from taking exception to our unannounced arrival, the Frenchman especially appeared delighted to see some white faces. As he drove us back to the fort, he explained that he was a doctor employed by the French Government and assigned to Mauretania as part of a technical assistance programme. He and his wife were the only Europeans for thousands of square miles and, after six months, felt they had exhausted the possibilities of the place. The outpost consisted of no more than a settlement of black nomad tents, crowded around the fort that stands on top of the sand dunes. The only sparse shade was provided by a dozen or so thorn trees; little else could stand the heat and the intense aridity of the air. Life at Boutilimit was sustained by a single well, sunk deep into the sand. Water was hoisted to the surface in a goatskin tied to the end of a 200 ft rope. The other end was attached to a donkey which drew the water to the surface as it was driven away from the well. The fort itself had been abandoned, except for a few rooms used by the French doctor and his wife, and the courtyard had become buried under several feet of rich yellow sand. Most striking of all was the silence of the place. There was nothing to be heard but the moaning of the wind – a hot, dry, dusty wind that had travelled perhaps 3,000 miles or more across the burning Sahara. Now and then it lifted a cloud of fine sand into the air, blinding and suffocating man and beast. This was indeed the wilderness – a wilderness that destroys the living, yet preserves the dead.

Mauretania is one of the most desolate countries in the world; it has an area more than six times larger than England, but a population less than one-sixtieth as great. We flew on to the country's newly designated capital of Nouakchott, where the sands of the Sahara reach to the very brink of the ocean and are pounded by the giant Atlantic rollers.

The next morning we made our peace with the authorities for arriving without visas, landing permission or overflying permission, before taking off for the Canary Islands. Just two and a half hours after leaving Nouak-chott, where the temperature had been 115°F, we were amazed to see snow rising up out of the deep blue waters of the Atlantic on the horizon ahead of us. We had flown across the Sahara for more than two hours before heading out across an equally deserted stretch of ocean. After the miles of the scorching desert we had overflown, the very idea of snow seemed incredible. It was no mirage but Tenerife's 12,000-foot snow-crested volcano, Mount Teide, still 200 miles away. After three relaxing days on Spain's Canary Islands we set our course northeast towards Morocco where we stayed overnight at Marrakesh, lying at the foot of the snow-shrouded

High Atlas mountains. Marrakesh was a favourite resort of my grandfather, who frequently went there in search of African sunshine to escape the cold of the British winter.

It was our misfortune that our visit the next day to Fez with its magnificent market, coincided with the official visit of the Italian President, Signor Segni. When we returned to the airfield to collect our plane we found the Moroccan Army everywhere and security was intense. A young officer appeared, who demanded to see our papers. Arnold produced his passport, which was promptly confiscated. I offered to fetch mine from our aircraft, which was only ten yards away, but was told very firmly to stay where I was. Unfortunately for me the officer then asked me my name. Naturally I told him. He immediately pronounced us drunk and ordered a soldier to arrest us both. We were forthwith unceremoniously removed to a nearby grass verge where we were held at sub-machine gun point for nearly two hours. Our guard, a corporal, who spoke excellent French, was deeply apologetic about the behaviour of his officer. 'You must understand,' he explained, 'this is not a European army. Here everyone gives orders and no one knows what is going on.' It was not until the Italian President had mercifully departed that we were released and allowed to take off ourselves.

After a final night stop on the African continent in a cold and fog-bound Tangier, we set course for home. By late afternoon we had landed at Oxford where everyone seemed most surprised to see us and quite astonished that we had brought back the Comanche from its 20,000 mile safari round Africa without so much as a scratch. My flying instructor, Jeremy Busby, rubbed his eyes and heaved a sigh of relief. He climbed aboard with us and we took off for Boxted, a disused airfield near my father's Suffolk home. It was already half an hour after sunset and Father was at the end of the runway with his car headlights on to guide us in, as we touched down just ten hours after leaving the shores of Africa. As the roar of the engine died and the propeller swung to a halt, he greeted us with the words: 'I have killed the fatted calf!' For the return of the prodigal son?

· XIII ·

A Pride of Kennedys

Soon after my return from Africa my father and I received a most exciting invitation from the White House. Plans set in train by Kay Halle, a close Washington friend of my father's whom, indeed, he had nearly married a year before he met my mother, had come to fruition and President Kennedy, with the approval of Congress, decided to confer honorary United States citizenship upon my grandfather. This signal honour had been granted on only one previous occasion, to the French Revolutionary leader, the Marquis de Lafayette who, in the American War of Independence, had befriended George Washington and fought with distinction alongside the American colonists against the British at the Battle of Yorktown. Grandpapa, who had always taken great pride in the fact that he was half-American by birth, was overjoyed and accepted the compliment with enthusiasm. Addressing a Joint Session of Congress on 26 December 1941, shortly after the Japanese attack on Pearl Harbor, he had prefaced his remarks by teasing his audience with the observation: 'I cannot help reflecting that if my father had been American and my mother British, instead of the other way round, I might have got here on my own!' Sadly, more than twenty years on and already eighty-eight years of age, he was not well enough to make the journey to Washington himself. He therefore asked my father and me to represent him. Father, on 4 April 1963, cabled our acceptance to the President and, the following week, we flew to Washington.

Jack Kennedy, unlike his father Joe, who had been Ambassador in London at the outbreak of war and had reported that Britain would be defeated, was a staunch Anglophile and held my grandfather in the highest regard. He went to great lengths to make the occasion a memorable one, arranging a splendid ceremony at the White House. Immediately following the formal signing of the Act of Congress by the President in the Oval Office, where Father and I had been received by him, we adjourned to the Rose Garden of the White House, where the President paid this heartfelt tribute to my grandfather:

Whenever and wherever tyranny threatened, he has always championed liberty. Facing firmly towards the future, he has never forgotten the past. Serving six monarchs of his native Great Britain, he has served all men's freedom and dignity. In the dark days and darker nights when Britain stood alone – and most men save Englishmen despaired of England's life – he mobilized the English language and sent it into battle. The incandescent quality of his words illuminated the courage of his countrymen. Indifferent himself to danger, he wept over the sorrows of others. A child of the House of Commons, he came in time to be its father.

It was a deeply moving moment and it was with pride that I stood between the President and my father as the latter read out in stentorian tones, Grandpapa's letter of acceptance:

I have received many kindnesses from the United States of America, but the honour which you now accord me is without parallel. I accept it with deep gratitude and affection ... I am as you know half American by blood, and the story of my association with that mighty and benevolent nation goes back nearly ninety years to the day of my father's marriage. In this century of storm and tragedy I contemplate with high satisfaction the constant factor of the interwoven and upward progress of our peoples. Our comradeship and our brotherhood in war were unexampled. We stood together, and because of that fact the free world now stands.

Following the ceremony at the White House, the President's younger brother Bobby, who was Attorney-General at the time, invited us to his home at Hickory Hill in Maryland, twenty minutes' drive from Washington. Though we had met on previous occasions, it was in the course of this visit that my father and I formed a close friendship with Bobby and his wife, Ethel, who has a bubbling sense of humour and had a full measure of the Kennedy *joie de vivre*. Visits to Hickory Hill were always a riot. There was no question of any formality. Children of all ages would spill out of cupboards and rampage through the house which was filled with shrieks of laughter. Visitors were regularly co-opted into lively games of Touch-football and both Bobby and Ethel were aces on the tennis court. Indeed, on one occasion I was soundly trounced by my hostess when she was eight months pregnant! They insisted that, should we be over later in the year, we visit them at Hyannisport, where the Kennedy clan spent their summer vacation.

That summer, while I was staying with friends at that mecca of sailing, Newport, Rhode Island, Father arrived and a plan was made to visit Bobby and Ethel at Hyannis the next day. They invited us to join them for a cruise aboard the family's large cabin cruiser, the *Honey-Fitz*, to Martha's Vineyard, an island off the New England coast, where we met up with a large number of their friends for a barbecue and a day on the beach. In fact we were all having such a good time that the decision was taken to stay on for dinner at a local inn. By the time we headed back to Hyannis night had fallen. A stiff breeze and choppy sea had got up, causing the *Honey-Fitz* to pitch and wallow in a most lively fashion. As I helped the young boatman with the navigation – he had confided to me that he had never navigated the boat at night before – the weather became rougher still and matters were not helped by the fact that there were no charts on board. Meanwhile, on the afterdeck Father, who could not sing to save his life, was, somewhat implausibly, leading Bobby and Ethel in choruses of 'Lloyd George knew my Father...' to the tune of 'Onward Christian Soldiers', as the waves crashed over the boat, drenching us all.

It was nearly midnight before we made harbour on the far side of the Sound and secured the *Honey-Fitz* for the night. Nearly all the lights were out at the Kennedy compound where the clan lived as on a commune, with each branch of the family having a holiday home of their own. Bobby suddenly remembered that they had the Chief of Naval Operations, who was there as the guest of the President, billeted with them in their only guest room. 'Don't worry, Randolph,' assured Bobby, 'I'll sneak you and Winston into Teddy and Joan's house. They have a spare room. But be sure not to make any noise otherwise you'll wake everyone up!' So saying, in the pitch black of the night, Bobby led us straight into a bed of tall and very prickly roses and started cursing and swearing in a loud voice. He took us into his brother Teddy's house and showed us up to a small twin-bedded room since our unwitting host and hostess were already asleep. It was not long before Father, exhausted by the exertions of the day and the rigours of the return journey, was fast asleep and snoring loudly, so loudly in fact that I was unable to sleep myself. After trying first with one slipper, then the other, aimed in the general direction of the offending noise, in a vain effort to persuade him to stop, I gave up, took my blanket downstairs and curled up on the living room sofa. With a determination to be up and back in my own bed at dawn, before being discovered by my host or hostess, I too fell into a deep sleep.

To my horror I was still there when Joan appeared in a dressing gown on her way to the kitchen. With considerable embarrassment I introduced myself and endeavoured to offer an explanation for my presence. But my hostess seemed totally relaxed about the matter and not in the least surprised to find a strange man sleeping in her living room. Evidently it was all part and parcel of life at Hyannis with the Kennedys to which she had long since become accustomed. In due course Teddy, by then already a Senator, appeared and, after a hearty breakfast, we all walked across to the main house where two large twin-engine helicopters were standing by to fly the President and his Secret Service detail back to Washington. Father and I could never have imagined that this would be the last we would ever see of the young President upon whom so many hopes – by no means only American – were founded.

Within three months he was dead, cruelly cut down by an assassin's bullet in the prime of his political career. The personal feelings of the British people for President John F. Kennedy were stronger than those they held for any other foreign statesman, past or present.

On learning the tragic news I wrote an article for the *News of the World* in which I recalled my last meeting with the dead President:

It was shortly after nine on a Monday morning. Two helicopters, each with twin jet engines, had just landed on the lawn in front of his father's house, ready to take the President on his way to Washington. He had instructed the helicopters to land here, rather than at a field nearer his own house, as he knew it would give pleasure to his old and infirm father.

The President arrived, driving himself in an open car. The helicopters were waiting with their engines running, all set to take him to Otis Air Force Base on Cape Cod, where he would board a Boeing jet liner for the 400-mile flight to Andrews Air Force Base near Washington. From there he would fly in yet another helicopter to the lawn of the White House, and by 10.30 he would be at his desk.

His life was busy, and his responsibilities grave. Nevertheless, he found time for a friendly word with everyone. Although I had only had the privilege of meeting him twice before, the President recognized me as I stood by the driveway and he came over to say good morning. As he boarded the helicopter with his brothers, Attorney-General Robert Kennedy and Senator Edward Kennedy, he added, 'Be sure and visit Jackie. It will cheer her up'.

I concluded with this tribute:

Never before in their history have the British people had to place their trust, for their present safety and future destiny so completely in the hands of a citizen of another land. Never before have they given that trust so willingly and with such confidence. And never was a trust so honourably and sagaciously kept as by the late President of the United States.

I had the honour of meeting President Kennedy in April of this year, when my grandfather, Sir Winston Churchill, was made an Honorary Citizen of the United States. The ceremony, which was held in the Rose Garden of the White House in Washington, was deeply moving. It was with great pride that I witnessed the signal and high honour paid by the American people to an Englishman. And it was with emotion that I listened to a young warrior in the middle of his battles, paying tribute to one whose battles were over.

The vile tragedy in Dallas, Texas, has robbed the United States of a leader, the world of a statesman, and Britain of a friend. Three United States Presidents, Lincoln, Garfield and McKinley, have been assassinated in the last 100 years. Immense security precautions were taken to guard against this ever happening again. Last Friday's shooting of President Kennedy proved them to be of no avail against a determined killer . . .

President Kennedy was a man of immense personal courage. He had shown this by his heroic exploits in World War II. He demonstrated it once again on the day of his death, when he insisted that the bulletproof glass roof of his car be removed. That a statesman, on whom the hopes of the whole free world were placed, could today be struck down in cold blood in a civilized land, is an appalling indictment of human nature . . .

No more fitting words can be said in epitaph of President Kennedy than those he himself used with such feeling when he conferred honorary United States citizenship on Sir Winston Churchill in April this year: 'Whenever and wherever tyranny threatened he has always championed liberty. Facing firmly towards the future, he has never forgotten the past.'

· XIV ·

My Best Decision

Within a week of my return from Africa I found myself in a queue at the local chemist's shop, round the corner from my mother's flat at Hyde Park Gardens. In front of me, to my disbelief, was a girl asking the elderly proprietor, Mr Hogg, for a screwdriver and fuse wire. The voice was familiar and I recognized it immediately as belonging to Minnie d'Erlanger, whom I had first met on the ski slopes of Kitzbuhel nine years before, when we had both been thirteen years old. I told her that she had come to the wrong place and would have more luck in the nearby hardware store but, as so often in the years that were to follow, she proved me wrong. Old Mr Hogg duly reappeared from a back room bearing the items requested, which he had produced from his own tool kit. On discovering that the problem was a blown fuse, I volunteered to fix it. Though we could not know it at the time, this chance meeting was to change our lives. It turned out that Minnie, with whom I had lost touch and whom I had not seen for several years, was literally 'the girl next door'. Her parents, who lived in Hyde Park Street, had bought her a small mews house nearby in Clarendon Mews, which turned out to be no more than two minutes' walk from Hyde Park Gardens.

With some hefty bills to be met for the hire of the aircraft and the huge quantity of fuel we had consumed on our 20,000-mile flight round Africa, I was hard at work fighting a deadline to produce a series of articles on our adventures for *Queen* magazine (now *Harper's & Queen*), whose editor Jocelyn Stevens had bought the rights to our story before we left. Jock Whitney, who had recently served with distinction as United States Ambassador to the Court of St James, and his wife, Betsey, both of whom I had come to know several years before in the course of my first visit to America, had generously loaned me Cherry Hill, their country home on

Wentworth golf course near Ascot. There I was able to write my articles without interruption and with the wonderful Mr and Mrs Ferris to look after me and provide my meals. I resolutely turned down all distractions and invitations, including one from Lindy Guinness, whose brother Billy had been a close friend of mine at Eton. Unbeknown to me, Minnie was helping Lindy with the arrangements for her dance and asked her if I would be there. When Lindy told her that I had declined, Minnie, with a sure conviction, declared: 'I'll call him – I *know* he'll come!' I duly appeared, as Minnie had so confidently predicted, and that proved to be the start of a romance which has already lasted over a quarter of a century, has given us four wonderful children and brought us untold happiness together.

As soon as my articles were written I had to fly to Paris for a couple of days. On learning of my plans, Minnie implored me to buy her dog, a beautiful border terrier called Tara, a new lead and collar which apparently could only be obtained from a shop called Aux Etats Unis in the rue de Faubourg St Honoré. In my innocence I did not realize that this was the Bond Street of Paris, where all the most expensive shops are to be found. I had taken with me £25, in those days an ample sum, to cover my hotel and incidental expenses for two days. To my horror I discovered that the pooch's lead and collar, albeit most elegant in green, black and gold, cost over £10, which was everything I had after paying my hotel bill. Since, on my return to London, Minnie was not at home, I slipped the lead and collar through her letterbox but, although she had asked for it, I decided not to give her the bill. As it turned out, this £10 dog lead proved the best investment of my life. With Minnie, it was definitely a case of 'Love me, love my dog!' We saw a lot of each other that summer and soon became inseparable. To my surprise I discovered that she had been living in New York for a year, working as a journalist under Eugenia Sheppard on the *Herald Tribune*. It turned out that we had been near neighbours there for a while, though our paths had never crossed. Indeed, when a mutual friend asked her if she would be going to my twenty-first birthday party, which my mother was giving at her Fifth Avenue apartment, she had replied with disdain: 'I haven't come to New York to see English people!' But, within a year of her arrival in the United States, she had to abandon her job on the *Tribune* to return to England to be with her father, Sir Gerard d'Erlanger, who was seriously ill.

'Pops' d'Erlanger, as he was known to his friends, was the scion of a French banking family and had made his life in aviation and the City. In 1935 he had founded British Airways and when, in 1940, the company merged with Imperial Airways to form British Overseas Airways, he had become one of its founding directors. By the outbreak of war, he had already created an organization called the Air Transport Auxiliary which employed civilian pilots, including many women pilots of distinction such as Amy Johnson, to ferry fighter and bomber aircraft from the factories to the RAF front-line stations where they were needed. Young women pilots working for ATA, with barely 100 hours' experience – and often none on the particular aircraft – would find themselves asked to fly massive four-engined bombers single-handed, in spite of the fact that the aircraft had no hydraulic or servo-assisted controls and considerable physical strength was required to retract or wind down the undercarriage. During the six years of war 1215 men and women from fourteen nations, ferried some 308,000 aircraft of 147 different types in all weathers and often in most dangerous conditions, with the loss of 173 lives, including sixteen women.

At the end of the war he founded British European Airways, becoming its first managing director and, a year later, chairman. In 1956 he was appointed chairman of British Overseas Airways Corporation and, two years later, was knighted by the Queen for his services in the field of aviation. By the time he retired from BOAC in 1960, he had supervised the airline's transition from propeller aircraft to jets and had introduced the airline's first nonstop service across the Atlantic. Like so many of his generation 'Pops' had been a heavy smoker – at a time when the dangers were not known – and, tragically, died of lung cancer in December 1962 at the age of only fifty-six.

Minnie's great-grandfather, Baron Frederick d'Erlanger, chairman for many years of the family banking house of Erlanger's in Paris, was a noted financier. He was the first in the commercial field to have the vision of a Channel Tunnel connecting Great Britain to continental Europe – a concept that can be traced back to the strategic thinking of Napoleon who, at the beginning of the nineteenth century, conceived of it as a means of invading Britain without the need for doing battle with the all-powerful Royal Navy. In 1884 Frederick sponsored the project for a Channel Tunnel, and two years later founded the Compagnie du Tunnel sous La Manche – a project that is only now, more than 100 years later, being carried forward to success. By an irony of history, while Minnie's great-grandfather was the visionary sponsor of this remarkable project, it was my own great-grandfather, Lord Randolph Churchill, who more than any other individual, was responsible for delaying its realization for a whole century when, on the spur of the moment, he intervened in a debate in the House of Commons on 27 June 1888. He heaped scorn on the proposal in a speech in which he conjured up fears of a military threat from France – Britain's traditional enemy with an army ten times as large – the difficulties of securing the tunnel against foreign invasion, and its exorbitant cost. It was a witty but lethal cocktail of a speech which sank the Channel Tunnel (Experimental Works) Bill and effectively killed off the project for 100 years.

Like my own great-grandfather, Minnie's had married an American, Mathilde, the daughter of John Slidell of New Orleans who was Senator for Louisiana and Commissioner for the Confederacy at the time of the American Civil War. Together with his fellow Commissioner, Mason, Slidell had been removed from the British ship, the *Trent*, when it was arrested on the high seas by the northern Yankees – an incident which had come close to bringing Great Britain into the Civil War on the side of the South. Eventually the Yankees, following a bout of British gunboat diplomacy conducted by means of the newly laid Transatlantic telegraph cable, had backed down, allowing Slidell and Mason to continue on their way to Europe. There Slidell proceeded to negotiate through Frederick's father, Raphael, a loan on behalf of the Confederacy on the strength of the next year's cotton crop, to finance the continuing struggle of the South. Thus it was that Frederick came to meet and, soon after, marry Slidell's daughter, Mathilde. It is intriguing to observe that, as in the case of the Churchills and the marriage of Lord Randolph to Jennie, daughter of Leonard Jerome of Brooklyn, New York, sometime proprietor of the *New York Times*, it was the introduction of American blood that had the effect of firing the ensuing generation with a burning ambition that carried all before it.

Frederick and Mathilde's son, Emile, born in Paris in 1866, was a citizen of France until, at the age of twenty-five, he became a naturalized British subject. Emile was a pioneer of the Victorian era in the grand mould of Cecil Rhodes. The two in fact met in 1892 and, as a result of their encounter, Emile, already chairman of the family banking house, became a director of Rhodes's British South Africa Company. He was responsible for the finance and construction of nearly all BSA's railway system in Africa, including the Cape Central Railway, the Rhodesia–Katanga Junction Railway and the Central Africa Railway; in addition he raised the capital for the Victoria Falls and Transvaal Railway. He was a tycoon financier with an amazing, buccaneering spirit. Long before the days of the first flight by the Wright brothers, he had a perspective of the world that was truly global, building railways across five continents – North America, South America, Europe, Africa and Asia. For more than half a century between them, Frederick and his son Emile held the chairmanship of the Channel Tunnel Company and owned the bore-holes at either end, where initial tunnelling had begun.

It was just a few months after her father's death that Minnie and I met once again, and it has always been a great regret to me that, by less than six months, I missed knowing my future father-in-law, whose passion for aviation and sailing I shared to the full.

Indeed that summer, while spending a few weeks with my mother and Leland at Mount Kisco, I completed my training at Flight Safety, La Guardia, and gained my US commercial pilot's licence and instrument rating. Armed with these credentials I felt it would be defeatist to travel back to England as a fare-paying passenger aboard a commercial jet.

Knowing that, at the time, all American light aircraft sold in Europe were ferried across the Atlantic by air, I telephoned the Piper Aircraft Corporation at Lockhaven, Pennsylvania, to enquire if, by chance, they had any aircraft requiring delivery. To my disappointment I learned that I had missed the opportunity of a Transatlantic flight with Max Conrad, the veteran pilot known to all in the world of light aviation as the Flying Grandfather. 'Too bad you didn't call us yesterday,' the Piper spokesman told me, 'Max Conrad left just this morning with three aircraft and two other pilots for England.' I cursed my luck but, just in case anything came up, I left them my number. Imagine my surprise and delight when, within an hour of my call, Max Conrad himself telephoned to say that his departure had been delayed by a minor mechanical problem and he would fly into Westchester Airport that very evening to pick me up.

I accepted with alacrity and, a few hours later, Max Conrad collected me in a brand new Twin Comanche – in fact the first twin-engined Comanche ever to be delivered to Europe. In Boston we were joined by two single-engine Piper Cherokees. After a night stop in Boston we flew northeast over the beautiful New England countryside, where the dogwood was already showing the first hint of its flame-coloured autumn hue, to the Canadian border, and from there across Prince Edward Island and the Gulf of St Lawrence to Gander in Newfoundland. There we were delayed for several hours by Hurricane Beulah, which had built up over the Caribbean before moving out to mid-Atlantic where she stood directly in our path. Max, who at the time held the single-engined round-the-world record and who had made over 100 crossings of the Atlantic in light aircraft, judged it prudent to wait overnight until what would have been a 100-mph headwind, became a 100-mph tailwind, as the hurricane passed north across our intended track. Over a meal I got Max to tell me something of his past, which had led him to become known as the most famous light-aircraft pilot in the world, and the holder of numerous world records for long-distance flights and endurance.

Max was a most remarkable man and, like almost all the old-time pilots that I have known, had a deep religious conviction. He made all his record-breaking trips alone – on one occasion staying aloft for sixty hours on a nonstop flight from London to Los Angeles – and, being so much at the mercy of the elements above deserts, jungles and the vast expanse of the oceans, he felt close to the Almighty and very much in His hands. As a young man he had been an enthusiastic pilot and, to finance his flying, had regularly given joy rides for a dollar a time in his native Winnetka, Illinois. One day, having just come in from a flight, he noticed to his horror a beautiful young girl with long blonde hair walking straight towards the propeller, which was still spinning. Max flipped the magneto switches, leaped out of the plane and threw himself bodily at the girl. Though he saved her life, it was only at the expense of fracturing his own skull. He was taken unconscious from beneath the propeller and it was to take him many years to rebuild his life. He suffered total loss of memory and had to learn to read and write again from scratch. But nothing could keep him out of the air, and it was then that he began driving himself to ever longer flights. His whole life after that had been a battle to regain the ground lost in the accident, and it was this that made his subsequent achievements in the field of aviation, including his round-the-world flights – by way of the Equator as well as over the North and South Poles – so truly amazing.

To save money we slept that night on the benches of the terminal building and were finally able to get on our way shortly before dawn. As we rolled down the runway for take-off I asked Max if he had the charts for our flight. 'Charts?' he replied, affecting surprise. 'What charts?' This was to be Max's one hundred and tenth Transatlantic crossing, and he had long since given up bothering with such niceties as charts. I was nonetheless glad that I still had with me in my pilot's flight bag a Transatlantic chart given to me by the captain of the TWA jet on which I had flown out from London the previous month. It was to prove invaluable later in the flight.

Setting course for Ireland with some 2500 miles of Atlantic Ocean ahead of us, we tracked out on the back-bearing of the Gander radio beacon, which we lost after about forty-five minutes. Max let me fly as captain in the left-hand seat and invited me to do the navigation and radio communication for all three aircraft. About an hour and a half after take-off, to my surprise, I saw Max holding the palm of his hand to the plexiglass of the windscreen. 'What are you doing?' I enquired. I was dumbfounded by his reply.

'Oh, I was just checking our position,' he answered in a matter-of-fact way.

'You were *what*?' I asked in disbelief.

'The windshield,' he explained, 'is colder than usual. That means that the polar airstream is probably rather stronger. I would say we are about four or five miles south of track.'

To one who had just completed an in-depth course in the mysteries of instrument flying and the arts of long-range aerial navigation, including astro-navigation with a bubble sextant and Loran – neither of which we had with us – this seemed quite preposterous. Half an hour later I succeeded in making contact with Ocean-Station Charlie, one of the two weather ships – in the days before weather satellites – positioned respectively one-third and two-thirds of the way across the Atlantic. Knowing that they were equipped with radar I asked for a 'fix' on our position. To my amazement the position they gave us placed us just six miles south of track, which meant that Max had been exactly right in his estimate.

The men manning the weather ships had lonely lives, stuck in mid-Atlantic for three months at a stretch. The pilots of the big jets, flying high above, were too busy to chat to them, and they were thrilled to have someone to talk to. They wanted to know all about our flight and what the view looked like from 10,000 feet above the water. Max was always very friendly with them and this, a few months later, was to save his life. It was one of the rare occasions when he made a westbound crossing of the Atlantic, having been asked to deliver an Italian plane to the United States. On that occasion he was busy talking to one of the ocean-stations as dawn came up and was describing to them the beauty of a large iceberg, bathed in the pink glow of dawn, some miles to the north. On the spur of the moment he decided to alter course so as to overfly the iceberg and give them a better description. Moments later the oil line on the single-engined aircraft fractured and soon the engine seized up and fell silent. Thanks to his having altered course, Max was within gliding distance of the iceberg and was able to crash land on it, being rescued some twelve hours later by the US Navy, alerted by his friends on the weather ship.

Max had pointed out to me, as we headed out over the ice floes of the North Atlantic, that a human being cannot survive long in such waters. 'If you're well covered, you might survive for a couple of minutes. If you're skinny like me, it is less than sixty seconds!' he observed laconically. Once over the southern tip of Greenland we started picking up the strong winds and fierce turbulence generated by Hurricane Beulah 100 miles or so to our north. Although each aircraft carried an enormous quantity of fuel in special ferry tanks in the cabins, we cruised at a speed of only 140 mph, so as to achieve maximum fuel economy and range. However, the hurricane-force winds, which had by now swung behind us, were boosting our ground speed by a further 100 mph.

The weather was clear for most of the way until about two hours from the west coast of Ireland, when a thick deck of cloud appeared beneath us. All three aircraft carried only temporary and very basic radio equipment, in fact no more than a VHF radio and an automatic direction-finder. We were relying on Shannon radar to guide us in to our landfall, and it was therefore with consternation that we learned from one of the jets flying some 25,000 feet above us that Shannon radar was out of service. At this point I produced my small TWA Transatlantic chart, covered in multi-coloured parabolic lines radiating from the handful of long-range Consol beacons which, for many years, had been the only system of long-range radio navigation and which I had recently learned about but never had the chance to use. Now it was my turn to amaze my flying companion. As I counted the dots and dashes transmitted by the different beacons and plotted our course to a landfall in the Shannon estuary, I could see the same look of bewilderment on Max's face as he must have seen on my own, when he had judged our position with the palm of his hand. We landed safely at Shannon just after sunset, having flown the Atlantic in 9 hours 52 minutes – the fastest of all Max's 110 crossings. In fact we had not used even half the fuel we had brought with us from Gander! We flew on at dawn the next morning to London's Gatwick Airport, where an anxious Minnie was on the tarmac waiting to greet us.

On my return to England I found an invitation from Aristotle Onassis, the Greek shipping tycoon, to join him, Grandpapa and my father for a cruise aboard his sumptuous yacht, the *Christina*. Grandpapa, in his later years, enormously enjoyed his cruises aboard the *Christina* and Onassis would treat him with all the reverence and love of a son for a father. 'Ari' was most certainly included among that category of my grandfather's friends of whom my grandmother did not wholly approve. Among some of the others who fell into this category were Max Beaverbrook and (in the earlier years) Brendan Bracken – both of them my godfathers – and many others besides. The cruise to Ithaca and the Ionian Islands was to be the last Grandpapa would ever make aboard the *Christina*. It was a memorable experience. Wherever we came into harbour a large crowd would immediately gather and Grandpapa was greeted with waves and heartfelt cheers by the local Greeks, no doubt in recognition not only of the fact that British forces had liberated Greece from the Nazis, but that, thanks to my grandfather's personal intervention when he visited Athens the last Christmas of the war, Greece was saved from Communism and consequent incorporation within the Soviet bloc.

The publication of my African articles in *Queen* magazine led directly to contracts from Heinemann in London and Random House in New York to write a book about my adventures. To get solitude to write the book I buried myself in a cottage in the Thames valley lent to me by Minnie's brother, Robin, called Thatched Cottage, at Shurlock Row in Berkshire. Minnie, who had a job in London at the time, valiantly volunteered to help type the book for me at weekends and, indeed, has typed every one of the books that I have written, including the present one.

While I was working on my book, my grandfather's Private Secretary, Anthony Montague-Browne, called to let me know that my grandmother was in hospital and that Grandpapa was all alone at Chartwell and would appreciate a visit. I wrote to him immediately to send him copies of the photographs I had taken on our recent cruise together aboard the *Christina*, and proposing myself for lunch or dinner. Grandpapa replied:

30 September 1963

My Dear Winston,

Thank you so much for your letter and for the excellent photographs.

Your grandmother is unwell and is having a rest cure in the Westminster Hospital, so I am alone, and it would be very nice if you would come and see me as you suggest.

Your loving Grandpapa,
Winston S. Churchill

I dined and stayed with him at Chartwell on 4 October and, a few days later, a magnificent box of Romeo y Julieta cigars arrived for me through the post as a birthday present.

When, at the end of the year, the book was finished, I took Minnie with me on a skiing holiday to Zürs, where I had an accident in which I nearly lost the sight of one eye. As I approached a bump at speed, the tips of my stiff racing skis suddenly dug into the snow, throwing me violently forward face first, and causing my rimless Polaroid dark-glasses to slice through my cheek, missing my right eye by a fraction of an inch. I picked myself up and made a snowball, which I pressed to my face to hold the wound together and staunch the flow of blood, before skiing to the bottom and walking to the local doctor, who stitched me up. He wrapped me in a bandage which completely covered my head with the exception only of my left eye, placing me under a firm injunction not to ski until the stitches were out. The next day, by way of diversion, we made an expedition to visit the spectacular, fairy-tale castles of King Ludwig of Bavaria, with whom my ancestress Jane Digby had sojourned for a while at Hohen-Schwangau a century before. Driving my old grey Jaguar with my head entirely bandaged up, it was perhaps not surprising that cars coming in the opposite direction would, as they approached, suddenly swerve sharply to the opposite side of the road, almost into the ditch. I must have looked rather like the man in the then recently released film called *The Man Who Never Was*. Evidently the very sight of me was sufficient to inspire terror.

In the spring of 1964 I proposed to Minnie. Having asked the consent of her mother, Smut, who gave us her blessing, we both drove down to East Bergholt to break the news to my father, who was equally delighted. We thereupon flew to the United States to tell my mother and Leland in Mount Kisco, where our engagement was announced.

The next few weeks were hectic in the extreme, with all the preparations for the wedding which was set for 15 July. No sooner back in London, I paid a visit on Grandpapa Churchill at 28 Hyde Park Gate, of which I gave my mother an account in a letter I wrote in the early hours of the following morning:

> 11 Hyde Park Gardens,
> London W2
> 27 June 1964 (3 am)

Darling Mummy,

A million thanks for everything . . .

I paid a visit on Grandpapa C. who has been ill for the last ten days, but today he was in spanking form. He was sitting looking at a book of sculpture in the garden of 28 H.P.G. It was a lovely sunny afternoon and he greeted me with the words: 'Congratulations and happiness.' He looked at me for a while, then returned to brooding over his book. After a few minutes he looked up and seemed surprised that I was there. After fixing me with his eyes for a second or two he

174

asked me if I would come to his room with him. His nurse and I helped him to his room. He got into bed and demanded his chequebook. This was brought by a secretary (but no pen). He browsed through the counterfoils (perhaps to see how much things cost today) and then asked for his pen. I gave him mine and he began writing. The secretary reappeared, glanced at what he was up to and announced that she would write it out. Having done this she presented it to him for his signature. He pondered over it for a while and then barked 'No!' The secretary then disappeared to consult Lady C., reappeared and proceeded to write out a second cheque. Again – rather more gruffly – he pronounced 'No!' Then he took his pen and set about inserting another 'o'. The secretary protested and asked if he wouldn't like to leave the whole matter to another day when he was feeling better. He was adamant. Eventually the secretary was prevailed upon to do as she was told and write a third cheque. This one he appeared to like the look of better and in a slow but steady hand he put his name to it. Then with a smile of triumph on his face he passed it to me, sitting at his bedside.

> Your loving son,
> Winston

I could not believe my eyes, the cheque was for £1000 – far and away the largest I had ever had in my life. I wrote that same day to thank him:

> 11 Hyde Park Gardens,
> London W2
> 26 June 1964

Dearest Grandpapa,

Thank you for your handsome and most generous present. I am particularly grateful to you for it as a token of your blessing upon my forthcoming marriage to Minnie. She is a sweet girl and I look forward to bringing her to luncheon with you next Sunday. We shall do our best to carry the name of Churchill, which you made great, with honour into the future.

> Your loving grandson,
> Winston

A vexatious problem arose from the fact that while Minnie was a Catholic, as her family had been for generations, I had been brought up a Protestant in the Church of England. Indeed, it had been my ancestor John Churchill, 1st Duke of Marlborough, who as Captain-General (or Commander-in-Chief) of James II's armies had, with a small body of conspirators, been instrumental in ending Roman Catholic ascendancy in Great Britain and effecting the Glorious Revolution of 1688. I have today, hanging in a place of honour, on the wall of my home, John's original letter of 4 August 1688 pledging his support to the Dutch King, William of Orange, and declaring that he was 'resolved to dye [sic] in that Religion that God has given you both the will and the power to protect'. While I did not feel I could insist that we should be married in the Church of England, I was not prepared to submit to what I regarded as the shameless blackmail then practised by the Church of Rome which required that I should, as a non-Catholic, sign a document agreeing to our children being brought up as Roman Catholics. In spite of the powerful entreaties of Minnie's delightful priest, Father O'Hagan, who was full of Irish charm and persuasive argument, this proved an insurmountable obstacle to our marrying in church.

As a result we were forced to contract a purely civil marriage before our immediate families in Kensington registry office, and it has been one of our eternal regrets that we were unable to have a 'white' wedding. The premises were furnished like a dentist's waiting room and the ceremony was virtually over before it had begun. As in a crematorium, we found ourselves hustled along because the next party was due just fifteen minutes later. We went on immediately to 28 Hyde Park Gate, to pay our respects to Grandpapa and Grandmama Churchill who had put on ice some Pol Roger champagne – without which no Churchill family celebration is ever complete – and where Karsh, the famous portrait photographer, who had flown in from Ottawa, lay in wait to take the wedding photographs, lured by my father's promise of a sitting with Grandpapa who, that morning, had written to me:

15 July 1964

My dear Winston,
I should like to mark the occasion of your marriage by giving you three pictures painted by myself. As you will know, most of my pictures are at Chartwell, but when I next go down there I shall select three and have them dispatched to you.

Your loving grandfather,
WSC

From my grandparents' we went on to the Hyde Park Hotel for a splendid reception for all our friends and relations which my mother-in-law, Smut d'Erlanger, had most generously arranged. Madame Floris, who each year made a wonderful cake, each with an original theme, to celebrate Grandpapa's birthday, had been commissioned to produce one of her splendid creations. Meanwhile Father had arranged through the Duke and Duchess of Buccleuch for the Sword of Ramillies – the very one with which John Churchill had led the charge in that famous battle more than 250 years before – to be brought down from Boughton in Northamptonshire for the occasion. When the moment arrived to cut the cake I drew the sword and, with Minnie's hand clasped in mine, plunged the blade into Madame Floris's cake. It soon became evident that the sword had been made for doing battle with softer targets than Madame Floris's cakes and – to my horror – began to buckle on the seemingly armour-plated icing. Leaving family, wellwishers and one slightly bent sword behind us, we flew off on our honeymoon to the South of France, where we spent a week, before travelling on to a tiny but exquisite island – little more than a rock in the Bay of Naples – called La Gaiola.

From the South of France, I hastened to thank Grandpapa for his letter – the last I was ever to get from him – and for the wonderful gift of his paintings, which I have always admired for their bright colours and translucent skies:

> Villa Fal'Eze,
> Eze sur mer, A.M.
> 22 July 1964

Dear Grandpapa,

Thank you so much for your very splendid wedding present to Minnie and myself of some of your own paintings. They will be our most treasured possessions and will hold the place of honour on the walls of any house we inhabit.

We are having a wonderful and most relaxing honeymoon here in the South of France and we look forward to seeing you again soon.

With fondest love from us both,

> Your loving grandson,
> Winston

Looking back on my marriage to Minnie after already a quarter of a century together, I have no hesitation in saying that it has proved the best decision of my life and our love remains as deep and abiding as on our wedding day.

Immediately on our return to England we set about finding a home. Having both spent much of our lives in London, we were determined to find a home in the country in which to bring up our future family. However, because of my commitments as a journalist, we decided we had to be within one hour of London. We were fortunate to find a lovely Sussex farmhouse, known as Broadwater House, on the edge of Chailey Common near Haywards Heath, some forty-five miles from central London. With twelve acres of fields and garden, Broadwater was to be our home for the next twenty-one years.

In September of that year, Sir Alec Douglas-Home who, in the wake of Harold Macmillan's illness and the political fallout from the Profumo affair, had taken over as Prime Minister, decided to call a general election for the following month. I had by now become closely interested in politics – an interest heightened by a day spent at the House of Commons reporting for the *Evening Standard* the critical debate which led directly to Macmillan's decision to quit as Prime Minister. The day before my marriage I had been interviewed by a panel under Paul Bryan and, as a result, was successful in getting my name on the Conservative Central Office list of approved candidates.

From the earliest stirrings of my political consciousness I held the firm conviction that Britain's duty and future lay in forging, with the other democracies of Europe, a European unity which would restore to those nations the self-determination and self-confidence essential if Europe was to have the economic strength and military capacity to prosper and defend itself in an age of superpowers.

At that time no one on the British political scene was doing more to champion the cause of European unity than Edward Heath. I therefore determined, though we had never met, to write to him, offering my services in the forthcoming general election campaign. I received a prompt reply asking me to come to his office at the Board of Trade, of which he was president, for an interview. The upshot was an invitation to become his personal assistant in the campaign. I had never before taken an active part in a general election campaign and working for Ted Heath was first-class experience, for there are few people who have got the running of their constituencies down to a finer art than he. Winning the London suburban seat of Bexley from Labour in 1950, he had steadily but relentlessly built up both his party organization and, with it the Conservative majority. With the help of his superb agent, Reg Pye, he had established a network of Party 'street wardens' so comprehensive that, by the eve of poll, a leaflet drop could be made to every home in the constituency in the space of two hours.

I might have been born with politics in my veins but it was nonetheless invaluable to watch from close quarters a seasoned and expert political campaigner at work. Among my tasks was to collect Ted from his home in the Albany, just off Piccadilly, and drive him to his constituency, as well as to public meetings throughout the south of England. Keeping the candidate on any kind of schedule – Ted had little sense of time – was a major challenge. I also soon learned that he had a secret vice: a passion for chocolates. Even when we were running late, he would ask me to stop the car and dive into a local shop to buy him a box. I was also to learn at his side some of the hazards of political campaigning. One morning, with a large team of party workers and a couple of journalists from the national press, we were canvassing a road of semi-detached houses in his constituency. I had gone up the pathway to ring a doorbell. To my amazement the door was opened by a very attractive young lady in a black diaphanous nightdress who, seeing Ted coming up the pathway hard on my heels, greeted us warmly with the words: 'Good morning, gents! Won't you please come in?' I looked over my shoulder to see the candidate fleeing down the path as fast as his legs could carry him.

All told, it was a fascinating three weeks. My appetite for a future political foray of my own had definitely been whetted. While Ted Heath managed marginally to increase his majority in his own Bexley constituency, the campaign at a national level proved disastrous for the Conservatives, who were narrowly defeated. As a result, Harold Wilson replaced Sir

Alec Douglas-Home as Prime Minister – a situation that was to persist until 1970 when Ted Heath, by then Leader of the Conservative Party, managed, in the teeth of the opinion polls, to carry off the victory. By that time I had myself entered Parliament, winning the industrial seat of Stretford in Lancashire from Labour.

Meanwhile, that same autumn, my book *First Journey* – an account of my adventures in Africa – was published. It received an especially friendly notice in the *Yorkshire Post* from Iain Macleod, one of the most senior political figures of his day, who remarked:

I do not regard myself as a nervous character and I have flown a good deal in that admirable aeroplane, the single-engined Piper Comanche. But to take off on a round-Europe-and-Africa trip with two pilots who had less than 250 flying hours' experience between them ... would seem to my middle-aged mind a splendid but highly dangerous adventure. It was a complete success, and Churchill writes shrewdly and directly of their travels. Perhaps he is as yet better as a journalist than an author, and better as a pilot than either ... His views on the policies of the ex-colonial powers, and of Portugal in Africa are mature and wise. Perhaps (for of course I am a prejudiced witness in this field) I really mean that in most matters my personal judgment agrees with his ...

It must be both a glory and a handicap to be called Winston Churchill. This is the first true personal achievement of the young Winston Churchill. And so, I would guess, it is all the more precious to him. He has shown that he can carve out his own route, more exciting and more adventurous than the journeys of his grandfather and great-grandfather. He has shown that he can tell a good story, as they could do. He has written a fine book. For him it is the record of his first journey. There will be many others. And I hope that soon he will try the endless adventure of politics. That is the true journey for a Churchill.

Publication of *First Journey* led directly to an invitation to act as anchorman for a new BBC Radio midday news and features programme called *This Time of Day* – the fore-runner of *The World at One*. My job was not only to host the programme, introducing each individual item, but also to go out as a reporter with a tape recorder to interview a wide range of personalities from visiting foreign statesmen to lorry drivers in transport cafés, depending on the story of the moment. I was wholly inexperienced in the art of broadcasting and, at least to start with, rather shy in front of the microphone. However, I was given great encouragement by the programme's creator and editor, Andrew Boyle, as well as by others in the team. The first person I interviewed was the most distinguished and, as was then thought, veteran broadcaster, Alistair Cooke, who I am glad to say is still going strong twenty-five years on.

One person in particular who went to enormous trouble to coach me was a delightful Austrian who had been with the BBC for many years, called Eric Stadlen. Each day after the programme had gone out Eric and I would have a snack from the BBC's meals-on-wheels trolley and he would then give me an hour or two of coaching. He taught me to pace my delivery and to project my voice at the right pitch and modulation. Frequently after a session, as we were walking down the labyrinth of passages in Broadcasting House, Eric would take a quick glance at his watch and seeing that some thirty seconds remained before *Radio Newsreel* was due to go out on the BBC's World Service, would lead me into a studio where some unfortunate newsreader was waiting for the green light on the desk in front of him to be extinguished before going 'on air'. Eric would ask him to step aside, sit me down in his chair and, with just ten seconds to go, would say: 'Right, Winston! You are now going to read the World Service news to Africa!' In an instant the green light had flicked out and I was 'live' to a whole continent. It was a daunting experience, but after a couple of weeks of this deep-end treatment I had left behind all trace of my microphone shyness.

Though my contract had only been for an initial three weeks, this was extended and I stayed on at the BBC for several months before leaving to embark on a mammoth coast-to-coast lecture tour of the United States. Many of my colleagues on the programme, male and female alike, have moved on from the congenial world of 'steam radio' to successful careers in the more competitive world of television reporting. My place was taken by William Hardcastle who anchored the programme for many years before, in turn, giving way to the doyen of British current-affairs broadcasters, Sir Robin Day. I look back on my time at the BBC with nostalgia for what was a very happy period of my life.

· XV ·

Operation 'Hope Not'

On 30 November 1964 we celebrated Grandpapa Churchill's ninetieth birthday with a family dinner at 28 Hyde Park Gate. It was a splendid occasion. Every member of the family was present including all his children – with the exception only of Diana, who had died the previous year – and grandchildren. Though by now very frail, Grandpapa presided benignly at the end of the table and clearly enjoyed the evening. On behalf of the entire family, Father proposed the toast to the 'Author of our being'.

But, early in the New Year, on 11 January, Grandpapa had a stroke. It soon became apparent that he was losing his valiant and long-drawn-out battle against the infirmities of old age which, due to his formidable constitution and, above all, to his indomitable spirit, he had managed to keep at bay since his first heart attack more than twenty years before in the war years, and through several subsequent strokes and bouts of pneumonia. Members of the family were alerted to expect the worst. We gathered round his bedside at Hyde Park Gate to keep vigil as he slipped gradually away. The lugubrious Lord Moran, his personal physician for a quarter of a century, clearly felt that the moment had passed for any heroic attempts to save him. He dozed on fitfully for several days and I would go each evening after finishing my work at the BBC to be with him at his bedside in the dimly-lit bedroom which had been made for him on the ground floor after he fell and broke his hip in 1962. Sometimes with Grandmama or another member of the family, at other times alone, I would sit for long hours at his bedside.

As he slumbered on peacefully in the shadows, the sound of his breathing and the slight heaving of his chest beneath the bedclothes the only signs of life, I reflected upon his remarkable and adventurous career in the army, in journalism and in politics. Above all, I thought of his mental power which, when harnessed to his literary talents and his gift for oratory, inspired his fellow countrymen – when it seemed that all was lost – to a heroic resistance and onwards through five long years of courage and sacrifice to victory. This was the man who, in his youth, rode his white horse along the skirmish line on the northwest frontier of India, charged with the 21st Lancers at Omdurman and escaped from the Boers at Pretoria. This was the parliamentarian who twice crossed the floor of the House of Commons (he once joked: 'Anyone can rat – it takes talent to re-rat!') and served six sovereigns from Victoria to Elizabeth II. This was the prophet whose warnings of disaster and calls for action, while time remained, went unheeded, and to whom – almost too late – the British nation turned in its hour of need. This was the 'Former Naval Person' to whom it fell twice in a quarter of a century to mobilize the fleet for war. This was the strategist who judged it prudent to attack the enemy on the periphery in North Africa until we had the strength to beat him in the heartland of Europe. This was the friend and ally who convinced the tortured nations of occupied Europe that the day of liberation would surely dawn. This was the historian whose writings fill fifty volumes, the builder who laid 10,000 bricks and the artist who painted 500 canvases. What a man! What a life! What a debt owed by all the world to one, as Duff Cooper so movingly put it in his heartfelt tribute to his chief and to his friend:

> When ears were deaf and tongues were mute,
> You told of doom to come.
> When others fingered on the flute,
> You thundered on the drum.
>
> When armies marched and cities burned
> And all you said came true,
> Those who had mocked your warnings turned
> Almost too late to you.
>
> Then doubt gave way to firm belief,
> And through five cruel years
> You gave us glory in our grief,
> And laughter through our tears.
>
> When final honours are bestowed
> And last accounts are done,
> Then shall we know how much was owed
> By all the world to one.

Yet he was also the grandfather whom I loved, who would get down on his knees to play trains with me on the nursery floor, who endeavoured to teach me to paint, who, even when Prime Minister, invariably found time to answer my letters from school. My thoughts went back to the days at

Chartwell when, together, we would feed the stately golden orfe in their shadowy pools, talk to the black swans on the lake and scratch the backs of the pigs in the farmyard; to the many lunches together when, if alone, he would hum a little ditty as Toby his budgerigar perched on the rim of his brandy glass; to the dashes – even when in his eighties – to his beloved House of Commons so as to be in his place by 3.15 pm for Prime Minister's Question Time. I remembered his constant solicitude for my welfare. 'Are you sure you are all right for money?' was a regular enquiry, as he remembered how constrained his own finances had been as a young man on army pay with an extravagant mother to help support. On one occasion, when I had driven up from Oxford to have lunch with him, he had enquired: 'You did not drive yourself, did you? I trust you had your man drive you. With the provision I have been able to make for you, you should certainly be able to afford that.' I told him that the provision he had made for me was indeed handsome, but that it did not quite extend to employing a 'man' to drive me, look after my clothes and generally attend to my needs, as he would have wished. He had been disconcerted to know that the grandeur of his ideas had, sadly, been overtaken by the depredations of inflation.

By mid-January, as Grandpapa slipped into unconsciousness, Lord Moran had ordained that he should be given no further sustenance or liquid. However, I could not bear to see how parched his lips had become and the way in which they moved involuntarily as if asking for a drink, so, in defiance of the eminent doctor's injunction, I gave him a small sip of orange juice from a jug that was still by his bed. As the moment approached when we knew he would not be with us for much longer, the family assembled around his bed to take our leave of him. We knelt in the lamp-lit room in silent prayer, each with our own precious memories of this being we loved so deeply and who had meant so much to us all. Thus, quite peacefully, on the morning of 24 January 1965, he went out on the ebb tide.

For many years plans had been laid for Operation Hope Not, the code-name that had been given to the arrangements for my grandfather's funeral. These had been conceived not by the family, though my grandmother and father had both been advised and kept informed of the plans, but by Buckingham Palace in consultation with 10 Downing Street. The Queen had decided that Winston Churchill should have accorded to him the exceptional honour of a State Funeral, granted to a commoner just four times in the nineteenth century – to Pitt (the Younger), Nelson, Wellington and Gladstone – and never at all in the twentieth. The Duke of Norfolk, Earl Marshal of England, had charge of the arrangements and I well recall my father asking him: 'Well, Bernard, at the end of the day, what *is a State Funeral?*'

'Why, you bloody fool Randolph,' the Earl Marshal had replied with the matter-of-factness for which he was well known, 'it's a funeral paid for by the state!'

It was not only the Buckingham Palace that had, long before, prepared plans for my grandfather's death. Charles Collingwood, of CBS News in the United States and one of the world's most respected television reporters, told me that Grandpapa had succeeded in burying at least three generations of CBS reporters who had been assigned to cover his funeral!

By order of the Queen, my grandfather's body lay in state in Westminster Hall for three days. In spite of the bitter cold of winter and a biting wind, the people of Britain – and many from overseas – queued round the clock for several hours, so as to file past the coffin and pay their last respects to the man they revered as saviour of his nation. The numbers were so great that the queue extended more than two miles from Westminster Bridge by way of the Lambeth Embankment on the east bank of the Thames, across Lambeth Bridge and along Millbank to Parliament Square and, finally, to Westminster Hall itself, the oldest surviving part of the Palace of Westminster which had been built in the eleventh century by William Rufus, son of the Conqueror. In the gaunt hall with its high hammerbeam wooden ceiling, Grandpapa's coffin was set on a catafalque. A Union flag draped the coffin on which his insignia as Knight of the Garter rested on a silk cushion. Candles flickered round the funeral bier, which was guarded at each corner by officers of each of the three services in turn, with clasped hands resting on their drawn reversed swords. People filed past in their thousands and tens of thousands to bid farewell. So many were to say: 'But for him . . .'

He had died on a Sunday morning, by a coincidence of history seventy years to the day after the death of his father, Lord Randolph Churchill. The next day tributes were paid in Parliament to one described, without hyperbole, as the greatest parliamentarian in 700 years. His seat, the corner seat below the gangway on the government side, was left symbolically empty as the tributes were paid; then the Commons adjourned for the rest of the day as a mark of respect.

Saturday, 30 January, the day set for his funeral, dawned steely grey with a searingly cold east wind. Already the streets on the route of the procession from Parliament Square to St Paul's were crammed, as the 7000 soldiers and 8000 police involved took up their positions. As my father and I together with other members of our family assembled in New Palace Yard, in the precincts of the Palace of Westminster, a bearer party from the Grenadier Guards lifted the coffin from its catafalque in Westminster Hall and lowered it on to the naval gun-carriage that was to carry him on his final journey through the streets of London. While my grandmother and the other female members of the family rode in carriages, Father and I, together with the other men of the family, walked behind the coffin. I was most concerned for my father as, less than a year before, he had had part of a lung removed and was far from fit. I sensed that he too was anxious about the one-hour march ahead of us, though he made no mention of it. But all anxieties were swept aside by his determination to honour his father by following the coffin on foot and, as he had brought me up to be on such occasions, he was very 'steady on parade'.

At 9.45 am, as the chimes of Big Ben – which thereafter were to be silenced for the rest of the day – rang out above our heads, the procession in the courtyard moved off. To the sound of the horses' hooves on the cobblestones and the muffled beat of drums, the cortège got under way as the guns of the Royal Horse Artillery, nearby in St James's Park, fired a ninety-gun salute – one for each year of his life. The great black gun-carriage drawn by 140 naval ratings turned into Whitehall as Father and I, in morning coat, top hat and greatcoats, followed immediately behind with the other members of the family. Some considerable way ahead the band of the RAF was playing a funeral march by Beethoven. The crowds stood tightly pressed together and watched in silence – many with tears in their eyes – as the procession wound its way down Whitehall to Trafalgar Square, up the Strand and Fleet Street to Ludgate. On the climb up Ludgate Hill to St Paul's, the naval gun-carriage crew were straining at their heavy load, the horses pulling the carriages were slipping and Father became very out of breath. I was worried for him, but he gritted his teeth and soldiered on. On arrival at St Paul's the Royal Navy gun crew made way for an eight-man bearer party of Grenadier Guardsmen, who hoisted the heavy lead-lined coffin to their shoulders and bore it haltingly up the steps of the cathedral.

The great cathedral was full as the Queen and the Duke of Edinburgh, before representatives of 110 nations, led the nation's homage. To 'Fight the Good Fight' and the stirring anthem 'The Battle Hymn of the Republic' – in deference to the fact that he had been half American by birth – the giant congregation poured out their emotion and their grief. All present sensed they were witnessing the passing of an era as, with finality, the link was severed with the man who had led them through the years of 'blood, toil, tears and sweat' to victory. As the service drew to its close trumpeters, high above in the gallery, sounded the Last Post which reverberated hauntingly under the great dome. Total silence followed as the echoes died away, before a single trumpeter sounded the answering call of Reveille.

The procession re-formed with the coffin once more on the gun-carriage. We marched down Cannon Street to Tower Hill, where sixty massed pipers from Highland regiments played a lament, and the Yeoman of the Guard in their brilliant red and gold tunics – a stark contrast to the Guardsmen in their tall black bearskins and grey-blue greatcoats – stood to attention with their ceremonial pikes. The guns of the Tower of London fired their salute. On reaching the river at Tower Pier, the bearer party placed the coffin on the deck of the Port of London Authority launch,

Havengore. With Grandpapa's flag of Lord Warden of the Cinque Ports, of which he was so proud, fluttering at the bow, and a Union Jack covering the coffin on the quarter-deck, *Havengore* headed up the Thames to Festival Pier, as the pipe bands on shore played 'The Flowers of the Forest'. Sixteen Lightning jets of the Royal Air Force flew overhead to represent the 'Few' who had stood between us and defeat in the Battle of Britain. Dockers manning the cranes at the wharves on the south bank of the river spontaneously lowered their giant booms in silent tribute.

At Waterloo the coffin was placed aboard a Pullman funeral train, and Winston Churchill began his final journey to Bladon, hard by Blenheim Palace where, just over ninety years before, he had been born. I recall that journey as the most moving I have ever made: the train took a route through the south and west of London before joining the old Great Western line towards the country and Oxfordshire. Outside their homes, at the bottom of their gardens or crowded at the level crossings, people of all ages and every walk of life had gathered to see the train pass. Old soldiers, some standing smartly to attention, others who could no longer stand in their wheelchairs, all with row upon row of medals proudly pinned to their chests, saluted in a final tearful farewell to their chief as we passed by. Women and children were gathered round too, many waving Union Jacks.

As we headed out into the country and the train gathered speed, I walked down the corridor and was astonished to come upon, in a nearby compartment, what appeared to be a farmer wearing bright red braces over a loud check shirt. I looked again and realized that it was the Duke of Norfolk who, as Earl Marshal, held responsibility for arranging every detail of that day's solemn tribute. He was cursing the Household Cavalry for the fact that they had taken forty-five seconds longer than they had said they would to make the one-hour journey from Westminster to St Paul's, thereby putting out of kilter his split-second scheduling of the ceremonial. When I remarked upon his strange attire he replied: 'The most important requirement on such an occasion is to be comfortable. The great advantage of being Earl Marshal is that there is no official uniform, therefore I was able to design my own!' The outfit which he had created was a double-breasted tunic that came well below the knee, covering everything beneath it, surmounted by a cocked hat with white feathers. Finally the train, pulled appropriately by a Battle of Britain class steam locomotive named *Sir Winston Churchill*, drew into Long Hanborough station.

From there, the mile-and-a-half route to the small village churchyard of Bladon, which stands within sight of Blenheim, was packed with onlookers. At a brief graveside service attended only by the family and closest friends, we committed him to the earth, surrounded by a mass of wreaths, including one of daffodils from the Queen, bearing the inscription: 'From the nation and from the Commonwealth. In grateful remembrance, Elizabeth R.' We laid him to rest beside his place, near his ancestral home where he had spent much of his childhood and close to the spot where he had proposed to his beloved Clemmie. So often foreigners, especially Americans, have expressed surprise, almost shock, that one so great can lie in a simple country churchyard. Perhaps they have never read Gray's 'Elegy'.

But in the midst of death, there was life. On 22 January, in the Westminster Hospital, Minnie had given birth to our first-born, a boy. Out of deference to family tradition which had alternated the Christian names of Randolph and Winston for four generations, we called him Randolph, after both his grandfather and his great-great-grandfather. For thirty-six hours, as Grandpapa's life ebbed away, the new generation overlapped with the old, like runners in a relay race, passing the torch from one to the other. By a strange quirk of fate the same issue of *The Times*, which devoted its front page to Grandpapa's death, recorded on the back page Randolph's birth. On the final evening of the lying-in-state, I took Minnie, who had overruled the objection of her nurses, to file past the coffin in Westminster Hall. She would not be strong enough to attend the lengthy state funeral the next day. As we passed by in the sombre half-light provided by six large candles around the catafalque, guarded at each corner by four officers of the Household Cavalry, heads bowed, hands resting upon their reversed swords, I silently thanked him for the warmth with which he had welcomed Minnie into the family and the blessing he had given to our marriage.

· XVI ·

Reporting Vietnam

In the autumn of 1965, together with Minnie, I embarked upon my mammoth lecture tour of the United States, which was to take us to forty-seven cities in fifty-six days, and in the course of which we drove 12,000 miles by car. Apart from a two-minute speech at the Oxford Union in which I had defended the Macmillan government's decision to purchase Polaris as Britain's new generation of submarine-based nuclear deterrent, I had never before made a public speech in my life.

In contrast to my father who, from an early age, was bursting with self-confidence and was a natural, indeed brilliant extemporaneous speaker – a gift which even my grandfather did not possess – I was by nature rather shy and reserved. However, with my sights set upon an eventual career in politics, I knew I had to overcome my fear of public speaking and concluded that there was no better way than to plunge in at the deep end.

Some months earlier, following publication of *First Journey* on both sides of the Atlantic, Robert Keedick, a prominent New York lecture agent, proposed that I make a speaking tour on the subject of my African adventures. However, before the ink was even dry upon the contract, Bob Keedick had turned to me and said: 'Say, Mr Churchill, most people here in the States have kind of had Africa. What do you propose as an alternative?' I was somewhat taken aback but, convinced that the agency would be pushing the subject of which I had first-hand experience, I agreed to his suggested alternative: 'The Changing Face of European Politics'.

It was not until our arrival in Boston, on the eve of the tour, when I started leafing through the forty-seven contracts – one for each lecture – waiting for me at our hotel that I discovered to my horror, that, by a margin of two to one, they had chosen 'The Changing Face of European Politics', which I had scarcely prepared. I dashed out to buy whatever books were available locally on the subject of the fledgeling European Community and sat up reading them through the night. Audiences ranged from 1000 elderly ladies some of whom, like the *tricoteuses* at the guillotine during the French Revolution, were merrily clicking away with their knitting needles, to 10,000 Mormon students in the Brigham Young sports arena in Provo, Utah. It proved an unrivalled way of seeing the United States and of overcoming my shyness of public speaking.

In the course of our tour we made a diversion to Washington to attend, at the invitation of President Lyndon Johnson, a White House reception to mark the presentation of an Epstein bust of my grandfather, which had been subscribed by some of his American wartime friends and admirers. Many friends were there for the occasion, including Ambassador David Bruce, Ed Murrow's widow Janet, Kay Halle, who had been the moving spirit behind the award to my grandfather of the US honorary citizenship three years before, and Averell Harriman who made the actual presentation. The President replied and then, without warning, Mrs Johnson called on me to say a few words. This caught me off-guard but fortunately, with half a dozen lectures under my belt, I was able to take it in my stride, even in the presence of the President of the United States – something I could certainly never have done ten days before. At the reception which followed, Mrs Johnson remarked to Kay Halle that I must be looking around to see how things had been changed since the Kennedy days and, moments later, she sought me out to tell me what a superb job she thought Jackie Kennedy had done in redecorating the White House, and to assure me that everything was 95 per cent as she had left it. That evening Minnie and I dined at the Metropolitan Club as the guest of David Bruce and were joined by Kay Halle and Alistair Cooke. David insisted that we try one of the few gastronomic delicacies unique to America, the terrapin – a form of small sea turtle – the like of which we had never had before.

The next morning, before leaving Washington, I had a meeting at the Pentagon with the Secretary of Defense, Robert McNamara, a remarkable and most able man. There are some public figures who seek to impress one with their importance by keeping their visitors waiting in an outer office long beyond the time of their appointment but, in my experience, there is nothing so impressive as those who organize their lives so efficiently that, although extremely busy and important, they stick precisely to their schedule. Arriving at Bob McNamara's office at the appointed hour, I had to wait no more than a minute before being shown into his office – the identical experience that I had had when I had visited him a year or two before in the company of my father. A tall, affable man, he received me in his huge office where his desk, flanked by the Stars and Stripes, was completely clear of paperwork. In the course of a most rewarding half hour he told me of the problems being encountered in Vietnam, where a major build-up of US forces was under way.

Following this meeting, I reported to my father in a letter of 10 October 1965 – my twenty-fifth birthday – that 'it's still invulnerable'. The cryptic reference was to Polaris. The Cuban missile crisis, just three years before, had highlighted the vulnerability of land-based systems and it had become apparent that the reason Khrushchev had been forced to back down was that, at the time, the bombers of the US Strategic Air Command would have been able to destroy the liquid-fuelled Soviet missiles on their launch-pads before they could be loaded with their liquid hydrogen propellant. In consequence of this, the United States and Britain have, ever since, placed special emphasis upon submarine-based systems because of their invulnerability to a pre-emptive strike – the nightmare of US strategists since Pearl Harbor. However, there has always been an anxiety that a technological breakthrough might suddenly render translucent the opaque waters of the deep, enabling hostile satellites to pinpoint the ballistic missile submarines on the ocean bed. Since this matter had become of more than academic interest to Britain following the decision to buy Polaris missiles from the United States and place them on British-built submarines, which were due in service later that decade, the first question that my father would invariably ask McNamara on meeting him was: 'Is it still invulnerable?' In his absence, I always accepted the duty of putting the question on his behalf. Even a quarter of a century on from our first meeting, the answer, Father would be glad to know, remains the same, though this situation is unlikely to endure.

In the same letter to my father I reported to him how invaluable it was having Minnie at my side: 'Thank goodness I have Minnie with me – she does all the work, I just do the talking!'

In my mother's New York home, at the conclusion of my two-month speaking tour, I met Gardener Cowles, the proprietor of *Look* magazine, who asked me if I would travel to Southeast Asia for *Look* to report the Vietnam war, where US forces seemed to be sinking ever deeper into a quagmire. Though Minnie was far from enthusiastic at the prospect, I accepted with alacrity and left for the Far East in mid-January 1966.

I first flew to Singapore to meet Premier Lee Kuan Yew, a staunch friend of the West, and on to Borneo, where I went on patrol through the jungle with forty-two Royal Marine commandos. They were at their forward position at Biawak, on the border of Indonesia, where they had been sent to protect newly independent Malaya from Indonesian incursions.

On the day after my arrival in Saigon, as I walked down Tudeh Street, convinced that I knew nobody in all of South Vietnam, I was amazed to be hailed by a familiar voice from the far side of the street: 'Hi, Winston! What are you doing here?' It turned out to be my friend Johnny Apple, with whom I had worked side by side on the copy desk of the *Wall Street Journal* six years before. By the time of this chance meeting he was working for the *New York Times* and for more than twenty years now he has been known to *Times* readers through his byline of R.W. Apple Jr. 'Come to my place tonight – we're celebrating!' he exclaimed. When I enquired the cause of the celebrations, he turned round and pointed to two distinct holes in the seat of his khaki denims. 'That's what we're celebrating! War Zone D – 0500 hours this morning. The bullet went clean through my pants, but I didn't get so much as a scratch!'

That evening, as the iced lagers were flowing at Johnny's place, I met a friendly and talkative Irish-American Air Force colonel by the name of McGinty, who was the US Air Force information officer at the main Saigon airbase of Tan Son Nhut. During the Second World War, before the United States had entered the conflict, he had volunteered to fly Hurricanes and Spitfires with the RAF, and was clearly quite a character. Having asked how long I was staying, he enquired: 'What are you planning to do during your month in-country?' Knowing that Britain had recently placed an order with the United States for Phantom jets and having, on my way out to the Far East, read a report by a British journalist who had been catapulted off the deck of a US carrier in a Phantom, I replied – without malice aforethought – that what I would most like to do would be to get on a Phantom strike with the US Navy. McGinty rose magnificently to the unintended bait and exploded: 'Hell! Those Navy guys don't know how to fly. If you want to fly – come fly with the Air Force. Call me tomorrow morning at noon and I'll fix you on a strike!'

Not believing that wars were fought in such a way, I suspected that he might have had a beer or two too many and that his offer was no more than Irish blarney. But I was mistaken. Sometimes it seemed that inter-service rivalry between the different elements of the US armed forces in the battle for publicity back home, was in danger of taking precedence over the war against the Viet-Cong and their North Vietnamese allies. If there was to be a report on an airstrike, so far as McGinty was concerned it had better be an Air Force strike. The next morning I was busy obtaining my press credentials and setting up a programme for the coming weeks. As a result I did not get round to calling the Colonel until about 12.30 pm. 'Get your ass the hell out here!' he exclaimed with a New World charm, 'I've got four Super Sabres lined up on the tarmac ready to go. The briefing starts in fifteen minutes.' I did not need asking twice. Hailing the first pedicab (a bicycle-drawn rickshaw) that I could find, I raced out to the airbase behind a fast-pedalling driver, who negotiated his way expertly through the heavy traffic.

An hour later I was wading out on to the tarmac in a US Air Force flight suit, weighed down with a parachute, life jacket, dinghy, G-suit, emergency radio transmitter, strobe flashlight, miniature flare gun, two daggers, survival rations, a jungle survival kit, fishing tackle and water purification tablets. I felt about as ungainly as any medieval knight in armour preparing to enter the lists. Before I climbed into the navigator–

bombardier's seat to the rear, the pilot, Major John Sercel from Cleveland, Ohio, handed me a holster and the butt end of a Colt .45 with the query: 'Mr Churchill, if we are shot down, do you want to try explaining to the VC [Viet-Cong] that you're only an English roundeye rather than an American roundeye? Or would you sooner have this?' Following the drift of his conversation, I accepted the proffered revolver which was loaded but uncocked, fully aware – from my grandfather's experience in the armoured train incident in South Africa during the Boer War, when he had been taken prisoner-of-war – how this might imperil my non-combatant status as a newspaper correspondent. Finally, I donned a helmet and oxygen mask with built-in microphone and earphones and slipped on a pair of black leather flying gloves, before being secured into my ejector seat.

On a thumbs-up signal from a ground engineer, Major Sercel fired up the engine with a cartridge blast. Then, with the other three F-100F Super Sabres at our wingtips, we taxied out to the active runway. Each plane was armed with two tanks of napalm and a pair of 500 lb bombs slung under their wings, as well as 20-mm cannons. Our aircraft, being a twin-seater for training purposes, was considerably heavier and therefore we carried cannons only. Taking our turn behind civilian jet traffic, we lined up in formation on the runway. On being cleared for take-off there was a roar from the lead aircraft, then a flash from its tailpipe as its after burner ignited in a plume of flame and the aircraft began to career down the runway.

We launched at ten-second intervals and soon Silver 21, as our flight was designated, was airborne and heading towards its target near Tuy Hoa (pronounced 'Tooey Wa') on the coast some 300 miles northeast of Saigon. We soon passed through a layer of scattered cloud and climbed in brilliant sunshine to our cruising altitude of 17,000 feet. For the next thirty-five minutes, until we were over Tuy Hoa, we formed part of a round-the-clock 'taxi rank'. Though we were heading towards a relatively low-priority target – some recently dug Viet-Cong trenches and a hut that might be an ammunition dump in the jungle nearby – our flight stood ready with its full war-load to be diverted at an instant's notice to a higher priority target. It was the existence of this airborne 'taxi rank' that gave American commanders in the field, finding themselves under serious enemy fire, the ability to call down from the skies within fifteen minutes hell-fire and damnation.

Some idea of the colossal scale of US air operations in Vietnam at the time may be gained from the fact that our flight of four aircraft was only one out of 125 such strikes each day. If the B-52s, which were making daily sorties from the distant Pacific island of Guam, each carrying forty times the bomb-load of our Super Sabre, are counted in the equation, the formidable strike power carried by our flight represented no more than one two-hundredth of the day's tonnage.

As we cruised in open formation, Major Sercel invited me to take the controls, warning me that it would be more sensitive than any of the light piston aircraft I had previously flown. While this was certainly true of the flight controls, jet engines – as I soon discovered – are in fact much slower to respond to changes in power-setting than the piston engines I had been used to. It was several minutes before I learned not to over-correct. Seeing that we were slipping behind, I applied more power. When we continued to slip back, I gave it a touch more. The next thing I knew we were sailing ahead of the rest of the formation and I had to touch the dive brakes to slow us down. I soon managed to tame the beast, but formation flying in a jet fighter was certainly a novel and exciting experience.

On reaching the coast at Tuy Hoa we made contact with our Forward Air Controller – a lone pilot flying low over the jungle canopy in a small, slow, unarmed, single-engine aircraft known as a Bird-dog because of its duty to 'point' the fighter aircraft on to their targets, enabling strikes to be made with a high degree of accuracy. Each FAC had his own parcel of real estate which he came to know like his own back garden. Targets would be selected on the basis of information received from captured prisoners or village headmen, or from observation. As we made a descending turn over the sea the FAC – whom we could not yet see – steered us towards our target some four miles inland. He then informed us that he was about to 'make smoke'. Some twenty seconds later, just ahead of us, we saw a puff of red smoke which grew rapidly in size. Our target was a building, partly concealed by the jungle, believed to be an ammunition dump, 200 yards due east of the smoke. We made a wide circle before coming in for our bombing run.

The leader peeled into the attack and, one by one, we followed suit. When it came to our turn we made a brisk roll to the left, passing through the vertical so that we were upside down and inclined at about 120 degrees to the horizon. The sky had disappeared under the cockpit of the aircraft. The altimeter began to unwind rapidly and the airspeed indicator spun round to about 450 knots. At this point there was a buffeting and a roar as Major Sercel deployed the dive brakes to hold us at that speed. The ground was rushing up towards us at a terrific rate and, suddenly, I saw two fireballs left by the first pair of aircraft in the jungle ahead. All at once he rolled us level with the ground as we came into the target close behind the third aircraft as it made its strike. Within seconds of the canister from the aircraft in front hitting the ground, the jungle was enveloped in an inferno. At the same instant, I felt myself being pushed down deep into my seat as we pulled out of the dive. As we circled, the FAC reported that we had been off target and gave us new instructions for our second run. This time we appeared to hit something for there was a sudden burst of flame among the trees and a fireball rose to 100 feet or more and continued to burn for a good minute and a half. The FAC, with satisfaction, reported the structure destroyed and next directed our attention to a nearby hill on the crest of which was a triangular network of trenches on which we dropped our 500-pounders.

Thus far Major Sercel had not opened fire, but now we all went in for our strafing runs with the 20-mm cannon. Flicking the stick to the left he rolled us abruptly on our side and we began hurtling towards the ground yet again. We were going faster this time, perhaps 480 knots (550 mph); there was a shudder and a roar as the dive brakes came out, the wings snapped level with the horizon and, suddenly, the trenches were immediately ahead of us. There was a deep growl from the machine guns and the bullets exploded in clusters of white stars in the network of trenches immediately ahead of us. When we were no more than 100 feet above the target, Major Sercel pulled back sharply on the stick. I felt that I was about to fall through the bottom of the aircraft, so intense was the pressure. Suddenly I felt my calves, thighs and stomach being squeezed in a vice-like grip. I looked down and saw that my pressure suit had inflated automatically, making me look like a Michelin man, so as to prevent the blood draining from my head and a consequent blackout, as we pulled seven or eight times the force of gravity coming out of the dive. With a quick half roll to the right and another to the left to avoid any ground fire, we climbed vertically at full power before making a tight circle and repeating the procedure in a second strafing run. As we climbed on course for home, we made a climbing barrel roll and Major Sercel handed me the controls once again. He let me fly the aircraft all the way back to base up to the point of our wingtip-to-wingtip formation landing at Tan Son Nhut.

Following meetings with the South Vietnamese Foreign Minister, Trang van Do, who was forceful in urging the US bombing of the North Vietnamese cities of Hanoi and Haiphong, as well as with President Johnson's representative, Ambassador Cabot Lodge, a diffident man who seemed reluctant to exert the authority vested in him, I flew south by US Army helicopter to Can Tho, the capital of the Mekong Delta region, where half the population of South Vietnam live and which was known as the rice bowl of Southeast Asia. The Delta consists of a rich, fertile plain rarely more than ten feet above sea level and intersected on every side by branches of the river and irrigation canals. The houses, standing for the most part on bamboo stilts with palm-leaf roofs and sides, lay stretched out along the banks of the canals.

Before leaving London I had taken the precaution of visiting Field Marshal Sir Gerald Templar who, in the 1950s, had successfully masterminded Britain's victory over Communist insurgency in the jungles of Malaya. One of the key features of his strategy involved moving all civilians into protected villages, where they would no longer be exposed to terrorist intimidation, while relentlessly pursuing those who remained in the jungle.

But it required only a glance at the Delta to realize that the strategies that had worked so well in the dense jungles of Malaya could not so readily be applied in this very different and open terrain. In the Delta of Vietnam the overwhelming majority of the population lived stretched out along the water's edge close to their rice paddies, which provided their sole means of economic and physical survival. Nearby lay their ancestors, whom they worshipped. As a result, they resisted most attempts to force them together into villages, which was the only way to afford them protection.

Another clear distinction between the conflicts in Vietnam and Malaya was that, in the latter, the enemy was a readily identified minority of Communist Chinese, entirely different in colour, facial characteristics and clothing from the majority of Malays. In Vietnam there was no such ready distinction that could be made and a patrol of GIs passing through a village had no means of knowing if the twelve-year-old raising his arm was waving or preparing to throw a hand grenade. In the circumstances it proved virtually impossible, outside the main centres of population, for the Americans and their South Vietnamese allies to provide effective security to the local population which, by night, was dominated by the Viet-Cong.

It is easy for those who were never there and who look back with the benefit of hindsight on the Vietnam saga and the humiliating circumstances of the subsequent United States withdrawal, to jump to the conclusion that the great majority of the Vietnamese population were against the Americans and on the side of the Communists: but this would be a facile and incorrect judgement. The Viet-Cong were never more than a sizable minority – but a ruthless and determined one – willing to use all the weapons of intimidation, terror and murder against their fellow countrymen, and prepared to suffer massive casualties in their struggle.

Before leaving for the Delta I had paid a visit to Saigon's thriving black market and, for just $17, I had been able to kit myself up with jungle-green denim trousers and shirt, cap, socks, belt, water bottle, backpack and a pair of boots. The latter were secondhand and I did not enquire what had become of their owner. In the Delta security was the responsibility of the South Vietnamese Army, with the Americans only providing advisers and helicopter transport, together with a Special Forces contingent along the Cambodian border, which was used by the Viet-Cong as an infiltration route from North Vietnam by way of Laos. In Can Tho, the main town of the Delta, I received briefings from US public information officials which, though I was assured they were identical to the ones given to visiting Congressmen, I found absurdly optimistic in their estimates of the percentage of territory and population controlled by the South Vietnamese government. As I recorded in my diary at the time: 'The major towns and many of the villages are relatively secure, as is Saigon, but anywhere else one can encounter the VC at anything up to battalion strength.' Many areas which were listed by the Americans as secure, were indeed relatively so by day but, by night, they would be swarming with Viet-Cong, leaving the civilian population with the difficult and often dangerous task of keeping their fences mended with both masters.

The suffering of the civilian population in the conflict was terrible. Areas of the country that were not designated as having been 'pacified' were declared 'free bomb zones' where pilots and ground forces were free to engage any 'target of opportunity' with little regard for the consequences to the civilian population. In fairness, it must be said that it was almost impossible to distinguish the Viet-Cong from the rest of the population as they all wore black pyjamas, unlike the distinctive uniform of the regular North Vietnamese battalions. Nonetheless many of the young American conscript soldiers and their South Vietnamese counterparts, who sought to emulate them, were trigger-happy and far too ready to call down artillery fire or airstrikes, in the event that their patrol came under even light rifle-fire from a village. Within fifteen minutes, the entire village was liable to be wiped off the face of the earth. This basic inability to differentiate between civilians and the enemy, combined with an often indiscriminate application of military power, had the effect of relentlessly pushing the civilian population into the arms of the Viet-Cong.

In Can Tho I asked to visit the local hospital where I was horrified to discover that civilian casualties were coming in at the rate of thirty or forty a week, many more than the number of military casualties. Among the casualties I was shown by Dr Kinh Hong Hanh, who acted as my interpreter, was a young woman, the wife of a South Vietnamese Army officer, who had been hit in the stomach by shrapnel from a Viet-Cong mortar bomb. In spite of my protests Dr Hahn insisted on ripping back the dressing to show me the horrific wound. I was appalled by the conditions that I found in the hospital and recorded my impressions in my diary immediately following the visit:

The mattresses were stained with blood and urine – there was no bed linen, only a thin blanket on which they lay and a cover over them ... The US Army has put in a team of military surgeons and the operating theatre seemed adequate – such as I saw of it through the half open door: there was a middle-aged Vietnamese man lying naked on the table and the operation was about to begin.

It seemed incredible to me that the United States was pumping so many millions of dollars into the country, including civilian aid, and yet that such conditions of squalor could exist in one of the country's main regional hospitals. I was bitter at what I saw and wrote in my diary:

One would have thought that hospital beds, mattresses, bed linen and blankets would have been given priority in any aid-giving programme. And why is there only one non-Vietnamese nurse (American)? Why don't any of the great ladies of America organize something – just as Jennie Jerome helped organize and raise funds for a hospital ship at the time of the Boer War? And what about the Red Cross in England and the other countries in Europe?

The South Vietnamese, in addition to their regular army, had Regional Forces, equivalent to Britain's Territorial Army or the US National Guard, and, at the lowest level, Popular Forces, akin to a Home Guard, who had responsibility for defending only their own villages. Through General Kwang, military commander of the Vietnamese Fourth Corps area as well as regional civilian governor, I arranged to visit the village of Bac Lieu. This was in a part of the Delta designated by the Americans as a 'two-ship' area, meaning that we would have to travel with two helicopter gunships because of the precarious security situation. In Bac Lieu, a tiny village surrounded by waterways and paddy fields, I found nearly 1000 refugees from a Catholic community some ten miles to the north, called Nang Reng, where they had been under relentless Viet-Cong attack for six months. Twenty-three of their houses and much of the rice they had just harvested had been destroyed by enemy fire. Sixty of the men of the village, all members of the Popular Forces, had retreated behind a stockade around their church, determined to stand and fight whatever the cost. But the rest of the community, including the women and children, had recently been moved to the relative safety of Bac Lieu.

So impressed was I by the determined spirit of the villages that I insisted on visiting the village from which they had been evacuated. As we came in to land at Nang Reng, I could see the Viet-Cong in trenches no more than three or four hundred yards from the village. Our helicopters scarcely stopped long enough in the hover for us to jump out, before they were airborne again. In addition to the remaining villagers, eighty members of the Regional Forces had recently been drafted in to help in the defence of the village, which came under attack almost every night. From the heavily damaged church tower, I was able quite distinctly to see the Viet-Cong forces a mere rifle's shot away. I could not help but admire the courage and tenacity with which these simple people, armed with a rudimentary assortment of weapons and without a single American to help them, were fighting to defend their homes and families. It certainly gave the lie to those who claimed that this was a purely American war.

From the Delta I flew by a C-130 Hercules to Da Nang in the very north of the country, close to the border of North Vietnam. Though Da Nang was then held by 26,000 US Marines, the Viet-Cong would come right up to the perimeter of their base at night and, just the night before my arrival, had nearly overrun an artillery position only six miles south of the town. At the vast American airbase, I discovered that the information officer was Colonel Coverley, whom Minnie and I had met three months before when we had visited NORAD and the US Air Force Academy in Colorado Springs in the course of my US lecture tour. I had still not got my Phantom strike and thought I would try my luck once again. To my amazement, this also was arranged. The Phantoms at Da Nang operated almost exclusively on what were termed 'out-of-country' missions, over North Vietnam. Because of the significant numbers of surface-to-air missiles, heavy anti-aircraft fire and the very great difficulties of recovering downed pilots from the north, journalists were forbidden to go on such missions. Nothing daunted, an in-country mission was set up, using an F-4C Phantom and two B-57s (the US designation for the British-built Canberra medium bomber). Having been kitted up as before with pressure suit, survival kit, parachute, dinghy, life-jacket and assorted gear, I was briefed on our mission by Lt Col. Pasqualicchio – 'Call me Pancho for short!' – a dark, lean, distinguished-looking fellow with a well-trimmed moustache, who commanded the US 480th Tactical Fighter Squadron.

I climbed into the rear seat of the Phantom, where, before take-off, I was given a full hour's briefing on the aircraft's controls and systems. The aircraft was equipped with four Sparrow air-to-air missiles which could only be fired from the navigator–bombardier's seat, which I was to occupy. Since we were so close to the North Vietnamese border and there was a danger that we might be engaged by North Vietnamese MiGs, I was given a detailed briefing on how to bracket a target on the radar so as to achieve 'lock-on', as well as instructions for the arming and firing of the missiles. In addition to our defensive missiles we carried on underwing pylons four pods, each containing sixteen rockets with high-explosive incendiary warheads, as well as an enormous cigar-shaped pod under the belly of the aircraft, known as 'the pistol' – a Gatling gun capable of firing 1200 rounds in the space of twelve seconds. Though the Phantom could fly at Mach 2, or twice the speed of sound, the vast array of weaponry that we carried restricted our speed to Mach .82 or 600 mph. In the event that we were engaged by North Vietnamese MiG-21s we would instantly jettison all the 'garbage', as the Colonel described our external war-load, so as to recover the full speed and manoeuvrability of the aircraft for a dog-fight.

Once our weapons had been armed, we taxied for take-off behind some Marine Crusaders and South Vietnamese F-5s, in company with the two B-57s that were to come with us. On this occasion I had a vivid demonstration of the way the taxi-rank concept for the deployment of air power was used by the Americans in Vietnam. No sooner were we airborne and climbing on track towards our destination than we were switched to a different target. Five minutes later we were reassigned to a third, even higher priority, target. This turned out to be a point on the Ia Drang River, just three miles from the Cambodian border, where a US Special Forces unit found themselves engaged in a 'fire-fight' with a sizable force of Viet-Cong on the far side of the river.

The Forward Air Controller met us over the target area and pinpointed where he wanted us to drop our munitions on the east side of the river. The two B-57s made a shallow dive into the target and we followed close behind. They seemed to make little impression on the dense jungle with their 750-lb bombs but, as we reached about 2000 feet, we fired one of our rocket pods, followed moments later by a second one – making a salvo of thirty-two rockets. We pulled 6.5 times the force of gravity as we came out of the dive and, as we made a steep left-hand turn, we could see the jungle in flames for 100 yards or more along the bank of the river. We came round for a second pass with our bombs and rockets. Finally we made four or five run-ins with our Gatling gun, which growled fiercely as we let fly two or three bursts on each pass, each time making a quick bank to left and to right, as we climbed away, so as to avoid the enemy ground fire which had been reported by the FAC. As we set course back to Da Nang we could see a pall of smoke rising from the smouldering jungle we left behind us. A couple of days later, when I visited the Special Forces base at Pleiku in the central highlands of Vietnam, I discovered that we had in fact killed no one in the strike but that it had had the desired effect of persuading the Viet-Cong to break off the action and make a tactical withdrawal. Shortly before we were due to touch down at Da Nang, Col. 'Pancho', who had let me fly the plane all the way to and from the target area, exclaimed: 'I don't think I've shown you how this bird performs!' We were at the time descending through 1500 feet on final approach to the runway, when he thrust throttles abruptly forward and pulled back sharply on the stick, cocking the Phantom on its rear end, almost vertical to the ground. At the same instant the two after burners kicked in and, with an incredible surge of power, we shot up through the clouds into the brilliant sunshine above, making climbing barrel rolls as we went. Within seconds we were at 22,000 feet: two minutes later we were on the ground.

My two air combat missions and a subsequent two-hour flight low over the jungle canopy at no more than 80 or 100 mph with a Forward Air Controller in his 'Bird-dog', gave me a first-hand insight into the lives and attitudes of fighter-bomber pilots in combat. Unlike troops on the ground the pilot is, to a large degree, divorced from the realities and discomforts of war. Hurtling through the sky at hundreds of miles per hour with incredible power at his fingertips and the ability, at the touch of a button, to decide the fate of hundreds of his fellow mortals, he can easily come to feel like a god of Greek mythology, unleashing deadly thunderbolts from the sky. As one dives towards the target at nearly 600 mph, it is difficult to appreciate that the black ant-like creatures scrambling for cover below are in fact human beings – each someone's son, husband, father or brother. Unless unlucky enough to be shot down by a missile or by ground fire – as indeed all too many were, especially over the North – one is back at base within an hour or two in a totally secure environment far removed from the squalor and hardship of the battlefield, sipping an ice-cold lager. It is a form of warfare which can readily lead to insensitivity and callousness.

As one who has on half a dozen occasions flown in fast military combat aircraft and felt totally exhilarated by the experience, I count it a salutary antidote that, three years later, while reporting the Nigerian civil war from Biafra, I found myself on the receiving end when a Russian-made Tupolev bomber of the Nigerian Air Force opened its bomb-bay almost directly over my head, dumping its weapon-load just a quarter of a mile away on what turned out to be a clinic for nursing mothers and their babies. Under such circumstances one is liable to get a more jaundiced – possibly truer – view of air power. It becomes easy to understand how simple people, who find themselves defenceless in the face of such awesome destructive power, have before now, when a plane has been brought down, literally torn the pilot limb from limb in expiation of their pent-up rage and hatred, 'a fate that has undoubtedly befallen several Israeli pilots shot down over Arab lands'.

There can be few experiences more memorable than to be aboard a large aircraft carrier engaged in combat operations, and I count myself fortunate to have had the chance of spending twenty-four hours aboard the USS *Ranger*, positioned on Yankee Station in the Gulf of Tonkin, opposite the coast of North Vietnam. *Ranger* was one of two carriers on Yankee Station at the time, each taking it in turn to operate for twelve hours nonstop. As I touched down on the deck of *Ranger*, our aircraft was brought to an abrupt halt by one of four arrester wires stretched across the deck. I arrived on board just in time for the start of *Ranger*'s twelve-hour operational cycle, due to start at noon. At midday sharp, a flight of Phantom F-4Bs, A-1 and A-4 fighter-bombers, a Vigilante photo-reconnaissance aircraft, an E-2 Hawkeye with early-warning radar and a couple of tanker aircraft were catapulted off the deck at 22.5-second intervals. One and a half hours later, a second wave of aircraft, almost identical in composition to the first, was shot off the carrier and, fifteen minutes after that, the first wave returned to be refuelled and re-armed, before being launched once again against the enemy. This routine was to continue until midnight when the other carrier, the USS *Hancock*, took over. I spent much of the time on the flight deck with the launch crews, who provided me with a helmet equipped with goggles and ear-pads against the deafening combination of the thunder of the steam catapults at launch and the high-pitched scream of jet engines at full power.

There is an especially generous streak in the American character which makes them eager to acknowledge their gratitude to others. I found this especially noticeable in Vietnam. On shore the Americans spoke unhesitatingly of their Australian allies as 'the finest jungle troops in Vietnam'. Aboard *Ranger* they made clear to me that the effectiveness and efficiency of their operation was largely due to three British inventions: the steam catapult, the angled flight deck and the mirrored light approach aid. I reflected with sadness on the decision of the British government of the day to build no more attack carriers – a decision that nearly led to disaster in the 1982 Falklands conflict, as it meant that Britain was unable to deploy either supersonic fighters or airborne early-warning aircraft to the South Atlantic.

But in spite of the immense power deployed in Southeast Asia by the United States and epitomized by the USS *Ranger* with its 5000-strong crew, the Americans by no means had it all their own way and the toll of human lives on both sides was relentless. During my brief time aboard *Ranger* two aircraft failed to return. One, an F-4 Phantom, disappeared at low altitude into a fog bank from which it never emerged; the other, an A-4, had been shot down close to the coast where the pilot had been picked up and taken prisoner by North Vietnamese in sampans before one of *Ranger*'s helicopters, which came under intense fire, could reach him. Many of those captured pilots were never to return and I found myself lost for words of comfort when, later that same evening, I was introduced to the captured pilot's brother, who also happened to be serving aboard *Ranger*.

Ground forces too were taking a heavy toll. When I visited the 1st Air Cavalry Division at An Khe and Bong Son, where they were engaged in the sixth week of Operation Mastiff, I was told that they had lost some 280 men in that one operation. Likewise, the US Marines whose base I had visited at Chu Lai had, in the previous week, lost over 100 'KIA', the jargon for those killed in action. The bodies were shipped home by way of Da Nang and Saigon in plastic body-bags to contain the terrible stench, due to the heat and the fact that there were no refrigeration facilities until they arrived in Saigon after three or four days. Though, in the same operation, the Marines claimed, by body count, to have killed 298 Viet-Cong – a 'kill ratio' of three to one in favour of the Americans – this was small consolation to those who had lost their friends, let alone the widows or children condemned never to know their fathers. It was abundantly clear to me that this was no longer the 'peanuts' war, as the hawks in Washington were continuing to claim.

On my return to Saigon from the north of the country, I discovered that the buzz among the Saigon-based international press corps was that a major operation, involving the US 173rd Airborne Division and a battalion of the Royal Australian Regiment, was getting under way that evening in War Zone D. Security at the time was next to nonexistent. Saigon's bar girls, many of whom had brothers or boyfriends among the Viet-Cong, knew of operations twenty-four or even forty-eight hours in advance. Many operations were compromised in this way, severely undermining their effectiveness and undoubtedly putting at risk US and Allied lives. When I asked the Australian ambassador if he would arrange for me to accompany the RAR on their search and destroy operation in War Zone D the following morning, he was aghast that I knew of it, and said that he could neither confirm nor deny the fact and was therefore unable to help me in my quest to join the RAR in the field. Undeterred, I went out to the nearby airbase of Bien Hoa, from where the operation was being supported. By going from helicopter to helicopter as they were about to take off – many, to my amazement, loaded with cases of ice-cold lager, clearly an essential war supply for American forces in the field – it did not take me long to find one going to the RAR on which I was able to hitch a lift.

My arrival late in the day was not particularly appreciated by the Australian colonel, who made no effort to conceal his distaste for the press. However, he agreed to let me stay and placed me in the hands of a major called Ken, who was in charge of press relations. So determined had I been not to miss out on the operation, that I had arrived without either rations or a sleeping bag – a sure way to make oneself unpopular in the field! But Ken managed to find me a spare bag, and he and a young corporal most generously shared their rations with me that evening.

As we were in close contact with the enemy, we were all instructed to 'dig in'. I took it in turns with the others to wield a pick and a trenching tool but the ground, which was hard and rocky, stubbornly resisted our efforts in spite of the perspiration pouring from us in the 100-degree heat and high humidity. By the time the sun was setting, our trench had got down to a depth of about three feet, whereupon a senior officer arrived on the scene, complimented us on our trench, and promptly announced in his Australian drawl: 'That will make a nice hole for one of my machine-gunners!' There were now four of us to share our inadequate trench and, during the alarms and excursions of the night – which were many, with mortar bombs landing on our camp and the whine of machine-gun fire ripping through the jungle trees around us – we would all dive into the trench. Invariably I would be on top of the pile and it did not take me long to conclude that I was closer to the ground staying in my sleeping bag, than in a heap on top of my three Aussie companions.

After a lively night in which our side had put out a lot of artillery, mortar and machine-gun fire, all fell silent as dawn broke. Suddenly, in the clear blue sky above, something silver caught my eye. Looking more closely I saw that there were a dozen vast aircraft at a great altitude above us – clearly the B-52s from the Pacific island of Guam. It turned out that their target was an extensive underground complex of tunnels and bunkers built by the Viet-Cong, who would regularly disappear into these intricate warrens with an entire division of troops, to the bewilderment and frustration of their US pursuers. Several minutes later, though their target was five miles from where I stood, the ground shook beneath our feet and leaves blew off the trees as more than 500 tons of bombs cascaded from the B-52s in a single pass before they set course for their island base 5000 miles away.

No visitor to Vietnam at the time could fail to be impressed by the incredible power, especially air power, deployed to Southeast Asia by the

United States. However, the overwhelming impression with which I left Vietnam was that the battle for the hearts and minds of the population – the key factor in achieving long-term success in Malaya, as Field Marshal Templer had explained to me – was being lost, despite the considerable pacification programme which the US was conducting in the villages of the Delta. But it is self-evident that, at the end of the day, you cannot bomb the husbands, sons and brothers of people by day and pursue their sisters, daughters and girlfriends by night, and still expect to be loved.

The evening of the same day that I had left the RAR in War Zone D, I arrived in Hong Kong. I checked into the Mandarin Hotel and, as I arrived for a late meal at the rooftop restaurant, I could not believe the sight that greeted me. There, lined up around the pool (which, at the time, was open air), was a band of the Brigade of Guards in full dress uniform, surrounded by the governor and ladies of the British Empire wearing their tiaras and finery. As I stepped out of the lift the band struck up with 'Rule Britannia'! It seemed so far removed from the mud and squalor of War Zone D that I thought I had arrived on another planet.

· XVII ·

Six Days that Shook the World

In mid-May of 1967 I rented a single-engine plane and flew up to East Bergholt to spend a couple of days with my father, who had not been well. Over dinner the conversation turned to world affairs. All at once Father remarked: 'It seems to me that the situation in the Middle East is warming up. Winston, why don't you go and visit our friends in Israel – so far you have only seen the situation from the Arab side?' Like many young men of my age – I was twenty-six at the time – I was reluctant to accept parental guidance and ever ready to assert an independent view. Far from accepting my father's suggestion, I disputed it. However, revolving the situation in my mind during the night, I concluded that Father was probably right. By the time he awoke, I had already booked myself to Tel Aviv on an El Al flight leaving London at 1 pm that day. I had called *The Times* to ask if they would be interested in having some articles from me on the Middle East, only to learn that they had, that very morning, sent their defence correspondent, Charles Douglas-Home, on an early flight to Israel.

Having drawn a blank at the quality end of the market, I decided to try the mass circulation end instead. I telephoned the *News of the World*, which at the time enjoyed a circulation of over six million and had a claimed readership of twenty million, and for which I had recently written a series of articles on the rise of the neo-Nazis in West Germany. I suspected that the paper's editor, Stafford Summerfield, had not been best pleased with my assertion that the neo-Nazis were unlikely to gain the 5 per cent of popular support required in order to secure political representation in the Bundestag, the Federal German parliament – a forecast which, happily, has stood the test of time. Before leaving for Germany, Mr Summerfield had left me in no doubt as to his, and the newspaper's, attitude – which were one and the same – towards Nazis and Germans, between which he evidently found it difficult to make any distinction. In a scene worthy of Lord Copper addressing his would-be war correspondent, Boot, in Evelyn Waugh's brilliant novel *Scoop*, Mr Summerfield, seated at one end of the long boardroom table and peering at me through his thick bifocals, had growled in tones of strongest condemnation: 'You must understand, Mr Churchill, that the *News of the World* disapproves of all this neo-Nazism!' Having failed to bring back reports confirming his view that most Germans were Nazi, I was not sure that Mr Summerfield would wish to avail himself of my services for reports from the Middle East, but I thought it worth a try.

I left a message for Mr Summerfield, who was not yet in the office, to the effect that I presumed they already had a correspondent in the Middle East to cover the situation but, in the event that they did not and he wished me to represent them, he could leave word with El Al at Heathrow before 1 pm. Meanwhile I bade farewell to my slightly amazed father, leaped into the single-engine Piper Super Cub which I had rented the day before, and flew it back to Redhill, where Minnie met me with a passport and packed suitcase and we raced from there to London Airport. Though we did not arrive until the scheduled departure time, El Al had held the flight and there was a message from Mr Summerfield commissioning me to write a series of three articles for them on the Middle East situation.

Father had given me but a single contact in Israel, a friend of his from Eighth Army days in North Africa, Eliav Simon, who was the Tel Aviv correspondent of United Press International. Though by the time I reached Israel the hour was already late, Eliav immediately invited me round to his apartment, which doubled for an office and contained a battery of more than half a dozen teleprinters, one or more of which would suddenly spring to life with urgent noisy chatter from around the world. I explained to him that I knew no one in Israel, had never been there before and had to file my first story assessing the situation within thirty-six hours.

'Who should I see?' I enquired.

He scribbled a number on a piece of paper saying: 'Call that number, Boss' – a term of endearment he has used ever since.

'Who is it?' I enquired.

'Moshe Dayan,' he replied. The name conjured up the familiar black eyepatch and the hero of Israel's Sinai campaign of 1956, but little else.

I looked at my watch and saw that it was already well past midnight. 'I can't call him this late,' I protested. 'He will be asleep.'

'It's the only time of day you'll catch him in – call him,' he said with insistence.

A very sleepy Moshe Dayan answered the telephone, doing something of a double-take when I tried to explain who was calling. Then in an instant he declared: 'I'll be at your hotel at 7 am and we'll breakfast together!'

He was as good as his word and it turned out to be just one of half a dozen meetings we were to have over the next few weeks, in the course of which we became firm friends. Dayan, at the time a civilian once again, was still two weeks away from being appointed Minister of Defence. The Middle East was plunging headlong into crisis, as Father had foreseen it would.

Dayan was Israel's hero, his career a matter of national pride. Born in Palestine in 1915, he had joined the Haganah (the Jewish underground defence organization) at the age of fourteen and in 1939 had been jailed by the British during the period of the British Mandate for his underground activities. Released after serving only a year of his ten-year sentence, he had joined the British Army. In the course of the Second World War he participated in a commando raid against the Vichy French forces in Syria, as a result of which he lost his left eye and acquired the eyepatch which was to become his trademark. In Israel's War of Independence of 1948 he fought as commander of a jeep commando battalion; but it was as Chief of Staff during the victorious Sinai Campaign of 1956 that Dayan won international fame and became a symbol of Israeli patriotism. In 1960 he was elected a member of the Knesset, Israel's parliament, and appointed Minister of Agriculture by Israel's first and great Prime Minister, David Ben Gurion. When Ben Gurion, no longer Prime Minister, seceded in June 1965 from the ruling Mapai party of Levi Eshkol to form the small but influential Rafi group, Dayan had followed him.

Dayan, who was instantly recognized by all Israelis and revered by the great majority, had a ready smile and an engagingly friendly manner. Even when discussing matters of moment, his quick sense of humour was never far away. His black pirate-like eyepatch, far from giving him a sinister appearance, served merely to emphasize his dashing good looks. I had the good fortune to get to know him at a time when he was out of office and had not yet been appointed Minister of Defence. He was therefore able to spare me much more of his time and was prepared to allow his thoughts on the situation and his assessment of the personalities involved much freer rein than could ever have been the case just a fortnight later when he was charged with the awesome responsibility of safeguarding Israel's security – indeed survival – in the face of a relentless military build-up by seemingly overwhelming Arab forces on all of Israel's borders.

In my first article for the *News of the World*, carried as a front-page banner lead, I reported that Israel's citizen army was mobilizing, in response to the large-scale concentration of Egyptian military forces in the Sinai Desert facing Israel's southern border. I had made my base at the newly built Tel Aviv Hilton – to the disapproval of my father who invariably stayed at the Dan, from where he had reported the Suez crisis and Sinai campaign of 1956. The disappearance, overnight, of the hotel staff had been most noticeable. The hall porter, the reception clerk, the bellboy had, one by one, gone off to serve their country. I had no doubt where responsibility for the crisis lay, reporting in the *News of the World* of 21 May: 'The situation is entirely of Nasser's creation – backed to an indeterminate extent by the Soviet Union ... The ignominious demise of the United Nations emergency force, when the UN flag was lowered at 1600 hours yesterday, not only puts another nail in the coffin of the world organization but also leaves a highly dangerous situation in the Middle East.'

The abrupt removal of the 3400-man UN force, in response to Nasser's demand, was a devastating blow to the stability and peace of the region. Their place was promptly taken by Egyptian troops who also took control of Sharm-El-Sheikh, the promontory dominating the Tiran Straits, through which had to pass all of Israel's shipping – including vital Persian Gulf oil supplies – to its only non-Mediterranean port of Eilat. I reported: 'It seems likely that Israel would regard closure of the Tiran Straits as an act of war: equally it is difficult to see how Nasser, the victim of his own propaganda, can afford to stand by and watch Israeli ships passing by under the barrels of his guns,' and added the prediction that 'Sharm-El-Sheikh could well be the flash point of a grisly explosion in the Middle East.' So indeed it was to prove.

Dawn on the morning of Monday, 22 May, found me in the company of Israel's former prime minister, David Ben Gurion, in his suite at the King David Hotel in Jerusalem. He had invited me to come and see him at 6.45 am in his room, which enjoyed a superb view over the Old City and East Jerusalem which was, at the time, under Jordanian control. The panorama of minarets, domes and spires, bathed in the brilliant pink glow of dawn beneath an azure sky, was breathtaking. The muezzin, from their lofty perches, were calling Allah's faithful to prayer and the bells of a dozen churches rang out across the city towards the Temple Mount and the garden of Gethsemane. Ben Gurion, who, following the creation of the State of Israel in 1948, had become her first Prime Minister and Minister of Defence, remained the acknowledged leader of the hawks on the Israeli political scene, though he no longer held ministerial office. He was regarded as Israel's Churchill, standing in fierce opposition to the Prime Minister, Levi Eshkol, whose appeasement policies cast him in the Chamberlain mould.

The old man, short and stocky with a powerful physique which belied his years, a wild white mane of hair and quick penetrating eyes, received me with great courtesy. As we drank tea together he told me of his high regard for my grandfather and their friendship over many years. All at once he glanced at his watch and, seeing that it was coming up to 7 am, told his bodyguard to turn on the radio news.

Seconds later the dramatic announcement came over his small radio set that Nasser had closed the Straits of Tiran. He motioned with his hand for the radio to be turned off. He was visibly shaken, but not surprised, by the news. He shook his head gravely and declared: 'This means war!' There then followed a lengthy silence before, with deep emotion in his voice, he went on: 'I am very frightened! Not for Israel – she will survive – but for the youth of our country. It is always the finest of their generation who never return.' He went on to expound his unequivocal conviction – as assured as had been my grandfather's in 1940 – that, come what may, Israel would survive. 'For the Arabs, what is military defeat?' he mused, before answering his own rhetorical question: 'It is the loss of an army. In ten years they will have another. But Israel can never afford to be defeated. Defeat for us would be the end – the end of everything, the end of our homes, our families, the end of the Jewish state, the end of the dreams of centuries. That is why we shall never be defeated!' His prediction proved all too true, except that the Egyptian Army, rebuilt with the assistance of the Soviet Union, was to be launched against Israel once again within just six years on Yom Kippur, the Day of Atonement, 1973.

Taking me by the forearm, the old man led me out on to the balcony where Jerusalem the Golden lay before us, and proceeded to give me a lesson in Jewish history which, seen through his mind's eye, stretched out in a seamless panoply of time. 'This,' he declared with a gesture, 'is the city of David – Jewish for 3000 years. But travel a few miles down that road,' pointing the way with his finger as he spoke. 'There you will find Hebron, the city of Abraham – 4000 years Jewish!' It was a moving and magical moment. As we parted I could see his eyes were moist at the prospect of the enormous casualties, both military and civilian, which he was convinced would be suffered in defending their homeland – a homeland to which they had so recently returned after being separated from it for nineteen centuries of diaspora following the sacking of the Temple by the Roman Emperor Titus in AD 70. Ben Gurion was the embodiment of the Israeli people's determination never again to be parted from their homeland. They would defend it whatever the cost.

Throughout the following week pressure mounted in Israel for the recall of the former Chief of Staff, Moshe Dayan, in the role of Minister of Defence, to take command of the military situation as the crisis deepened. Dayan was spending an increasing amount of time visiting the troops, all fully mobilized and at their battle stations. His progressive change from civilian to military dress was most noticeable. He began the week in civilian clothes, then he appeared in khaki but without any insignia of rank but, before the week was out, the transformation was complete and he was dressed in his uniform of general. Wherever he went he was acclaimed by the soldiers, one of whom remarked to me: 'Dayan, with his one eye, sees more than most people with two.'

With Nasser's boast on 27 May that 'We will destroy Israel', there were few left in Israel who believed that the path of appeasement could lead to anything other than disaster. Conviction was mounting that unless the Arab armies miraculously withdrew – something which appeared increasingly unlikely – Israel would have no choice but to go to war regardless of whether or not she was herself attacked. The fact that the overwhelming majority of Israel's armed forces were civilian reservists made it impossible for Israel to keep her forces mobilized on an indefinite basis, while business and industry ran down and the crops stood unharvested in the fields. Nor could she afford to demobilize while an Egyptian army of 100,000 men and 1000 tanks stood poised on her southern borders in Sinai and while Jordan, Syria and Iraq were pouring in armour and artillery along her eastern and northern borders.

That weekend I reported to the readers of the *News of the World* from the Negev desert, South of Beersheba:

The army of Israel is coiled like a tightly wound spring awaiting the moment of release. Here, amid the dunes and scrub of the desert, the tension is as oppressive as the heat. There is an eerie silence in the air. Nothing moves except a lizard or chameleon scurrying across the road to the sand where his natural camouflage makes him as invisible as the Israeli armour.

This is in direct contrast to the activity a week ago when the roads in this area were alive with armour on the move, interspersed here and there with bus loads of little old ladies of the American-Jewish Congress who had come to visit the Holy Land. There is now little sign of military activity – the troops are at their battle stations; the armour is deployed and heavily camouflaged waiting for the word 'go' ...

While the military, snug in their foxholes and sure in the knowledge of their own capabilities, exuded self-confidence, the same was not true of the civilian population. They, understandably, had become increasingly alarmed as, listening anxiously to their radios throughout the day and much of the night, they heard the blood-curdling threats being issued by Nasser and by Yasser Arafat of the PLO, declaring that the hour had come when the Jewish people would be put to the sword. For them it brought flooding back in their full horror the taunts and threats of the Nazis, before six million of their immediate relations and coreligionists had been herded into the gas chambers of Nazi Germany.

It is impossible adequately to describe to anyone who was not in Israel the mood of the nation in those critical days of late May and early June 1967 when the fate of Israel, indeed the very survival of her people, hung in the balance. It is also easy to forget how tiny Israel was in those days and how vulnerable she seemed both to her own civilians and, increasingly, to her enemies in the Arab world who, from Algiers to Baghdad, were mobilizing for the final reckoning. At one point close to Netanya, Israel was no more than ten miles wide, from the Jordanian border to the Mediterranean coast. Even Tel Aviv, by far the largest centre of civilian population, was within range of Jordanian artillery and Israeli-held West Jerusalem could easily be cut off from the rest of the country. The civilian population was expecting to take terrible casualties both from air raids and artillery. The authorities had begun digging thousands of graves. Strict blackout, so familiar to me from my childhood days, was enforced. Urgent appeals were made for blood, to which, among many others, I readily responded.

For visits to the front line I had assigned to me as escort a reservist officer who in civilian life was a lawyer. A man already in his fifties and clearly no longer fit for front-line service, he lived in Tel Aviv with his young wife and baby daughter. I asked him what he would do in the event that Israel should lose the coming war and Tel Aviv should be on the point of being overrun by the Arab armies. Without hesitation and with grave sincerity – it was obviously a matter which troubled him deeply and to which he had given much consideration – he replied: 'I would kill my wife and child rather than allow them to fall into the hands of the Arabs.'

On Friday, 2 June, the Air Attaché from the British Embassy, Wing Commander Goring-Morris, with whom I had made friends since my arrival in Israel, invited me to join him on a trip south to the desert in the hope of gleaning some inkling of what was going on. As Goring-Morris correctly surmised, the principal watering hole for the Israeli Air Force in the Negev was the Desert Inn in Beersheba. In the course of the evening several officers dropped into the bar for a drink. All were predictably uncommunicative. But one, Col. Abraham Yoffe, while revealing no secrets, at least gave me food for thought. Being deliberately provocative I had asked him: 'With the Arabs having so many more fighter and bomber aircraft, including many of the latest Russian MiGs, Tupolevs and Sukhois, how come you Israelis are so cocksure of the outcome?'

'You have got to understand,' he replied, 'that there is no policy of discrimination in our Air Force between European and Oriental Jews – pilots are recruited purely on aptitude and merit. But the fact is that 97 per cent of our pilots are, by origin, European Jews. We reckon that in mental and technical ability the Oriental Jew is roughly the equivalent of the better class of Egyptian. So, when we are scraping the barrel, for the Arabs it is *la crème de la crème*. We are not talking merely of a few hundred front-line pilots but of the radar controllers, the weapons specialists and the army of other ground technicians required to refuel, rearm and turn round an aircraft in the space of *seven* minutes.'

This exposition set me thinking and I tried to envisage an Egyptian Air Force ground crew turning around a squadron of combat aircraft. With the best will in the world, I doubted they could do it in under an hour. The moment of truth proved it in fact to be three hours. Indeed, it was doubtless this stark disparity in the efficiency of the two air forces that was to lead Nasser, in the course of the war, to claim that the Israeli Air Force had attacked with 'three times their known strength', convincing him that the Israelis had been assisted by the combat aircraft of the United States, Britain and France.

My contract for the *News of the World* was for a series of three articles, and the moment had arrived for me to file my third and final one. I therefore determined to invoke my newfound friendship with Moshe Dayan who, three days before, on 1 June, had been appointed Minister of Defence. The *Shabbat* or Sabbath is observed as religiously, even by non-religious Jews, as is the weekend by gentiles. Offices close at midday on Friday and all self-respecting Israelis retreat to their homes for thirty-six hours. On the afternoon of Friday, 2 June, I telephoned Dayan at his home and asked if I might come and see him. As if he had not a care in the world, he said that would be excellent and enquired if I would join him and his wife Ruth for supper at their home. I made my way to Zahala, a leafy garden suburb on the outskirts of Tel Aviv which is home to many of Israel's senior military officers. Dayan's was a modest bungalow set in a garden full of pots and urns of great antiquity. Archaeology was his passion; indeed he had even found time to do some digging before returning from the headlong dash of the Sinai campaign of 1956, which he had so brilliantly conceived and executed.

As I entered the garden I nearly tripped over a figure on all fours on the ground on top of an Egyptian mummy, which he was laboriously piecing together. Hearing my approaching footsteps, he looked back over his shoulder and, to my amazement, I saw that it was none other than Israel's new Minister of Defence, instantly given away by his Puckish grin and black eyepatch. It was certainly a remarkable – and, no doubt, calculated – display of *sang-froid*. Israel that weekend found herself surrounded by some 400,000 hostile troops equipped with 2200 tanks and over 800 combat aircraft, yet here was her Minister of Defence painstakingly putting together the remains of a 4000-year-old mummy. Not since the famous day in 1588 when Sir Francis Drake, on learning of the approach of the Spanish Armada while playing a game of bowls on Plymouth Hoe, had quipped, 'There is plenty of time to win this game, and to thrash the Spaniards too,' has a military leader been known to display quite such coolness at the approach of the enemy. Tearing himself away, albeit with reluctance, from the delights of antiquity, he led me to a table on the terrace where we sat down with a glass of wine in the evening sunlight to discuss the critical situation that confronted Israel.

I congratulated him on his appointment and remarked that it had taken Hitler to make my grandfather Prime Minister. He laughed and added: 'Yes, and it took Nasser and 80,000 Egyptian soldiers to get me into the government!' He proceeded to spell out the scale and gravity of the military build-up along Israel's borders to the north, east and south which Shimon Peres, many years later to be Prime Minister and, like Dayan himself, a disciple of Ben Gurion, had described to me as surrounding Israel like 'a vast banana stuffed full of Russian weapons'. But when Dayan tried to deploy the argument then being fed by Israeli spokesmen to the world press that, because of the scale of the military build-up along her borders, Israel had lost the initiative and was powerless to take decisive action, I took issue with him.

'I don't believe you,' I told him boldly, 'for the outcome of the coming conflict will be decided overwhelmingly in the air, as it was in the Battle of Britain. So far as concerns the balance of air power, far from being a setback, it is a positive advantage to you that several of the Egyptian squadrons have been deployed forward to bases in Sinai, where they will be all the more vulnerable to a pre-emptive Israeli airstrike. Therefore it is simply not true to claim that Israel has "lost the initiative" – I don't believe it for a minute!'

There followed a lengthy pause – the significance of which I failed fully to appreciate – in which Dayan took a deep breath before replying in Delphic vein: 'Winston, things are rarely so black or so white – they are much more often grey. It is most unlikely that any one side could achieve total air supremacy as you suggest.' Having no formal training in the arts of war or of military strategy, it had been a brave attempt to call his bluff. Regarding him as my friend and acknowledging his vastly superior experience of military matters, I wrongly allowed him to persuade me to set aside my own long-held conviction that, in conditions of modern conventional warfare, overwhelming air power can decide the outcome of a conflict – the one exception being in jungle conditions, as in Vietnam, where it proved impossible to bring that power effectively to bear. In retrospect I should have paid greater heed to the inordinate length of time and the depth of the breath he had taken before answering my assertion. Later, when the war was all over, he apologized to me in his disarming way. 'What else could I tell you? You had hit the nail right on the head, but I could not afford to let you broadcast your assessment at such a critical time in the life of my country. I had no choice but to tell you you had got it wrong!'

The following evening, after telephoning through my final article to the *News of the World*, I spoke to the editor, told him that war was imminent though I could not say when it would be, and asked whether it was his wish that I stayed on in the Middle East or returned home. He asked me to return and, accordingly, I flew back to London on Sunday, 4 June, getting home to Minnie and our two children in Sussex late that evening.

On waking the next morning, I reached out to switch on the radio shortly before 8 am, and was just in time to hear the BBC interrupt its broadcasts to announce that war had broken out in the Middle East.

Though at the time I cursed my friend Dayan for so calculatedly misleading me – the decision to attack having clearly been taken before our relaxed meeting at his home on the Friday evening – it proved a blessing in disguise. First and foremost I was able to make several broadcasts in which I gave the lie to the general conviction, prevalent among the noted proponents of the Arab cause invited to participate in the BBC's coverage, that Israel would be crushed by the superior numbers and military power of the Arabs. I asserted that, on the contrary, the outcome would be decided by air power within the first few hours, and in Israel's favour. Secondly, thanks to the best literary agent I knew – my father – I was able to negotiate to report the war for the London *Evening News*. I knew that to be stuck working only for a Sunday paper would have been hopeless – since the war was unlikely to last that long, and there could be nothing more frustrating, in such a rapidly developing situation, than to be left biting one's fingernails unable to file a story. The great advantage of writing for an evening paper in such circumstances was that, between 9 am and 6 pm, the paper ran through five or even six different editions, enabling one to file constant updates as the situation unfolded.

But my immediate problem was how to get back to Israel now that war had broken out. The Monday afternoon El Al flight for Tel Aviv was still due to leave London Heathrow on schedule and I, together with half of Fleet Street, managed to secure a booking on the flight. However, at the very last minute, word was received from Israel that it was 'unsafe' to land in Tel Aviv and that the flight was cancelled. This, I subsequently learned, was all part and parcel of Israel's skilful deception. For civilian Boeings to be landing as normal at Lod Airport on the very first day of the war would have totally undermined Nasser's magnificent propaganda – which Israel was only too anxious to sustain – that the Arabs were winning and that Egyptian forces were advancing to crush Israel. In fact it would have been perfectly safe for us to have landed, for the air war had already been resolved in the space of the first 170 minutes following Israel's pre-emptive airstrike at 0745 hours (Israeli time) that morning.

In the first minutes of the war the Israeli Air Force had simultaneously attacked ten Egyptian airfields including, as I had surmised, the four forward Egyptian bases in Sinai. Each airfield had been attacked by four aircraft flying in pairs which first smashed the runways with special runway-cratering bombs and then shot up with cannon the aircraft which, with military smartness, had conveniently been lined up in rows on the tarmac. By delaying their attack until three hours after dawn the Israelis knew that the two Egyptian MiG-21 airborne patrols, which took off just before dawn each morning, would be back on the ground and that the several flights of MiG-21s waiting at the end of the runway on five-minute alert against the possibility of a dawn attack would have been stood down. The Egyptians were even in the habit of switching off some of their radar scanners before going to breakfast and the Israelis knew that by 7.30 am (8.30 Cairo time) the Egyptians had lowered their guard. The other key factors dictating Israel's choice of timing had been the need to give Israel's pilots a reasonable night's sleep before what might be thirty-six hours of sustained combat, the fact that the morning mist over the Nile, the delta and the Suez Canal would by then have burnt off, and that by striking fifteen minutes before most Egyptians get to their offices, generals and air force commanders would be caught incommunicado on their way from their homes to their offices.

General Mordechai Hod, Israel's Air Force commander, was in his command centre as the last of the Egyptian dawn patrols had got airborne and appeared on the Israeli radars. He pressed his stopwatch with a smile knowing that by 0745 when the attack was due, the patrol would be almost out of fuel and on the point of landing. Thus eight formations of MiG-21s were destroyed in the first few minutes as they taxied to take off. Earlier the Israelis had, by deception, persuaded the Egyptians to move twenty of their front-line aircraft from the area around Cairo and the Canal, where Egypt's main airbases were concentrated, to Hurghada in the south, where they were effectively *hors de combat*. By the time the Egyptians realized their mistake and had ordered the aircraft north again, they had nowhere to land and fell easy prey to the Israeli Air Force. Apart from these, only two flights of four MiGs were able to get airborne, and these succeeded in shooting down only two Israeli aircraft before being shot down themselves.

As the first wave of Israeli aircraft struck their targets, the second wave was already on its way and the third had just got airborne. They were spaced at ten-minute intervals and each flight of four aircraft was given seven minutes over their targets – enough for one bombing run and two or three strafing passes. In consequence of their incredibly fast turnaround time, which averaged seven and a half minutes, the Israeli aircraft were over their targets for a second time within an hour of their first attack. Israel had committed virtually every aircraft to the attack. Only twelve aircraft – eight flying top cover and four on standby at the end of the runway – had been left behind to guard Israel and her home bases. Israel was playing for high stakes and it had become a question of win or lose all. But Israel's leaders had weighed the risks with care and played their hand with confidence and decision. In the first 170 minutes of their offensive, Israel's pilots broke the back of the Egyptian Air Force, destroying over 300 out of some 340 serviceable Egyptian combat aircraft at nineteen airbases, all of whose runways were put out of action – the only exception being the Sinai airfield of El Arish which the Israelis deliberately kept intact as they intended to have it in use already by the following evening as an airbase of their own.

By nightfall on the second day of the war the Israeli Air Force had flown more than 1000 sorties with the loss of twenty-six aircraft, but for that price they had knocked out five Arab air forces – those of Egypt, Syria, Jordan, Iraq and Lebanon – destroying a total of 416 aircraft, including 393 on the ground. Not since Pearl Harbor had there been such a devastating surprise attack.

When, on the Monday, my return flight to Israel had been cancelled, several Fleet Street colleagues urged me to join them on a flight to Nicosia with the aim of chartering a boat to get from Cyprus to Israel. I wished them luck but told them I preferred to take my chance with El Al. My faith in El Al proved well founded, for the next day there was indeed a flight to Israel and I was fortunate to be the only passenger allowed to board in London. Apart from some fifteen Israeli surgeons and anaesthetists who had been working in Boston at the Harvard Medical School and had boarded the flight in New York, every other seat in the Boeing 707 was stacked to the ceiling with gas masks from Fort Bragg, North Carolina. Immediately before the start of the war, the Israelis obtained intelligence that the Egyptians had shipped rail-tankers, loaded with chemical warfare agents, to their troops in Sinai, and an urgent appeal had been made to the United States for gas masks. Indeed, within a week I was to find myself the proud possessor of a brand new Soviet-made chemical warfare suit of latex rubber, which I picked up from among the military debris in the sand dunes of the Sinai desert. The presence of this equipment – and there were many other such suits left lying around – provided sinister proof of the intent of Nasser and his senior officers to use chemical weapons against the Israelis, had they been given the chance, and tended to confirm the reports I had heard that Egyptian forces had used these barbaric weapons against the hardy tribesmen of the Yemen, whom I had visited five years before.

As we approached Israel under cover of darkness, all the cabin lights were extinguished. There had been virtually no news received from Israel before we had left, and tension and excitement were mounting among the Israeli medical men as we flew in low over the coast to an Israel that was totally blacked out. Only at the very last minute were the carefully shielded runway lights, at very reduced power, switched on to enable us to land.

Returning to the Tel Aviv Hilton after an absence of only two days, I found that all was drastically changed. There were no street lights in the town, the plate-glass windows of the hotel lobby had been crisscrossed with adhesive tape to guard against blast, and the hotel was almost completely enveloped in darkness. I arrived back just in time to witness an amazing bust-up between a vociferous contingent of the US press corps and the distinguished and cultured Israeli colonel, Moshe Perlman, a retired officer who had been placed in charge of press relations for the Israel Defence Forces. Perlman was being berated in the most peremptory terms by more than half a dozen furious American correspondents who were demanding to be allowed to ride in the 'lead tanks across Sinai' and fly with Israeli pilots in 'strikes against Egypt' (all of which were long since over). In stark contrast to the attitude towards the press adopted by the American military in Vietnam – a largesse of which I had myself been one of the beneficiaries – the Israelis, like the British, regarded the press as surplus baggage to be kept well to the rear, while they got on with the war. I felt it difficult to restrain a smile as, one by one and sometimes simultaneously, the Americans gave account of what they had been allowed to get away with by their own military in South Vietnam, and Colonel Perlman quietly but firmly replied: 'That is of course all very interesting, but this is Israel and here we do things our way.' The pressmen seethed with outrage and frustration at the imposition of such unwonted constraints on their supposed rights.

With President Nasser's propaganda machine turned up to full volume on the airwaves of the Middle East, it remained Israeli policy to say nothing. In the absence of any official statements by Israel's military spokesmen, it was difficult to piece together the jigsaw of what was happening at the front line. However, working through the night at the press centre in Beit Sokolov Street, I was gradually able to build up a picture and, all at once, I got wind of the fact that the progress of Israel's ground forces on the southern front in Sinai had been much greater than anyone had, thus far, appreciated. By 10 am on Wednesday, 7 June, the *Evening News* carried my first report for them under a front-page banner headline:

FLAT OUT TO THE CANAL

It looks as if the Israelis are achieving one of the greatest victories of all time. The defeat for Nasser seems to be massive and overwhelming, and it is a defeat not only for Nasser but also for his supporters in the Arab camp and in the Soviet Union. Having routed Nasser in the air, the Israelis have been routing his forces on the ground in the last twenty-four hours. The Israeli armour and infantry, with the benefit of close air support, is thrusting westwards in a great headlong rush to the Suez Canal . . .

By midday I was able to report that the Israelis were already on the banks of the Suez Canal and had retaken Sharm el Sheik, the fortress controlling the entrance to the Gulf of Aqaba; it had been the Egyptian seizure of that fortress three weeks before which had provoked the original crisis. but not all my press colleagues were as sanguine as I was about the extent of the Israeli victory. Indeed Charles Douglas-Home of *The Times*, a first-class journalist, later to become a distinguished editor of the paper, remained distinctly sceptical.

Like myself, Charlie was staying at the Hilton, which stands in a prime position on Tel Aviv's shoreline, and he had a room looking out over the sea. That morning he awoke to find the sun attempting to break through a thick sea mist and, as he rubbed his eyes in the bright sunlight, he suddenly saw looming through the mist a destroyer which he instantly recognized as Egyptian. Seconds later he heard the explosion of a shell which fell some way away on the outskirts of Tel Aviv, followed by a second and a third. He dashed indoors and proceeded to attack his typewriter with a fury, producing a story to the effect that, contrary to misleading reports from certain correspondents that the war was all over bar the shouting, he had seen with his very eyes an Egyptian destroyer shelling the Israeli capital. Armed with his piece, he raced to the press centre at Beit Sokolov, where all foreign dispatches had to be submitted to Israeli military censorship under the auspices of one of the three colonels. One of these, having glanced at the story, turned to Charlie and enquired: 'Are you sure you are feeling quite all right today, Mr Douglas-Home?'

Charlie who, like all of us, bridled at any form of censorship, exclaimed irately: 'I *knew* you would not let me send the story!' – to which the censor replied: 'We merely wanted to save you from embarrassment!'

Charlie's experience should be an object lesson to all foreign correspondents how one cannot rely even on the evidence of one's own eyes. For, by an amazing set of coincidences, the situation had been far from what it had appeared to be. The destroyer had indeed been Egyptian – at least until 1956, when it had changed sides after being captured by the Israelis – but the shells which he had seen landing on Tel Aviv had come, not from the destroyer with which he had understandably linked them, but from Jordanian Long Tom guns in the villages of Kalkilya and Tul Karm, twenty miles away, out of sight in the hills of Jordan's West Bank.

Already, in the first forty-eight hours of war the Israelis, by their lightning and daring thrust through Sinai and by making the most of the advantages which flow from total air supremacy, had routed the Egyptian Army with its force of 1000 tanks. Time and again the Israelis outflanked their enemy, positioning troops by helicopter or taking routes across the desert which they had surveyed in 1956 and which the Egyptians believed to be impassable, thereby establishing blocking positions behind the Egyptian forces who proceeded to retreat headlong into them, with disastrous consequences.

It had been the Israeli hope and indeed, until the fateful kiss between Nasser and King Hussein in Cairo on 30 May, their belief that Jordan would not involve herself in any conflict between Israel and Egypt. In 1956 Jordan had held aloof and the Israelis firmly believed that she would do so again. Brigadier-General Uzzi Narkiss, the Israeli commander on the central front facing Jordan, was under instructions to maintain a strictly defensive posture. However, in the days immediately preceding the outbreak of war Jordanian forces, consisting of an infantry and an armoured brigade with 80 Patton tanks, were reinforced by the arrival of an entire Iraqi infantry division backed by some 150 tanks. Even after the Iraqi division had crossed the River Jordan on to the West Bank and after the Israeli airstrike had been launched against Egypt on the morning of 5 June, the Israeli Prime Minister, Levi Eshkol, had sent a message to King Hussein via the UN Force Commander in Jerusalem to assure him: 'We shall not initiate any action whatsoever against Jordan. However, should Jordan open hostilities, we shall react with all our might and he [King Hussein] will have to bear the full responsibility for the consequences.'

Later that morning, following a radio broadcast in which King Hussein declared 'The hour of revenge has come . . .', Jordanian forces and heavy guns opened fire along the entire length of the Jordanian border and it became evident that their forces had been placed under Egyptian command. The Israelis were surprised but not dismayed. For them it represented the opportunity of a lifetime to seize East Jerusalem and so unite the Holy City, which is sacred to Christians and Moslems as well as to Jews. It also gave them the excuse to gain control of Jordan's West Bank, from which Israel could so easily be threatened. General Narkiss had already been told the week before by Dayan: 'Don't bother the general staff with requests for reinforcements. Grit your teeth and ask for nothing.'

Just after midnight, in the early hours of 6 June – the second day of the war – Israeli forces launched their counter-attack, prompting the Army Chief Rabbi, General Schlomo Goren, to tell Narkiss: 'Your men are making history – what is going on in Sinai is nothing compared to this!' Narkiss told him to prepare his trumpet. By midday on Wednesday, 7 June, Israel had control of the Old City. At the Wailing Wall – supposedly the last remains of the temple destroyed by the Romans – Dayan, following an old Jewish tradition, scribbled a prayer on a scrap of paper and slipped it between the stones of the wall. It read: 'Let peace reign in Israel.'

The Jordanians, with far smaller armed forces and incomparably less sophisticated equipment than many of her Arab neighbours, were the only ones to inflict damage on Israel. Neither the Egyptians nor the Syrians, in spite of all their bluster and bravado, undertook any aggressive action of significance in the course of the entire war. The Jordanians who had, against their own interest, taken the path of duty as laid down by the dictates of Arab nationalism were the only ones, of the dozen Arab states that declared war on Israel, to acquit themselves honourably on the field of battle. But it was an unequal struggle. Jordan was fighting against impossible odds and, in spite of the sacrifice of several thousand of her men, she lost nearly half her territory. Thus, by nightfall on the third day of the war, the Israelis had in their hands all of Jerusalem, the city of David, and Hebron, the city of Abraham – of which Ben Gurion had spoken to me with such fervour just two weeks before – and all the Holy Land. Few Jews believed they would see any of those places in their lifetime and, for the Jewish nation around the world, this represented the fulfilment of the dreams of centuries. After the fighting was all over, Brigadier-General Ezer Weizmann, son of Chaim Weizmann, one of the most prominent Zionist leaders in the early part of the century and a friend of my grandfather's, told me: 'You must understand why Israel was built here rather than in Uganda or Canada – both of which were seriously suggested at various times by the British Foreign Office. We could never have fought for a Jewish state in any other part of the world the way we have here. Jerusalem, the West Bank of the Jordan, indeed the whole of Palestine holds the deepest religious, historical and emotional significance for us, and it is this which forms the basis of Zionism.'

On Thursday, 8 June, with the Egyptian Army in full flight in Sinai and Jordanian forces smashed on the West Bank, the Israeli Air Force began devoting its attentions to the Maginot Line of underground bunkers, tank-pits and gun emplacements on Syria's Golan Heights, which dominated the low-lying plains of Israel and the settlements around the Sea of Galilee. The Syrian defences here were more than ten miles deep and their artillery was able to launch more than ten tons of shells per minute from the 265 guns along the ridge. In addition they had Russian-made Katjusha missiles mounted on vehicles, capable of firing twenty-four rockets per minute. Meanwhile the Israelis were switching vast quantities of armour and manpower from Sinai, where their work was done, to the Syrian front.

On Friday, 9 June, I reported to the *Evening News* that the attempt by the United Nations to secure a ceasefire at 0300 hours that morning had come to nought and that a fierce battle was raging along the Syrian Heights. At about 6.30 pm Israeli time (4.30 pm in London), having filed my final dispatch of the day, I went down to the Hilton hotel bar for a drink. I was closely followed by Arnaud de Borchgrave, senior editor of *Newsweek* magazine, whom I had first met eighteen months before in Vietnam. He breezed in, in a state of considerable elation.

'I've just come from the Israeli War Room,' he confided with as much modesty as he could muster, 'and the assault on the Syrian Heights has just gone in!' Trying hard to sound unimpressed, I asked him if he was absolutely sure. On the strength of his confirmation, I walked briskly behind the bar, grabbed the telephone off the wall and asked to be connected to London as a matter of urgency. Within two minutes I was through to the copy-taker of the *Evening News*, where the final edition of the day was already rolling on the presses. Officially we were supposed to send our dispatches by telex, having had them vetted by the Israeli military censors, but on this occasion there was no time for such proprieties. As soon as I had identified myself, I began my report: 'The long awaited Israeli assault upon the Syrian Heights has just gone in.' At this point I was interrupted on the line by a man's voice saying 'Change the subject, Mr Churchill – speak about the weather!' With that, the line went dead. But it had been enough. The presses were stopped and an entire extra edition was run with billboards across London proclaiming: ISRAEL STRIKES SYRIA – CHURCHILL.

The official end to what has come to be known as the Six-Day War –

the title which my father and I were to give our book on the subject – came at 1930 hours on the evening of Saturday, 10 June, when firing ceased, after both the Syrians and the Israelis finally accepted the UN Security Council's repeated call for an end to hostilities. By a feat of arms unparalleled in modern times, surrounded by enemies superior in quantity and quality of equipment and overwhelmingly superior in numbers, Israel had fought a war on three fronts. She had not only survived but had won a resounding victory. As one Israeli paratrooper remarked to me: 'This is an interesting country – there's never a dull moment. You have a war: in six days it is over and you have turned the whole world upside-down!'

On the Wednesday of the war I had received a telegram from my father which read:

SUGGEST WE DO JOINT RUSH BOOK STOP WHAT DO YOU SAY STOP
LOVE = FATHER

This had been an idea which Minnie and I had discussed the day before at Heathrow airport as I was waiting for the departure of my flight to Israel, and I immediately cabled my agreement. Father promptly negotiated a deal for the book rights with Heinemann and for serialization in the *Sunday Telegraph*. Meanwhile Minnie volunteered to fly out to type the book, and arrived in Israel on the last day of the war. Though six months pregnant with our third child, Marina, she gamely insisted on accompanying me on a visit to the newly occupied West Bank. We travelled in an Israeli Army jeep, which seemed devoid of springs, on one of the hottest days of the summer, with the temperature reaching well over 100 degrees. We made our way through the Old City of Jerusalem down to the town of Jericho on the banks of the river Jordan, where we found Israeli troops in roisterous mood 'liberating' a Bata shoe shop. From there we followed the valley northwards before heading west up into the hills towards Nablus.

Just a week before the outbreak of war I had walked through the Mandelbaum Gate which, since 1948, had separated Israeli-held West Jerusalem from Arab East Jerusalem, and had driven down across the river Jordan to Amman, where I had met my Palestinian friend from Oxford days, Farouk Toukan. I knew that he had been intending to visit his family in Nablus so, on arrival there after the conflict, we went immediately to his home, a lovely old house set high on the hillside above the town. My friend was not there, but his mother and sister greeted us with great emotion. Though they had not been threatened in any way by the occupying Israeli forces, they were desperately anxious about their situation, convinced that they would be raped and their possessions plundered by the occupying soldiery – fears which no amount of reassurance from us was able to allay. Mrs Toukan could not believe that the Israelis would not behave like any other Middle Eastern army and was begging us to take with us for safekeeping the family jewellery and Louis XVI furniture, 'otherwise the Jews will steal it'. It is perhaps impossible for those who have not had to suffer the pain and humiliation of having one's home, one's land and one's country occupied by a hostile power – however correctly behaved – to appreciate the anxiety, trauma and unhappiness to which it inevitably gives rise. Though we knew that neither she nor her family would come to any physical harm, there was nothing whatever we could do or say to persuade them of this, and it was with hauntingly deep looks of despair that they waved us goodbye.

As soon as the war was over I seized the opportunity of flying down to the Sinai to see, at first hand, what had been going on there. I arranged to fly in an Israeli Army Super Cub to Bir Gifgafa, an airfield and military base in the heart of Sinai captured by the Israelis. We flew by way of Gaza and El Arish, through which had passed the main thrust of Israel's 'mailed fist' of armoured forces, as their commander, General Tal, had described it to me. The scale of destruction and devastation of burnt-out tanks, armoured vehicles, self-propelled guns and rocket launchers was stupendous. On all sides lay a full inventory of the most modern and powerful weapons that the armaments factories of the Soviet Union could produce, in quantities quite unimaginable for a Third World country such as Egypt. In fact, thanks to Russian munificence, Egypt had acquired significantly more tanks, artillery and modern military hardware than Great Britain possessed at the time. But nowhere was the devastation so concentrated as at the Mitla Pass, the narrow track through the mountains which had become the jaws of death for vast columns of Egyptian armour fleeing headlong towards the Canal and – as they must have thought – to safety, unaware that their path had been blocked by a force of Israeli paratroopers positioned by helicopter with large quantities of anti-tank weapons at their disposal. Meanwhile the Fouga Magister trainer aircraft of the Israeli Air Force, specially equipped for tank-busting, had mercilessly wreaked their toll on the stranded armour as it lay helplessly trapped in the greatest military traffic jam since the Falaise Gap in Normandy in 1944, unable to advance or reverse because of the hundreds of vehicles blocking them front and rear, and sinking immediately into the desert sands if they tried to leave the narrow roadway. In places the bodies of tank crews still lay beside the burnt-out hulks of their vehicles. Elsewhere one merely saw footprints disappearing into the desert.

On arrival in the Bir Gifgafa I was conducted to Brigadier-General Ariel Sharon's tent, where I found him in expansive good humour, attended by Ya'el Dayan, the beautiful daughter of Israel's Defence Minister, looking extremely smart and efficient in her army uniform.

'We now have peace,' declared Sharon grandiloquently, 'a piece of Egypt, a piece of Jordan and a piece of Syria!' After outlining to me his capture of the Egyptians' heavily dug-in strongpoint of Abu Agheila, in northeastern Sinai, and his headlong dash across the desert with a large force of armour and infantry to take the retreating Egyptians in the rear, he offered to show me something of the surrounding country. Accompanied by a driver and three or four Israeli soldiers, we climbed aboard his jeep, on which was mounted a heavy machine gun. In addition to further quantities of charred vehicles, I was amazed at the number of boots to be seen lying here and there in the desert, evidently abandoned by their owners who found them either too cumbersome or too painful in their precipitate flight towards the Canal and home. Suddenly we saw in the distance two or three forlorn figures making their way on foot westwards across the desert. In the instant Sharon was on his feet. He grabbed the handles of the machine gun with both hands, and as we flew across the rocky desert in pursuit, he fired bursts of machine-gun fire to 'speed them on their way'. Fortunately the bouncing of the vehicle was so intense that his quarry was unscathed and the unfortunate Egyptians, who had long since abandoned their weapons, were left to flee towards the Canal.

On my return to Tel Aviv I presented one of the colonels in the military censor's office with a list of more than a dozen of the principal military commanders whom I wished to interview for my book, starting with the Minister of Defence. I detected from his amused smile that I would be lucky to see even one or two of those on my list if I relied solely on his good offices. I therefore set about making direct contact with them, making full use of the numerous contacts I had made in the course of the two and a half weeks I had been in Israel before the start of the conflict. For several days on end, we had a stately procession of army, air force and navy commanders, as well as chiefs of intelligence and government ministers, passing through our suite at the Tel Aviv Hilton. At one point, while Minnie was transcribing a tape on to the typewriter in the bedroom and I was debriefing a general in the living room, two other military commanders were cooling their heels in an anteroom eagerly awaiting the opportunity of telling me how *they* had won the war. I was especially fortunate in my timing. In the euphoria of victory – a victory which, like so many before it, was erroneously believed to be the 'war to end all wars' – everyone who had played a major part was determined to secure his place in history and was only too eager to give an account of the heroic exploits of the men under his command.

Some three weeks after the end of the war, I received a telephone call from one of the colonels in the military censor's office asking if he could come and see me. This was certainly a turnaround, for it was invariably the press who had, hitherto, been the ones seeking the interviews. I agreed with good grace. However, I was taken aback to find that I was being waited upon by a deputation consisting of all three colonels from the military censor's office. In a state of some anxiety one enquired: 'We understand that you may have seen some of the individuals on the list which you presented us some two weeks ago. Is this so?' I told them that I had indeed seen everyone on my list and a few more besides and that it had certainly not been thanks to their efforts. Evidently embarrassed and ill at ease, one of them rejoined: 'We presume that you will be submitting your book to Israeli military censorship?' When I replied that that consideration had not been uppermost in my mind, the censors made clear that they would not allow any of my chapters to leave the country without their going through them with a fine-tooth comb, deleting whatever they felt was necessary. When I told them that the chapters relating to the military side of the conflict were already in my father's hands at his home in East Bergholt, looks of consternation and dismay came over their faces.

They could not know that, as each couple of chapters was written, I had shipped them back to England by the safe hands of Sir Isaac Wolfson and other distinguished members of the British Jewish community, who visited Israel immediately following the war. Realizing that the horse had bolted, they had no choice but to accept my terms. I acknowledged that I had been given access to a considerable amount of sensitive details and that many of those whom I had interviewed had been very free in what they had told me. I therefore told them that while my father and I could not accept submitting the book formally to Israeli military censorship, we would be happy to allow the Israeli Military Attaché in London to have sight of the galley proofs and that we would be willing to entertain any specific points of concern they might have. In the upshot, the only request that was made, to which I was happy to accede, was to round the number of aircraft in the Israeli inventory to the nearest five and insert before it the word 'about', as they did not welcome my precision on this sensitive subject.

While Minnie and I had been at work recounting the steps that had led Israel and her neighbours down the path to war, and uncovering the military secrets behind Israel's spectacular victory, Father, with a team of gifted researchers, temporarily diverted from their principal task of working on the great biography of my grandfather, was at home in Suffolk writing the chapters dealing with the historical perspective and the global view of the crisis in terms of East–West relations and the UN. Within a month of the start of the war the book was written and with the publishers, Heinemann. Precisely two months after the end of the war it was on the bookstalls.

The collaboration with my father – never the easiest person to work with – went amazingly well although he could not bring himself to believe that anyone could actually stay at a Hilton Hotel. In Tel Aviv he had always stayed at the Dan, and he categorically refused to accept that there could be any other. In consequence of this a bellboy would each day be dispatched from the Dan in the early evening with a sheaf of half a dozen telexes – five of them demanding to know why I had not replied to the first! It was several days before we were able to persuade him to address the telexes, with which he bombarded us with queries and suggestions, to the hotel where we were actually staying. Even in the final three weeks when we were all at Stour buttoning up the book the harmony was remarkable, due in large measure to the pressure of our tight deadline and the judicious, clear-cut, division of responsibility between the two of us.

Meanwhile Father had negotiated eminently satisfactory terms for the syndication of the book. Very soon after the war was over he had telephoned Harold Evans, the editor of the *Sunday Times*, and informed him: 'Winston and I are going to do a book on the Middle East War. You can have the rights for £15,000.' Harold Evans replied that they had just run the story in a single issue and had no plans to amplify their coverage, to which my father rejoined: 'Very well – I will sell it to Hartwell!' Lord Hartwell was the proprietor of the *Sunday* and *Daily Telegraph*. It is one of the great advantages that British authors and journalists enjoy over their American counterparts, that there are in Britain a multiplicity of quality Sunday papers enjoying nationwide circulation, which makes for an intensely competitive situation. He did indeed, as threatened, sell the syndication, at the full asking price, to Lord Hartwell's *Sunday Telegraph*, which ran the story in five successive issues. For a whole month our faces peered down from hoardings all over the country advertising the *Sunday Telegraph*'s serialization under the slogan, 'The Churchills go to War Again'.

Considering the speed with which it was written, the notices which the book received were, by and large, very friendly. The distinguished military historian Sir Basil Liddell Hart wrote:

The Six Day War, the combined work of Randolph S. Churchill and Winston S. Churchill, is a remarkable achievement, and a much better blend than most books produced under joint authorship. It is very well written on the whole, and in parts brilliantly, with a turn of phrase as superbly apt as that of Sir Winston Churchill himself, while free from any rhetorical note. It is a fine piece of journalism and some of the chapters can rightly be termed fine contributions to historical literature, even though they be classified as 'instant history' because of the shortness of time since the event.

Among the letters I received following publication was one from General Arile Yariv, who had been most helpful to me in my researches. In a PS he made me an intriguing proposition: 'As Director of Intelligence I can't refrain from adding, that you got a hell of a lot of information from our people. How about joining Israeli Intelligence?' I was also especially pleased at the letter I received from the American author Irwin Shaw, who wrote in most generous terms from his mountain home at Klosters, Switzerland:

It's a book to be proud of. The writing is sober but swift, the facts clear, the judgements sound, the people plausible but human. The descriptions of the military actions models of precision. So often when writers try to reconstruct battles they bog the reader down hopelessly, so that the fog of war that the soldier feels engulfing him on the battlefield becomes an even more impenetrable fog in the library . . .

It gives me great pleasure to write this letter to someone I first knew as a little boy pedalling a bicycle in front of the Château de la Garoupe.

I was thrilled, above all, to have the opportunity of working in such close harness with my father. It made me understand my grandfather's plea on leaving school to *his* father, Lord Randolph, to be allowed to work with him as his right hand and ally, something that was never vouchsafed to him. But I value our collaboration all the more in retrospect, for – though I could never have guessed it at the time – my father had less than a year to live.

Meanwhile, at our Sussex home of Broadwater, my own family was becoming more numerous. Young Randolph, already two and a half, with blue eyes and a shock of blond hair, was charging noisily about the garden and developing a strong character of his own. We had him on skis before his third birthday and he was quite adamant that he needed no help or advice. Pushing me aside with his tiny elbow, he boldly declared: 'Randolph do it by his own!'

Jennie, born the year before on 25 September 1966, was also growing fast and becoming quite a personality. She had large hazel eyes, tinged with green, and her mother's dark hair. Minnie and I were both extremely proud of our respective American ancestry and we decided to name her after my great-grandmother, Jennie Jerome of Brooklyn, New York. Indeed it is through her that I can claim not only American blood but Red Indian blood too. For her mother's great-grandfather had married an Iroquois squaw by the name of Meribah. In a portrait I have inherited of Jennie Jerome's mother, Clara Hall Jerome, the Red Indian influence can quite clearly be discerned in her facial characteristics. Amazingly, though separated by four generations, Jennie Jerome's raven hair and striking looks have been inherited by her namesake.

That same year, on 11 September 1967, Minnie gave birth to our third child, Marina, who weighed in at a little more than 3 lbs and had to spend her first three weeks in an incubator at the Westminster Hospital, where all our children were born. Having married Minnie barely three years before, I was astonished at the speed with which my responsibilities had multiplied, for besides three children our family now consisted of two dogs, a King Charles Cavalier and a border terrier (with a litter of puppies), two donkeys and a budgerigar.

· XVIII ·

Foray on the Hustings

Father had, initially, sought to dissuade me from a political career, suggesting, while I was still at school, that in a technological age I should consider becoming an engineer or scientist. In retrospect I recognize it was his way of saying that I should not feel under any obligation to go into the family business. But the suggestion did not appeal to me and, in the course of my time at Oxford, I became increasingly attracted to the prospect of a career in journalism, above all because I felt I had so much to learn about the world and, indeed, about my own country. I saw journalism as providing the passport to that knowledge, as well as the means of establishing my political bearings. I was determined that any political views or convictions I might hold would be my own, derived from my own experience and not merely the hand-me-downs of my father or grandfather.

One of the first steps in this process of political self-education had been to visit more than forty countries of the Middle East and Africa, especially hot-spots like Yemen, the Congo and Angola, in each of which conflicts were raging, and getting to know at first hand many of the leading political figures such as King Hussein, Emperor Haile Selassie, Jomo Kenyatta, Tom Mboya, Julius Nyerere and Ian Smith. Writing articles and a book about my experiences, which in turn had led to an invitation to make a lecture tour of the United States, had provided invaluable experience in the fields of journalism and public speaking.

Subconsciously at least, I had been working towards a career in politics, but first I was determined to acquire some weapons for my armoury and lay in a stock of ammunition, having had drummed into me by my father the maxim of Napoleon: 'Never do battle without a 100 per cent reserve of ball ammunition.' Having once failed to interest me in an alternative career, Father was only too eager to help and encourage me in the fields of both journalism and politics. Indeed when I was still only twenty-three and not yet back from the jungles of Africa, runners were arriving through the jungle with cleft sticks bearing multi-page telegrams from him urging me to stand for the constituency of North Paddington, where the candidature was about to become vacant. Voluminous briefing material started arriving, detailing election results in the constituency going back to 1924 and pointing out that Lord Randolph Churchill had been elected Member for South Paddington in 1885 by a majority of two to one – a seat which he had held until his death in 1895 at the age of forty-six. Father gave me a thumbnail sketch of the North Paddington constituency as 'largely populated by black men, Irish, railway workers, tarts and building contractors, adding that 'much of the property is owned by the Ecclesiastical Commissioners of the Church of England'. In a letter dated 10 February 1963 he wrote: 'It has the smallest Labour majority (786) in London and if you were to win it mischievously, it would probably be the only Tory gain from Labour in the election. If you lost there would be no discredit and you would have gained considerable experience. My advice is to have a go. It would be 4 or 5 to 1 against your winning but you would not be fighting a hopeless seat...'

But I was not prepared to be rushed and I declined the suggestion, determined to get some experience under my belt first. Only after I had gained experience first as an author and radio journalist, then on the US lecture circuit and as a war correspondent in Southeast Asia and the Middle East, did I feel ready to take the plunge. In the summer of 1967, just as the final corrections were being made to the proofs of *The Six Day War*, I learned that there was to be a by-election at Gorton, following the death of the Labour MP Konni Zilliacus, who had had a majority of 8308 in the March 1966 general election. Manchester, Gorton, an industrial seat in the heartland of Britain, was a very safe seat for the Labour Party. It had been Socialist for thirty-six years and had returned the most left-wing Labour MP in Parliament for the previous twelve. It was just the sort of electoral challenge I had been looking for, and I seized the opportunity with alacrity. On 26 July I informed the *Manchester Evening News* that I had asked Conservative Central Office to forward my name to the Gorton Conservative Association as one of two or three hundred potential candidates anxious to be considered.

There is no doubt that bearing the name of the most famous Englishman of all time was a distinct asset, at least in the early stages of the selection process. In fact it more or less guaranteed that I would be among those selected for interview, if only for curiosity's sake. Thereafter, I was strictly on my own and it was certainly no advantage to face endless comparison with the greatest political figure of his, or any, generation. I was determined to enter Parliament not, as some might expect, as the grandson of the former prime minister, by way of a safe country or seaside seat in the

Conservative heartland, but by winning a Labour-held seat in the industrial north. Knowing little of the industrial heartland of Britain, I recognized this as a weakness in my armoury. I had come to realize from an early age that the name of Winston Churchill, which I was so proud to bear, was both a lot to live up to and a lot to live down. Conscious, perhaps too conscious, that there would be no shortage of people to criticize if they thought that I was looking for or expecting any unfair advantage, I went out of my way to seek out the hardest battles in the hope that I might be judged on my own merits rather than on the strength of what my grandfather, referring to *his* father in his maiden speech in 1900, had called 'a certain splendid memory'.

Eighteen candidates were eventually selected for interview by the Gorton Conservatives, my name among them. This was then further reduced to a shortlist of three, from which the final selection was to be made. I was fortunate in being the one invited to fight the seat and, in a state of great elation, hastened to telephone the news through to Minnie at the Westminster Hospital where she had just given birth to our youngest daughter, Marina.

There are few enterprises so lively or so hectic as a by-election campaign. At a general election an individual constituency – unless the fortunes of a political heavyweight are at risk – is just one of more than 600 seats where the battle is being fought, and merits no media attention beyond the local press. But by-elections take place singly or with no more than a couple of other seats being contested at the same time and, as a result, the arc-light of publicity and media interest focuses on the struggle as a barometer of the government's popularity, giving the campaign a national dimension. This is especially so when the election is in a government-held seat at a time when the fortunes of the government are flagging. The fact that I happened to bear the most famous name in the world served only to accentuate the interest. TV crews homed in on the dingy back streets of Gorton from as far afield as Los Angeles, Sweden and Japan and, at one stage in the campaign when all five candidates were sharing a public platform at a meeting organized by a local Methodist minister, there were demands from outside from those Gortonians who could not gain admission to the hall, which was bursting at the seams, to 'heave the press out and let the people in!'

If Gorton was an important part of my own political education, it was also quite an eye-opener for the visiting press. The *Sun* newspaper described it as consisting of 'grim acres of Coronation Streets'. The *Guardian* called it:

The kind of place that the promised brave New Britain is really all about. It is no twilight zone; the dark came down over most of it a long time ago ... its main shopping street would need little alteration to fit into a film about the Great Depression. Slap bang in the centre of it now, is a red-painted Bingo Hall, shuttered like a winter-closed stall on Blackpool's Golden Mile. There is a pub laughingly called the Suburban Hotel; a supermarket where a fly couldn't crawl between the bargains painted on the windows; Marcia's Café; and a settee-spattered emporium with a sign announcing it as the 'Working man's furnishers'.

Auberon Waugh in the *Spectator* commented:

If there is anything in the world more depressing than Gorton on a wet, cold, foggy afternoon, it is Gorton when the sun shines. The sun, one feels, has no business to illuminate the rows of drab houses all kept impeccably clean and tidy, the terrible wide streets and the seedy daintiness of Denton, on the posher side of the constituency. Whatever happens at this by-election – and I am not going to risk gratuitous error by making a prophecy – let there be no mistake that Gorton belongs to Labour in much the same way that lemon belongs to port, or lime juice to lager beer.

Whereas the general election the previous year attracted only two candidates, the by-election drew a field of five, some of whom reckoned that the £150 deposit was well worth the large amount of free publicity for their views. The Labour Party judiciously settled for a solid local man, Kenneth Marks, the widely respected headmaster of a local secondary school, as their standard-bearer. The Liberals chose twenty-two-year-old Terry Lacey, Chairman of the Union of Liberal Students, who was characterized by the press as one of the 'Red Guards' of the Liberal Party. Wearing jeans and a khaki denim jacket bearing a lapel badge inscribed with the slogan *Make Love not War*, he made a hilarious contrast to his party leader, Jeremy Thorpe, who came to campaign for him in the more traditional political garb of dark pinstripe trousers, dark overcoat and black Homburg hat. The Communist Party fielded Vic Eddisford, Secretary of the party's Manchester branch, who was supported in his campaign by John Gollan, the party's general secretary. Completing the field was John Creasey, a prolific author who had just published his 461st thriller and was calling for the country to be run by an All-Party coalition, which he believed should include the Duke of Edinburgh.

I was by no means the first of my family to fight an industrial Lancashire seat; indeed my father and my grandfather had each fought four elections in Lancashire. Grandpapa had fought Oldham, as Conservative candidate, in the 'Khaki' election of 1899 at the start of the Boer War. He had been unsuccessful at this first attempt but won it, a year later, at the age of twenty-six. After he 'crossed the floor' of the House of Commons, he won Northwest Manchester in 1906 and was returned as a Liberal MP. He lost his seat two years later when, after being appointed president of the Board of Trade, he was required under the rules that then applied to Cabinet Ministers to submit himself for re-election. My father, at the age of twenty-three, had contested the Wavertree division of Liverpool in 1935 as an Independent Conservative and, later the same year, the East Toxteth division, in both of which he scored a large number of votes though not enough to be elected. Finally he entered Parliament as member for Preston in 1940 during the party truce, only to be swept away in the Labour landslide of 1945. A more important consideration than family tradition in my decision to stand for Gorton was the fact that, having been brought up all my life in London and the southeast, I was determined to acquire a first-hand knowledge and understanding of the North, Britain's political heartland and industrial backbone.

Just ten days before I learned of the vacancy at Gorton, I had allowed my name to go forward for Brighton Pavilion, a safe Conservative seat within half an hour of our Sussex home. No sooner had I done so than I realized I had made a mistake and that it was not for me. I knew I had to win my political spurs in a more challenging way. Thus, as soon as I heard about Gorton, I withdrew my name from Brighton Pavilion without even meeting the selection committee, so determined was I to secure the Gorton candidature.

Feeling one's way in a new constituency, having never fought a seat before, is not the easiest task; but to do so under the minute scrutiny of the press and the gaze of the television cameras was definitely an ordeal. The first few days, knowing neither the geography of the constituency nor the people, were not easy, especially since at that stage few local people had heard of my candidature. Thus, every time I went up to people in the streets or on their doorsteps and introduced myself, I was potentially riding for a fall. The press loved it and could not wait for me to come a cropper. They were naturally delighted when, on introducing myself to a lady in curlers leaning on her broom handle, she had replied: 'Oh, yeah? Well, I'm Marlene Dietrich!'

On the very first day, the area where we started our canvass was one of the few more prosperous parts of the constituency and the accompanying press were discouraged at the amazingly high number of favourable responses I was getting from housewives whose husbands were out of work. On hearing one of the press grumble to another that it was clearly a 'put-up job' and that they had been brought to a solid Conservative area unrepresentative of the constituency, I produced a map and invited them to pick another area to canvass. They chose Gorton Cross, in the heart of an area regarded as solidly Labour. After two or three not unfriendly reactions there, a reporter from the New Statesman, a socialist weekly, spying a rough, tough-looking man in his fifties coming down the street towards us in shabby workman's overalls, tapped me on the shoulder and pointed – 'Him! Ask him!' – convinced by his appearance that he was a staunch Labour man and that I would finally get the rebuff which he evidently felt I so richly deserved. I waylaid the gentleman as he came down the street, offered an outstretched hand, and introduced myself, explaining that I had just been selected as Conservative candidate for the forthcoming by-election and asking: 'What do you think of the present crowd that's in?' I was apprehensive about his reply, while the press watched with eager anticipation, convinced they would finally get the quotable quote they had been waiting for. To their amazement and dismay, the man grabbed my hand in a vice-like grip and confided with what passed for a smile: 'Them two booggers, Wilson and Brown [the Prime Minister and his Deputy] – I wouldn't trust them to run a cloakroom raffle!'

The blunt frankness of Lancashire folk about their politics was refreshing in contrast to the more prim, reserved responses of southerners that I had noticed three years before while campaigning for Ted Heath in Bexley, where many were embarrassed to discuss politics on the doorstep and were coy about revealing their voting intentions. In the industrial north, on the other hand, they enjoy their politics and positively relish calling a spade a spade. Although in the course of the campaign a couple declined to shake my hand, declaring themselves bluntly to be communist, a more common reaction among some of the men whom I talked to in the factories and in their pubs and clubs was: 'I wish you luck, lad, but yer wasting yer time here – I've been rank Labour all m' life, always will be!' But the women were less solidly Labour than their menfolk and, more times than I can remember, housewives with their hair in curlers or women factory workers wearing head-scarves would declare: 'Y' know what they say around here, luv? Put a pig in a red coat up for Labour and he'll still get in!'

Having myself now fought no fewer than seven election campaigns in Lancashire, I never cease to be amazed at how deep my family's political roots go in that part of the world, and at the length of people's memories. In the course of the Gorton campaign I came across a man of eighty-five whose father, a coachman, had driven my grandfather to the polls in Oldham in an open horse-drawn carriage on Election Day 1900. He related that, for the occasion, the horses had some 'lovely plush material' on their backs and, after the election was over, the owner of the carriage, a local brewer, had given the material to his father, which his mother had used to make pretty dresses for his two little sisters. Indeed, as recently as the 1983 general election, I found a gentleman in an old people's bungalow who made the proud boast to me: 'I voted against your Grandad when he put up as a Liberal in Northwest Manchester in 1906 – I voted Tory!' For him to have been qualified to vote in that election, when the minimum voting age was twenty-one, meant that he had to be over ninety-eight years of age at the time of our meeting.

But by no means all the reactions were so friendly. Very early on in my campaign in Gorton, as I was canvassing a dismal street of terraced houses, an elderly but powerfully built man, wearing no more than a vest and his workman's trousers although it was a cold, wet, November day, came down the steps of his front door and bodily picked up one of my Young Conservative canvassers by his lapels and started shaking him vigorously back and forth, bellowing: 'Your bloody Grandad murdered everyone on the beaches of Gallipoli!' Amazed that such a charge should still be hurled on the political hustings more than half a century after the event, I raced up the street to rescue my young supporter and to explain that it was my 'bloody Grandad', not his, and that anyway he had his facts wrong. Lancashire people have not lightly forgotten the appalling sacrifices made at Gallipoli, most spectacularly of all by the Lancashire Fusiliers who, uniquely, can make the proud boast of having won 'six VCs before breakfast'. In many people's minds my grandfather's name remained bound up with the failure of the landings on the Turkish Dardanelles coast. His idea of breaking through to Constantinople and linking up with our Russian ally had undoubtedly been the most brilliant strategic concept of the entire First World War and, had it succeeded – as it so very nearly did – would have significantly shortened the conflict, sparing the lives of hundreds of thousands condemned to 'chew barbed wire', as he had so vividly put it, on the Western Front. Indeed it might well even have forestalled the Russian Revolution, with all the profound consequences that would have had for later history. Intriguingly, few among those who actually fought in the campaign blamed the failure on my grandfather who no longer had charge of the direction of events at the time the slaughter began, being dismissed as First Lord of the Admiralty soon afterwards. Indeed, such was the regard that the survivors of the campaign had for my grandfather, that, many years later, they made me an honorary member of the Gallipoli Association.

Despite the decline and dereliction all around them and the very real hardship faced by countless thousands, the spirit of the people of Gorton was magnificent to see. In my experience of Lancashire people over more than twenty years, there are none so naturally warm-hearted and few so stalwart in the face of adversity. They were the same people who had soldiered on through the horrors of two world wars, borne the brunt of the Great Depression in between and still come up smiling. There were still in those days many pubs or clubs where, in a packed, smoke-filled atmosphere, they would drown their sorrows and banish their woes around an old honky-tonk piano playing the old tunes, which were sung with gusto by all, from the oldest to the youngest. Invariably, whenever I arrived, regardless of political differences, I was given the warmest of welcomes for the very fact that I had come to be among them. Men in the dirtiest working clothes would insist on buying me a pint which proved the curtain-raiser for many a lively political argument. Sometimes I would be greeted with the words: 'Give us a song, lad!' It is to this that I attribute my downfall in the election, for I cannot sing a note and I would usually end up with a staccato rendition of 'It's a Long Way to Tipperary' or 'Pack up your Troubles in your Old Kit Bag'! Occasionally, out of devilment, my arrival would be greeted with the playing of 'The Red Flag' but, even then we would as often as not finish up with 'Land of Hope and Glory'. Their songs were the marching songs of two world wars as well as those of the music hall. Many were my grandfather's old favourites which often, when we lunched alone together at Hyde Park Gate, he would hum or even sing towards the end of the meal, drumming lightly with his fingertips on the scrubbed deal dining table, such ditties as 'Daddy Wouldn't Buy me a Bow-Wow' and 'Run Rabbit, Run Rabbit, Run, Run, Run'!

A quaint relic of the past was the large number of men-only pubs, known as 'vaults', where men in their dirty working clothes would stand around in their boots on the sawdust-covered floor, drinking beer or playing darts. But, most noticeable of all to one coming from the more prosperous south, where people for the most part keep themselves to themselves, was the wonderful community spirit to be found in the close-knit back streets. Everybody knew their neighbours, and housewives would pass the time of day chatting to each other on the doorstep. If there was sickness or a death in the family, the neighbours would invariably rally round and offer their help.

Sadly all this has long since gone, swept away by the bulldozers, at the behest of remote and faceless 'planners'. Instead of repairing or rebuilding these homes street by street, an unyielding, anonymous bureaucracy ordained that whole square miles be flattened so as to accommodate their grandiose and ghastly schemes comprising a jungle of high-rise blocks and 'overspill' developments devoid of all character and most amenities. In the process whole communities were broken up and the spirit which gave those communities their soul, destroyed. It was a crime of giant proportions, the consequences of which, in terms of alienation, vandalism and rampant violence, are with us to this day.

For the campaign Minnie and I, together with young Randolph by now aged two and a half, moved into a semi-detached house in Aldwyn Park Road, Audenshaw, at the posher end of the constituency. We soon learned the hard way the inconveniences of the open coke fire in the living room, which was supposed to provide hot water and heat the three radiators in the house. Invariably each night it would go out, leaving the house freezing cold by dawn when, before setting out at 7 am to canvass bus queues of workers on their way to the factories, we would have to scoop out all the clinker and ash from the grate, re-lay it and laboriously endeavour to bring it to life again. At one stage, with the house freezing cold and with the Shadow Chancellor of the Exchequer, Iain Macleod, due to arrive for dinner with us before addressing two public meetings, Minnie in desperation used up all the wooden clothes pegs as kindling in a valiant effort to get the fire going. To young Randolph's great delight, the main Manchester to Sheffield railway line ran past the back garden not twenty yards from his bedroom, and we would hear the steam engines thunder past in the night with their whistles blowing.

To defend their stronghold the Labour Party wheeled in all their biggest guns save only the Prime Minister Harold Wilson, who wisely refrained from engaging his prestige in the contest in case the result proved a disaster. James Callaghan, the Chancellor of the Exchequer and future Prime Minister, came up, as well as a whole raft of senior Cabinet Ministers, including the sharp-tongued red-headed Transport Minister Barbara Castle, Minister for Education and Science Shirley Williams, and the youthful Minister of Technology Tony Benn, who declared portentously that 'The age of technological revolution has come!'

On my side I had the support of Sir Alec Douglas-Home, Shadow Foreign Secretary and former premier who on a cold wet night drew 750 people to the two meetings which he addressed; Tony Barber, the Party Chairman; Peter Walker, Shadow Transport Secretary; Keith Joseph whose portfolio was Trade and Industry; and Iain MacLeod, the Shadow Chancellor. The campaign was a lively one. Conservative Central Office drafted in no fewer than six agents to help with the election. A thousand Young Liberals were brought in from universities all over the country to support the 'Red Guard' Liberal, Terry Lacey, and the Labour Party mobilized the phalanxes of the trade union movement which had massive muscle in Gorton as well as in Manchester as a whole.

Stagnation in industrial production, crippling levels of taxation, rising unemployment, the weakness of the pound, the balance of payments deficit, deflation at home and lack of confidence abroad were among the key issues in the election, but most damaging of all to the Labour government was the lethal combination of a 10 per cent inflation rate and a statutory wage freeze.

The spirit among my campaign supporters was magnificent. School-teachers would get up at 5 am to do their housework so that as soon as they had finished their work in the evening, they could join me 'on the knocker' for the evening canvass which, in spite of the lashing rain and bitter cold, would not end until after 10 pm. Meanwhile, well-wishers crowded in from neighbouring constituencies in Lancashire and Cheshire, and some from much further afield, to lend their support. For sixty-one years, the seat had consistently returned a Labour candidate, with the exception only of 1931, when a Conservative had been elected. My supporters knew that the by-election provided the best chance in two generations of winning what had come to be regarded as an impregnable Labour stronghold. The mood, though not euphoric, was nonetheless strongly optimistic, and the bookmakers who had opened the betting at evens were quoting six to four on a Conservative victory by the end of the campaign.

By polling day at the end of a hectic, noisy but for all that enjoyable three-week campaign, I felt that victory was within our grasp and that we might just carry it off. The fact that it was a dark November night and heavy rain set in as Gortonians in their thousands poured home from their factories and shops seemed to favour the Conservatives. But the Labour Party did a superb job of pulling out their supporters on the trade union register and the sight of so many voters standing patiently in the driving rain in queues up to 100 yards long outside the polling stations was a disturbing sign. Whereas, when my supporters made a 'car call' to take a disabled or elderly supporter to the polling stations, the driver would wait to bring them back, the Labour drivers unceremoniously dumped their voters at the end of a long queue and told them they would have to make their own way home.

The count in Manchester's Town Hall was a tense and exciting affair, as the bundles of votes piled up on the tables for each of the candidates. It was clear from an early stage that, despite the five candidates, it was a two-horse race between Labour and Conservative. The battle raged to and fro between the front-runners. Now and then my bundles would edge into the lead, only to be swamped a few minutes later by bundles from a box in a heavily Labour area. Shortly after midnight, following one recount, the result was declared. Joseph Minogue in the *Guardian* of 3 November 1967 reported:

> After a cliff-hanging recount, Mr Ken Marks, the local Labour candidate, scraped home in Gorton with a majority of 577.
> In an exceptionally high poll of 72.5 per cent – only 1 per cent below the voting in the general election – there were times when it looked as though the Conservative Mr Winston Churchill was going to romp home...

Though the Chief Constable had warned me that there was a large and hostile crowd waiting for me outside the Town Hall and had recommended that Minnie and I, together with our supporters, should leave by a rear exit, I – mindful of my father's decision in similar circumstances at the Devonport election sixteen years before – declined the offer and said we would go out the front door. The *Daily Mirror* reported:

> Tory candidate Winston Churchill and his wife were jostled by a fist-shaking crowd after the Gorton result was announced last night. About twenty policemen had to go to their aid as they left Manchester Town Hall. About 250 people had surged forward as the couple walked down the Town Hall steps to their car. Police formed a 'wall' round them as the crowd jeered and shook their fists.

The Conservative Clubs in Gorton and Denton were jam-packed with supporters when we arrived there in the early hours of the morning. They had had the champagne on standby for a victory celebration, but insisted on opening it nonetheless. I knew that it had been their best chance in thirty-five years of winning the seat from the socialists, and how bitterly disappointed they were that we had so narrowly failed to win. Though everyone was wonderfully kind in congratulating me on the campaign and the narrowness of my defeat, I felt that I had let down the hundreds of people who had worked so tirelessly and eagerly on my behalf. We had needed a swing of 10.1 per cent to topple the Labour Party and, in the event, secured just 9.5 per cent. Iain Macleod pointed out that, though it had been a five-cornered contest, we had succeeded in increasing the Conservative vote by more than 2,200 and reducing the Labour vote by some 5,500, and that 'the Gorton result was the equivalent of the Conservative majority of 150 seats at a General Election', adding quite rightly: 'There are no prizes for finishing second and no one knows this better than a Churchill.'

A few weeks later I was amused to receive a letter from Averell Harriman, writing from the Department of State in Washington on 19 December 1967: 'You may be interested to know that I met one of the Labour Party Ministers recently [I suspect it may have been Roy Jenkins]. He told me that you had done extremely well since the Labour Party had been determined not to permit a Churchill to win for psychological reasons, and had made an unusual effort to beat you...'

Within ten days of the by-election, the Labour government was forced to devalue the pound, making clear for all to see the serious straits into which Labour's economic policies had brought the country. James Callaghan, the Chancellor of the Exchequer, appalled his own party by stating that unemployment would have to rise and that a 'somewhat larger margin of unused manpower' was desirable. The socialist weekly *New Statesman* of 10 November, in a piece entitled 'Jim's Appalling Frankness', commented acidly: 'If Mr Callaghan's latest speech had been made a fortnight earlier, it is safe to say that Mr Churchill would be the MP for Gorton...'

Though bitterly disappointed in the result at the time, in retrospect it proved a blessing in disguise. It would have been impossible to sustain a swing in excess of 10 per cent in the general election that ensued, and I would have found myself without a seat just as Tory candidates up and down the country were winning theirs. I had the good fortune, two years later, to secure the nomination for the Labour-held seat of Stretford, some five miles away on the west side of Manchester – a seat which I was able to win from Labour in the 1970 general election and which, in spite of a major alteration of its boundaries and the change of its name to Davyhulme, has returned me to Parliament for nearly twenty years.

· XIX ·

Last Days at Stour

Contrary to the belief of all his White's Club friends and in spite of my grandmother's doubts, my father ardently espoused country life and it soon became clear that he intended Stour to be his home to the end of his days. He proclaimed himself to be a confirmed 'Country Bumpkin'. He pitied his townee friends for their impoverished existence in not possessing, as he now so proudly did, rolling lawns, colourful borders and distant views across an unspoiled countryside. He rejoiced in having a multitude of dogs – three black pugs, a King Charles Cavalier and a Jack Russell – and filling his house with roses, peonies, dahlias and other fragrant blooms from his garden and, above all, in being able to have his many friends to stay.

His garden – a hay field when he took it over – became his passion. He planted a wonderful variety of trees, including wisterias, walnuts and a mulberry tree. At one point, on discovering the glory of the tulip tree, he became one of its most avid fans, scouring the land to find the finest of the species for an article which he dedicated to the subject, naturally planting one in his own garden 'for posterity'. But nothing excited him more than the vision, planning and realization of his gently sloping avenue of pleached lime trees, which rapidly grew to form a leafy tunnel where he could stroll with his dogs and his friends in the cool half-shade. Each arch of the avenue on the valley side framed the unblemished view to the church tower of Dedham and the River Stour, whether on a crisp winter's morning or across a shimmering summer heat haze. At the midpoint of the avenue the trees opened out to form a broad circle where he strategically placed oak benches to capture the view both across the valley – his 'Constable', as he dubbed it – and, in the other direction, to the village church of East Bergholt, whose fine clockface he restored, framed under a canopy of tall cedars.

237

Under the expert guidance of his friend Xenia Field, the gardening correspondent of the *Daily Mirror* who was a regular visitor to Stour, one corner of the garden after another was tamed and embellished and the area of overgrown woodland at the end of the lime avenue was transformed into a carpet of polyanthus, the 'Blue River' as he called it, leading down to a dirty patch of water which he cleaned up and made into an attractive pond. The very first summer that I spent at Stour, at the age of fifteen, Father acquired a heavy but powerful machine called an Allen scythe, with which I would spend long hours 'bush-whacking' to reclaim the lawns and tame the woodland. Meanwhile roses and dahlias were planted close to the house, together with thousands of daffodils and snowdrops in the wood.

One day, while taking me out for lunch from Eton, he took me to the home of Sir George Bellew, former Garter King of Arms, whom he had befriended in the course of writing his books on the Coronation, *They Serve the Queen* and *The Story of the Coronation*. As we walked round the garden of Sir George's house at the edge of Windsor Great Park, Father spied four splendid white-painted eighteenth-century pinewood columns lying in a heap against a wall, apparently unused. He promptly made an offer for them, having just backed the Derby winner, Hard Ridden, at eighteen to one at Epsom. These he proceeded to erect on his stone terrace at Stour to form a pergola, shaded by a vine and cascading with climbing roses, wistaria, honeysuckle and clematis. On the terrace walls he placed some beautiful lead statuettes of nymphs which we have to this day on the terrace of our garden in Kent. Here, from the earliest spring sunshine until a late Indian summer of autumn, we would eat lunch out whenever the sun was shining. For long hours we would sit round the circular marble table beneath his lovely pergola, while the plight of the government was discussed or the hottest news from the crisis points of the world debated, amid blazing rows and uproarious laughter, which would follow each other as swiftly as the threatening dark clouds and brilliant sunshine would chase each other across the broad Suffolk landscape.

For one who did not know a plantain from a primula, Father took to gardening like a duck to water. The principal bait to attract his friends from London or abroad was: 'You must come and see my garden,' and it was not long before he was liberally dispensing horticultural advice, both verbally to his friends, and in articles in women's magazines. In an essay for *A Book of Gardens* he expatiated his views of the art of gardening:

The first rule is 'do it yourself'. On no account fall into the hands of a landscape gardener, any more than you would into those of your doctors, lawyers or interior decorators. Of course you pick the brains of all your clever gardening friends. In fact you don't have to pick them: they thrust their advice upon you. But don't get rattled; take the decision yourself after due thought. This does not mean, necessarily, that you need do much manual labour yourself. Apart from being the watering boy, I regard my functions in the garden as those of the constitutional monarch, as defined by Bagehot: 'to be consulted, to encourage and to warn'.

For most of his life my father's finances were precarious in the extreme. Though undoubtedly the best-known and probably the highest-paid British journalist of his day, he was forever in debt due to his determination to live in a style to which he had allowed himself to become accustomed from an early age. He had a retinue of three or four 'young gentlemen' researchers, an equal number of secretaries and – whenever they could be persuaded to stay – a complement of domestic staff. The situation was not improved by his lavish hospitality and his great generosity towards his friends. We would go through periodic crises when petrol could only be bought two or three gallons at a time and purchases of whiskey and tobacco had to be restricted to a single bottle and two or three packs of cigarettes. This latter was a tiresome constraint for it necessitated at least two visits to the pub per day, since Father, even when he was not entertaining, would put away by himself a bottle or bottle and a half, together with 100 cigarettes a day. Most mortifying of all – certainly to me – were those occasions when the local shopkeepers – the butcher, the baker, the green-grocer and newsagent – would form themselves into a desultory queue outside the back door to request payment of their accounts which were many months overdue. The only one not of their number was the publican, who sensibly and invariably required to be paid in cash.

It was at one such moment of financial constraint that my father came to learn of what was then the latest and most popular quiz show on American television, *The $64,000 Question*. In those days, $64,000 was a great deal of money and the prospect of winning such a sum was quite irresistible to my father, who readily convinced himself that he would win the jackpot and started behaving as if he had already done so, purchasing a few more magnolias for his garden or a *pâté de foie gras* to feast his friends. I recall a large part of one of my holidays being devoted to rehearsing him on Kipling, which it had been agreed with the programme's producers was to be the subject. Father, like my grandfather, had a remarkable memory for poetry. He knew his Kipling and could quote lengthy passages from memory. Each night we would sit up until two or three in the morning in his smoke-filled drawing room with its splendid if a trifle vulgar apricot flock wallpaper, as he declaimed great passages or was cross-examined by me and his 'young gentlemen' on others. Even well past midnight there would be a stenographer on hand to take notes or type any memos which might be required. If any of the team, myself included, showed signs of flagging, we would be abruptly galvanized into action once again with a *fortissimo* rendition of one of Father's favourite injunctions:

> The heights achieved by men and kept
> Were not attained by sudden flight
> But they, while their companions slept
> Were toiling upwards through the night.

It sometimes seemed to me that he would have made an admirable seventeenth-century slave-driver.

By the end of a fortnight, Father knew his Kipling backwards and had every confidence that the $64,000, on which he had set his heart, was in the bag. However, with less than a week remaining before he was due in New York for the contest, disaster struck. The producers telephoned to say that they had decided that, after all, Kipling was too narrow a field and would he mind extending the field to include the entire English language. Father had little choice but to agree, and anyway he prided himself as being the equal of any man on the subject. But, how do you mug up the English language? Where does one begin? In spite of the last-minute switch, he headed off to the United States with the highest hopes. Sadly, he came a cropper at the second fence. The first, 'What English nobleman, addicted to gambling, gave his name to a form of food?', he sailed over with the reply 'Lord Sandwich'. But the answer to the second question eluded him: 'What agent of an English landowner in Ireland so provoked his tenants by his repressive behaviour that his name entered the English language?'

Struggle as he might, and though he knew the answer, he could not recall the name of Captain Boycott. Father was mortified by his failure, returning not only with his fierce pride wounded but – to add insult to injury – a mere $64, instead of the $64,000 he had set his heart on winning. Soon afterwards a friend, by way of consolation, made him a present of a black pug dog and – so that he would never forget it again – he named him Captain Boycott. When, in the fullness of time, the good Captain took a wife, the *Dictionary of National Biography*, always to hand on his library shelf, had to be consulted. From this it was established that his wife should be called Annie and their male progeny, Cunningham.

Sad to relate, the Captain did not survive to a ripe old age, but was found upended among the dahlias with a hundred bites to his body, having been savaged by Father's fiendish Jack Russell terrier dubbed 'Little John' after Lord John Russell, who was twice Prime Minister in the nineteenth century. Nor was this the only misfortune to befall the latter-day Boycott family. Father had also acquired a beautiful King Charles Cavalier spaniel, whom he named Orlando. Unbeknown to anyone, the gallant Orlando had seduced the Captain's wife, Annie. Meanwhile my father had promised the pick of his next litter of baby pugs to Janet Auchincloss, Jackie Kennedy's mother. Full of pride, he took the adorable puglet with him on his next trip to the United States and, with great ceremony, made the presentation to Mrs Auchincloss, who was thrilled. However, after a few weeks had passed, she reported that the strangest things were happening. The baby pug's silky black coat was turning brown, its legs were getting longer and it had grown a brown bushy tail. Suspicion rightly turned upon the handsome and entrancing Orlando, whom my father, in a moment of weakness he was subsequently to regret, had given me.

In addition to his dogs, Father acquired a Shetland pony, originally for Arabella to ride. Because of its independent, determined and often intractable spirit he called the animal Macleod, after his friend Iain with whom he had fallen out over his column in the *Spectator*. When, one autumn day, the dogs uncovered, under a pile of leaves, a baby hedgehog, Father rescued it and dubbed him Quintin after another of his great friends, Quintin Hogg, later Lord Hailsham, who subsequently became a most distinguished Lord Chancellor. Taking pity on baby Quintin on what promised to be a cold November night, he tucked him up with him at the bottom of his double bed. The experiment was not a success. Father woke up in the early hours of the morning, itching all over, to discover the bed hopping with fleas.

Residential staff were a perennial problem. When asked by his friends: 'How is your new cook?' he was fond of quoting the dictum: 'She was good as cooks go: but, as cooks go, she went!' The only permanent retainers were a small army of daily women from the village.

These apart, the most loyal and long-surviving of the staff at Stour were his secretaries, Barbara Twigg and Eileen Harryman. When all else failed – as it often did – Miss Twigg, besides her secretarial duties, would be asked to meet trains at the local station, make the beds, and even on occasion do the cooking. Whatever she was asked to do, she always had a smile on her face. Miss Harryman, who was grandly styled the Archivist, found that her responsibilities included arranging the flowers and clearing up after the dogs. Nor were the 'young gentlemen' researchers exempted from activities outside their sphere of employment. They would find themselves 'volunteered' to mow the lawn if there was no one else to hand to do so. Among his many researchers – mostly high-flying Oxford history graduates – was Michael Wolff, who went on to be Director of Research at Conservative Central Office and occupied a senior position under Edward Heath for several years at Downing Street before, tragically, dying at an early age. Others included Alan Brien, who became a successful novelist, Tony Howard, subsequently editor of the *New Statesman* and later of the *Observer*, and Martin Gilbert, who was to carry forward to completion the great biography of my grandfather. For each one their time at Stour proved an unforgettable experience and, in spite of the ups and downs – and there were plenty of both – there were few who regretted the experience or who do not look back with a certain fondness on the time they spent working for my father.

The visits of friends were an important part of life at Stour and they were many and various. Of the family, besides Arabella and myself who would come for our school holidays, my father's sister Sarah, and his cousin Peregrine Churchill together with his delightful French wife Yvonne, were regular visitors. His mother would make occasional visits but, ever wary of being cornered in some argument or other, would confine herself to day trips from London, usually in the company of her lifelong friend Sylvia Henley. Among friends who came to stay were his comrades-in-arms David Stirling and Julian Amery; from the world of politics Iain and Eve Macleod, Woodrow Wyatt, Alec and Elizabeth Douglas-Home and Aidan Crawley with his wife Virginia, who was my godmother; from the fields of publishing and journalism George Weidenfeld (who commissioned this book), Charles Wintour, Norman and Jean Mailer and Bernard Levin; from the arts Paul Maze and Feliks Topolski; and from the world of television, Clive Irving, Ned Sherrin and David Frost.

Each human being is endowed with his or her share of virtues and vices. In my father's case, these were writ larger than most. He could be loud, boorish, offensive, bellicose and downright rude, often without just cause. These traits were not helped by his immoderate consumption of whiskey. But those who were not initially put off by such tantrums and who made clear that they were not prepared to be hectored or bullied, became devoted to him. He had a large heart and was ever ready to spring to the assistance of his friends, or even those he did not know but for whom he felt aggrieved. On one occasion, outraged at the way in which Lord Rothermere's *Daily Sketch* had published a story falsely reporting to be written by Mrs Jeremy Fry, the wife of the best man at Princess Margaret's marriage to Lord Snowdon, about her marriage, he had promptly contacted her and placed his very considerable experience of litigation at her disposal. It was at a time when he had been seeking single-handedly to clean up the Augean stables of Fleet Street and was endeavouring to insist that the press barons should have regard to basic standards of honesty and decency in journalism. Not only had Mrs Fry not written the article that purported to be by her, but she had not even given an interview to the newspaper. At one stage in the proceedings, as a result of the personal intervention of Lord Rothermere (father of the present one) who betook himself one weekend in his motorcar down to Lewes in Sussex, where Mrs Fry's mother had an antique shop, to warn her that her daughter was making a grave mistake which would cost her dear, Mrs Fry's lawyers urged her to settle the matter – a course of action which would have involved the loss of her case and considerable expense. The lawyers took the view that for Lord Rothermere to travel such a distance in his Rolls-Royce at a weekend must mean that he was in deadly earnest about defending the case. My father's reaction was quite the opposite. 'Windy old bugger!' he proclaimed. 'We've got him on the run – don't give an inch!' When Mrs Fry went on to win exemplary damages, she very generously sent my father a case of 1911 brandy – the year of his birth. Father was delighted with what came to be known as the 'libellous brandy' and bequeathed a bottle to his grandson and namesake with which to celebrate his twenty-first birthday.

At the height of the Profumo crisis, with Fleet Street in full cry – an unlovely spectacle at the best of times – Jack and Valerie Profumo found themselves besieged in their London home by the world's press who were camped on their doorstep. It was a low point in their lives and, at a time when other friends were seeking to distance themselves, my father insisted on publicly demonstrating his abiding affection for his friends by forcing his way through the throng of press and television reporters to visit them. He then launched Operation Sanctuary, enabling them to go to ground at Stour for five days at the end of June 1963 without the press having any idea where they were, while the furore subsided. Though Father could often be trying and argumentative, there was no friend more loyal or more dependable in a crisis.

There were also times, it has to be said, when my father would awake on a Sunday morning and at mid-morning, when there was no sign of his guests, he would enquire if they were still asleep, only to discover that they had packed their bags and left. He would no doubt recall that they had had a 'jolly' row but, forgetting the fierceness of the argument or how barbed had been the insults, he would find it quite incomprehensible that his guests should take offence and leave so unceremoniously. Alan Brien, a journalist and novel-writer who had once been one of my father's researchers, brought his pretty American bride-to-be, Nancy Ryan, to stay for the weekend. The cook had departed in dudgeon the night before, so we dined at the lovely old Sun Inn at Dedham. Before the coffee had arrived Alan, whom I had not suspected of being so sensitive, declared that he had had enough of the blazing row which had erupted and left the table, taking Nancy with him. I was at Oxford at the time and had a car of my own so, shortly afterwards, I slipped out to retrieve them. I found our guests hoofing it on foot in the darkness, already a mile on their way back towards the house, intent on catching the first available train home. For a man who in his good moods could be the most delightful, amusing and entertaining of companions, it was tragic that my father's brief bouts of uncontrollable bad temper made him his own worst enemy. It sorely tested the patience of his friends and effectively ruled out his ever holding down a parliamentary constituency, the workings of which are entirely dependent upon the goodwill and voluntary work of local supporters who, understandably, do not accept being shouted at.

In the closing years of his life at Stour, Father formed a deep friendship with Natalie Bevan, a Suffolk neighbour who lived some eight or ten miles away in a lovely house in the village of Boxted. She was a lady of great charm and beauty, with long blonde hair which she wore up. She was a talented artist – an accomplished painter and especially skilled in the art of pottery. She had a delightful husband, Bobby, and they and my father would spend long hours in each other's company around the dinner table or eating out in the summer months on the terraces of their respective homes. Father placed Natalie, with her fine artistic eye, in charge of selecting the photographs for the great biography from among the thousands he had inherited. It was she, too, who arranged the flowers for my marriage to Minnie, and no one could have done them better. Natalie became adept at handling my father who, as both my mother and my stepmother June had soon discovered, was not the easiest person to live with. It was a distinct advantage that Natalie lived some miles away and this was doubtless a major reason why their friendship was so enduring. She brought sunshine and serenity to his closing years.

The biography of his father became the most fulfilling of all the tasks to which my father set his hand, as he laboured with enthusiasm and filial devotion to erect a literary memorial worthy of the man he worshipped as 'the author of our being' and the greatest Englishman of all time. There was, of course, the odd diversion, when he felt impelled to intervene with an article for the *Evening Standard* or the *Spectator* in some domestic political row which had flared as a result of a nonsense perpetrated by 'our Socialist Masters', as he called the Labour government of Harold Wilson. He would still make occasional, though much less frequent, sallies across the Atlantic to 'take the temperature' of 'those' United States. He also, but only briefly, set aside his great work to write 'quickie' books on *The Fight For the Tory Leadership* following Macmillan's resignation in 1963, *Twenty-One*, a brief autobiographical essay, and to collaborate with me on the writing of *The Six Day War*.

Though robust in constitution, he was plagued with ill health, much of it self-inflicted. Surprising as it may be to many taken in by popular myths, my grandfather was not a heavy smoker and drank only in moderation. It is true that for much of the day he would have a cigar in his mouth and a glass of whiskey and soda on a table to hand. But, for at least half the time, the cigar would be out and anyway its effects are not so noxious as those of the cigarette, which he abandoned as a young man following a visit to Cuba at the time of the Revolutionary War against Spain. His fancy had apparently been taken by the sight of the Cuban women, their skirts pulled up high, rolling the tobacco leaf on the inside of their thighs to make cigars. His whiskeys were invariably weak – at least half the strength of that preferred by most confirmed whiskey drinkers – and one glass would keep him going a long time. Regrettably, my father's consumption was much less moderate. So addicted was he that he would scarcely go five minutes without a cigarette, and he bore heavy nicotine stains on the fingers of his right hand. Though the link between cigarette smoking and lung cancer was unknown at the time, Grandpapa urged him more than once to moderate his consumption, as he strongly suspected it was doing him no good. As early as November 1944 Grandpapa had written to him in Yugoslavia to warn him of the dangers:

I had a hope that the difficulties of your commissariat would enforce abstention from the endless cigarette. If you can get rid of your husky voice and get back the timbre which your aged father still possesses, it might affect the whole future of your political life. It may be that abandoning cigarettes may not be the remedy, but it is in my bones that it is worth trying. Your sisters told me that it was in the Liverpool election that, with a very sore throat and against the doctor's warnings, you bellowed for a considerable time in the market place. Weigh these counsels of a friend, even if you are unwilling to receive them from a father.

But the advice was in vain. Father's greatest concession was, in later years, to only half-smoke his cigarettes before discarding them. Nor was he any more restrained in his consumption of whiskey, which he had embarked upon in consequence of his visits while an Oxford undergraduate to his godfather F. E. Smith, later Lord Birkenhead, at his nearby home of Charlton. 'F. E.', who became Lord Chancellor and was the finest advocate at the bar as well as the greatest orator of his day, was responsible for convincing my father and a gilded circle of his Oxford friends who had political aspirations that, to make a proper speech, it was necessary to be half-inebriated.

I owe it to my father that I have never had any desire to smoke cigarettes, or touch a drop of whiskey. The way in which the wreaths of smoke which surrounded him would sting my eyes as a child whenever I entered his library or his bedroom and the bouts of coughing and spluttering which went with it, were enough to cure me of any temptation in that direction. Furthermore, living at close quarters to one addicted to the demon whiskey, which so readily transformed irritability into full-blown rage, left me firmly biased against it.

In my father's case, it was a close-run race between cigarettes and whiskey as to which would strike him down first. At the age of fifty-three he had to be operated on for the removal of part of a lung, which the doctors pronounced to be non-malignant. When this piece of information came over the ticker-tape of White's Club and was conveyed to the bar it provoked the immortal comment from his erstwhile friend Evelyn Waugh, who had not spoken to him for years: 'Trust those damn fool doctors to cut out of Randolph the only part of him that wasn't malignant!' This, when reported to my father, provoked an instant reconciliation between the two.

After that he had to take life more easily and, for two or three months when the cold and mists of winter threatened at home, he would retreat to the sunshine of Barbados or, more often, Marrakesh, which had been such a favourite resort of his father's. He would load up his car with a huge number of tin boxes containing his father's papers so that work on the book could go ahead at full steam. Taking with him Andrew Kerr – who, besides being an able researcher, became a close friend and companion in his later years, travelling with him almost everywhere he went and making all the necessary arrangements for his comfort and convenience – as well as his most loyal and efficient secretary, Barbara Twigg, he would set forth on the three- or four-day journey to Morocco.

There he would establish his forward base at the spectacular oasis of Marrakesh, standing beneath the snow-capped splendour of the High Atlas mountains. Its arid atmosphere and warm sunshine invigorated and restored him, enabling him to labour on with his writing. He would be visited for weeks at a stretch by Natalie, who would fly out to join him, or by Michael Wolff who, for a considerable time, was his magisterial Director of Research and whose company he greatly enjoyed. Michael, together with his wife Rosemary and their daughters, were close friends and frequent visitors to Stour. While in Marrakesh they would from time to time dine with 'Boule' (Comtesse) de Breteuil, at the Villa Taylor, her magnificent Moorish palazzo set in a subtropical garden, where my grandfather had once entertained President Roosevelt during the War, following the Casablanca Conference. They would also find time for jolly picnics in the rocky foothills of the Atlas mountains.

He would return from his winter sojourns suntanned and in good heart, but the various ailments that assailed him continued to take their toll and he was noticeably less robust than before. He was greatly excited by my decision to fight the Labour stronghold of Gorton and was anxious to come up and help, as his father had helped him in his contests at Wavertree and Toxteth in Liverpool in the Thirties. Knowing that he no longer enjoyed the best of health and conscious of his unrivalled ability with a few brusque words to offend platoons of volunteer workers, I dissuaded him from coming, determined to fight the battle myself. Nonetheless he dispatched the ever cheerful Barbara Twigg to the battlefront to help, and kept in close touch by telephone throughout the campaign.

Following my articles in the course of the Middle East war for the London *Evening News*, I received an invitation to become their roving correspondent, an offer which I accepted with alacrity. One of my first assignments for the paper was to cover the visit to Washington early in 1968 of Harold Wilson. I had up to that point never met the Prime Minister and I found myself in the amusing position of being introduced to him by the President of the United States, Lyndon Johnson, who happened to include me among the guests at the large state dinner he was giving for his British guest at the White House. It was a splendid and very grand affair but, given the hospitality of his host and the fact that the Labour government had been only too eager to borrow billions of dollars from the United States to sustain the British economy, I found it embarrassing to listen to the Prime Minister's insensitive and critical references to the US involvement in Vietnam, where the casualty toll was rising.

Soon after my return from Washington Minnie and I visited my father at Stour. He was as eager as ever to know the latest news from the United States and to have word of his many friends there. I found him in a reflective mood and, late at night, as he and I sat up talking alone together, he suddenly declared, certainly apropos nothing that I had said: 'You should never boast about your conquests!' I was taken aback and could not think what on earth he could be alluding to. Evidently my mention of the fact that I had lunched with Averell Harriman in Washington had reminded him of their first meeting in Cairo more than a quarter of a century before. He described how his father had sent him a telegram stressing the importance of Averell's forthcoming visit to the Middle East to assess the situation on behalf of President Roosevelt. In compliance with his father's request to do what he could to make Averell's visit enjoyable, he had one evening chartered an Arab dhow and given a small party in his honour as they cruised up the Nile under a moonlit sky. Telling the story against himself without bitterness or rancour, he confided: 'We had had a fine dinner and [speaking no doubt for himself] rather too much to drink, which led me to do the unforgivable. I boasted to Averell of an affair I was having with the American wife of a senior British officer in Cairo.' He added, somewhat wistfully: 'I had no idea what was going on in London.' He would have been as astonished, as, indeed would I, to have been told that, within barely three years of our conversation, shortly after my stepfather Leland Hayward's death in the spring of 1971, Averell and my mother would be married. Considering that Averell was on the point of celebrating his eightieth birthday when they married, he and my mother were fortunate to enjoy fifteen years of happy marriage together.

Following publication of my book with my father on the Six Day War I found myself – without so much as a day's military service to my name – being sought out as one with some pretension to military knowledge or expertise. To my amazement I was invited to address a group of eighty majors and lieutenant-colonels at Chelsea Barracks on the subject of Israeli tactics and deception in the war. I opened my remarks with a disclaimer of having had any formal knowledge or training in military matters beyond what I had been able to pick up along the way as a journalist in such places as Yemen, the Congo, Angola, Borneo and Vietnam. Afterwards an officer on the course, David Webb-Carter, who had been a friend and contemporary of mine at Eton, expostulated that he, in ten years' service with the Army, had not heard so much as a shot fired in anger, and was most envious of all the wars I had managed to get to as a correspondent.

Our book had sold out in the first fortnight and quickly ran into second and third editions. Meanwhile foreign editions were rushed out in more than a dozen languages including Hebrew, Russian (published in Israel),

Japanese and most European languages, as well as special editions for the Indian and Pakistani armed forces, which were eyeing each other with distrust at the time. I was disturbed to hear reports of people being jailed in the Soviet Union for possessing a copy of our book, which was on the index of forbidden literature. As the royalties poured in, the first thing I did with the proceeds was to plant an avenue of standard Peace roses in our garden at Broadwater. Not only do I love their brilliant golden colour and heavy scent, but I felt that enjoyment of them would make a pleasant respite from my career as a war correspondent. I interspersed the roses with flowering Japanese cherries – a reminder of the cherry avenue in the garden at Minterne, which I had so admired in my childhood days.

I had always wanted a sailing boat, so I used the success of the book as the excuse to acquire an International Tempest two-man keel-boat capable of speeds up to nineteen knots. I called it *Mercury*, after the messenger of the gods who had wings on his heels. The boat was not Minnie's favourite since the crew, wearing a trapeze harness, had to be suspended by a wire from the top of the mast, outboard of the vessel, with both feet against the outside of the hull to prevent it capsizing. We kept it nearby at the Channel port of Newhaven and, going out for a blow in a stiff breeze off Beachy Head, even wearing wetsuits, was guaranteed to be an exciting and invigorating experience. Fortunately I had a partner in crime, willing to go out with me any time the wind was too strong for Minnie's slender frame to keep the boat upright: our close friend and neighbour Christopher Davy, a solidly built six-footer who had done his National Service in the Royal Navy. I was amused to discover that we had been in the same house at Eton, but he had been asked by our housemaster, Tom Brocklebank, to leave a term early to make way for a boy who was due to arrive in the house the following term who, he later discovered, was me. Although our paths never crossed then, by the time we met he had long since forgiven me and we became the best of friends.

Whenever, at a weekend, I heard the wind blowing up in the night, I would make sure of listening to the shipping forecast on the radio just before the 6 am news. If there was a good breeze of Force 6 or 7 forecast, I would telephone Christopher to join me, and together we would launch the trusty *Mercury*, which was little more than a sailing dinghy with a keel made of a quarter of a ton of lead in the shape of a torpedo suspended beneath the hull. On one occasion we were the only boat putting to sea. Even the cross-Channel ferries to Dieppe were not sailing because of the high seas and the strength of the wind. We flew with the wind eastwards down the coast towards Beachy Head. But when, opposite the Beachy Head lighthouse, we tried to turn about to head back for harbour, we ran into difficulties. It was a raw day in early March with a biting cold wind, which was so strong that it proved impossible to go about. In spite of Christopher's considerable strength and weight, I could not get her to turn into wind. We failed more than a dozen times, including once when the boat was blown so flat to the water that Christopher, on the end of the trapeze-wire, found himself catapulted from the outside of the hull on the windward side, head first through the sail into the sea, making a terrible bloody mess of the sail. All the while, I had at the back of my mind the reassuring thought that at least if we found ourselves in serious difficulty, we were in full view of the lighthouse-keeper who would swiftly be able to call a helicopter to our rescue. Only subsequently did I discover that the Beachy Head lighthouse had recently been automated and was in fact unmanned!

That spring proved hectic from a journalistic standpoint. In mid-March I flew out at no more than three hours' notice to Central Africa to report developments there. It proved a particularly interesting visit as it afforded me the opportunity to meet political leaders both north and south of the Zambesi, including the Rhodesian Premier Ian Smith, Dr Hastings Banda, President of Malawi, as well as President Kaunda of Zambia. Minnie and I then travelled to Scandinavia where I addressed students at Oslo and Copenhagen Universities, before going on to report the Vietnam peace talks which were just getting under way in Paris, where Averell Harriman, leader of the U S delegation, briefed me on the many difficulties with which he was confronted.

Following a further journalistic sortie, this time to the Middle East, I returned in late May to find an invitation from our Sussex neighbour, Harold Macmillan, to lunch with him at Birch Grove, where my father was to be his guest. It was a sunny day in late spring and, at Harold's suggestion, Minnie and I brought young Randolph, aged three, Jennie, one and a half, and Marina, just six months, with us to see their grandfather. As we sat on the terrace before lunch Father, frailer than I had seen him before but nonetheless in good heart, took his grandson on his knee, put his arm around him and declared with feeling: 'I am very proud of this boy!' He proceeded to produce the large, beautifully engraved gold Breguet pocket watch which had been his father's and which has now been passed down to me. Dangling it on its gold chain, he made it chime the hours, quarter-hours and minutes, to young Randolph's great delight.

Though the possibility did not even cross my mind, that day at Birch Grove was to be the last time I ever saw my father. Within a fortnight he was dead. I had not appreciated, perhaps because it was not in his nature to discuss such matters, how seriously ill he had been. He had lost a considerable amount of weight and, for some time, had been eating very little. Though no one told me of it, at the beginning of June he became gravely ill and took to his bed. He was deeply distressed to learn the tragic news of Senator Robert Kennedy's assassination on 4 June. He had long had a deep admiration for Bobby, whom he often said he loved 'as a brother'. The following day, as his own life was slipping away, it was reported to him that Bobby's assassin had been caught. Feeling in close communion with Bobby, Father in his last words, as his life ebbed away, declared, pugnacious to the end: 'Good! But have they caught the fellow who's done me in?' He died on the morning of 6 June – D-Day – at his home at Stour with his faithful pug dogs at his side.

By the time of his death, he had already completed two volumes of his great biography of his father, which he intended as a five-volume work, but has since been extended to eight volumes by Martin Gilbert who succeeded him in the task. Those two first volumes stand as a worthy monument not only to the memory of my grandfather but also to the power and prowess of my father as a biographer. It had been far from a foregone conclusion that the privilege of writing the definitive life of his father would fall to him. It was an accolade which came to him only late in his life, after he had demonstrated his potential with his life of Lord Derby. His own had been a life of many disappointments, especially in the field of politics to which he aspired with such eagerness. He had been haunted by what Harold Macmillan's grandson, Alexander, the 2nd Viscount Stockton, has justly called 'the demons of ancestor-comparison'. But it was the Great Biography which gave purpose to his life and had been its theme in his closing years. He passionately wanted to be granted the time to complete the mammoth task and, thereafter, to accomplish 'Project K' – as he code-named the biography of President Kennedy, which the late President's family had asked him to write and which he regarded as the greatest compliment of his life. Sadly, none of this was to be.

He was a man who shared his father's courage and strength of character in full measure, but who proved less capable of exercising the self-discipline necessary for a career in public life. Because he had such a natural facility as an orator – unlike his father – he neglected to take the trouble over his speeches that might have made them great.

His life was full of paradoxes. He was never backwards in asserting his views nor, to use a Biblical metaphor, reluctant to 'kick against the pricks'. Here was the schoolboy who reprimanded his housemaster, the candidate who fought against the power of his own party's political machine, the lieutenant who would lecture generals and call for their dismissal, the journalist who publicly attacked the press barons of Fleet Street for 'romping in the gutter', and the litigant who reminded learned counsel of the finer points of the law. With relish and panache he had crusaded against spiritual wickedness in high places.

Father had given me clear-cut instructions about his wishes in the event of his death. I was to invite all his friends to drink up whatever might be left in his cellar and, as to his mortal remains, I was to 'have the dustman' take him away. This latter injunction – which anyway might not have been easy to fulfil – was subsequently modified to a request that his ashes be scattered at Stour in the garden which he had created and which he loved.

We held his funeral at East Bergholt. After the service, at which Harold Macmillan read the lesson, family and friends returned to Stour where we gave a luncheon. Afterwards, as we walked in the leafy shade of the already fine pleached lime avenue, Harold Macmillan, talking of my father, turned to me and said: 'You know, Winston, your father was the last to live in the grand manner!' I knew precisely what he had in mind. Even until the early hours of the morning Father would have a whole team of young gentlemen working away at his bidding and a secretary standing by to take dictation. I well recall how, following his last visit to Macmillan at Birch Grove, Father had telephoned me to let me know how shocked he had been to discover how poorly served was the former prime minister although, unlike himself, he was a wealthy man. 'I asked Harold, around midnight,' he recounted, 'if he would kindly have one of his secretaries or young gentlemen look up a train for me for the morning and order me a taxi to take me to the station. Would you believe it?' my father enquired in a shocked tone. 'The old boy got up, went to the bookcase, proceeded to look up a train in *Bradshaws* himself, before telephoning the station to book a cab for the morning. I just couldn't believe it!'

Though in the previous three years I had lost both my Churchill and my Digby grandfathers, I had never faced up to the possibility that my father might not have much longer to live. Ever since he came back from the War, he had been an important part of my life, and I could not believe that he would not be around for many years to come. Suddenly – too late – I received a telephone call to say that he was failing fast. It is no doubt the case in too many human relationships that one takes the other for granted but, as the Bible tells us: 'Death comes as a thief in the night, and none may know the hour when he cometh.' It was only when I saw the simple oak coffin before the altar in the village church, that the true finality of what had happened was borne in on me. Only once he had gone, did I realize how much he had meant to me and how deeply fond of him I had been. There was still so much that I wanted to ask him and learn from him ...

I now found myself the head of the cadet branch of the Churchill family and with a sizable family of my own. In the four years that we had been married, Minnie had produced three wonderful children, all within three years of each other. A fourth, Jack, was to come as an afterthought some eight years later. Meanwhile we had sunk our roots deep into the Sussex soil at Broadwater, which was to be our home for the first twenty-one years of our married life. Father had been passionately keen that, after his death, we should move to his beloved Stour and enjoy the garden he had created. Sadly, although I was myself by then one of the best-paid journalists in Fleet Street, we were forced to conclude that its size and the cost of the staff required to run it were beyond what we could afford. We were forced to place it on the market and, after death duties, the sale realized barely

£10,000. Not wishing to leave him behind when we were selling the house to strangers, I defied my father's wishes about scattering his ashes in the garden. We took the casket containing them to Bladon in Oxfordshire, where we buried him alongside the graves of his father and his grandfather, beneath the church tower which can be seen from the lawn at Blenheim.

Index